# Reducing Vulnerability
# and Increasing Opportunity

## About This Book

*Orientations in Development* was launched by the World Bank's Middle East and North Africa Region in 2001 to share analysis of the multifaceted development issues facing the region and to offer practical and innovative solutions. From managing scarce water resources to preserving cultural heritage to enacting policies that promote equitable growth and reduce poverty, the region confronts a broad range of challenges. Each contribution in this series seeks to deepen the knowledge on these topics and enrich the policy debate among development practitioners both within the region and worldwide.

Cover design by Naylor Design, Inc., Washington, D.C.
Photos by Guillermo Hakim.

# Reducing Vulnerability and Increasing Opportunity

## Social Protection in the Middle East and North Africa

The World Bank

Middle East and North Africa Region

ISBN 0-8213-5145-1

Library of Congress Cataloging-in-Publication Data has been applied for.

# Contents

## Appendixes

## Notes                                                                155

## Bibliography                                                          159

## Boxes

## Figures

## Tables

# Foreword

I am pleased to present *Reducing Vulnerability and Increasing Opportunity: Social Protection in the Middle East and North Africa.* This report presents an integrated framework for social protection in the Middle East and North Africa (MENA), assesses various formal and informal social protection programs, and discusses future reform options. This is the third volume in our series, Orientations in Development.

During the 1970s and early 1980s, most countries in the MENA region established a comprehensive structure of social protection programs ranging from cash and in-kind transfers and consumption subsidies of basic goods and services to pensions, disability, and health insurance. These programs played a key role in expanding access to basic social services to the population and promoting the accumulation of human capital. Changes in the international and domestic socioeconomic environments, however, are making governments reconsider the logic and structure of current social protection mechanisms. Indeed, the integration of information and capital flows brings new opportunities for growth and development, but also higher uncertainty and vulnerability. Demographic changes put pressure on labor markets to absorb expanding cohorts of young workers while threatening the financial sustainability of pensions and health systems in the future. Transformations in the socioeconomic structure, urbanization, an increase in the share of women who participate in the labor force, and the weakening of informal social protection systems also increase vulnerability. At the same time, fiscal restraints necessary to ensure macroeconomic stability limit the resources available to cover the growing financing needs of current social programs.

The proposed social protection framework expands the traditional view of social protection as a set of social assistance programs to help the poor, to include the wide array of mechanisms that reduce vulnerability by helping individuals to manage social risks. These risks can be man-made (for example, economic cycles, work accidents) or natural (disease, losses in agricultural production resulting from bad weather). The report argues that better economic management constitutes the main ingredient in reducing social risks and expanding opportunities for the poor and vulnerable. Hence, prudent macroeconomic policies, better governance, and more efficient regulatory institutions are necessary elements of an integrated social protection strategy. If these reforms are implemented, then traditional social protection systems could be relieved from some of the current mandates, and scarce resources and reform efforts could be focused on select cost-effective programs in labor markets, social insurance, and social assistance.

I believe that this new framework for social protection will contribute to a better informed and more focused debate on social protection reform options in the MENA region. I hope it will ultimately lead to a better and more equitable distribution of the benefits from economic growth, and a sustained reduction in poverty and vulnerability.


JEAN-LOUIS SARBIB
VICE PRESIDENT
MIDDLE EAST AND NORTH AFRICA REGION

# Acknowledgments

This report was prepared under the overall guidance of Zafiris Tzannatos (Adviser to the Managing Director Human Development) and George Schieber (Sector Manager, Health and Social Protection). It was written by a core team comprising Setareh Razmara, David Robalino, Iqbal Kaur, and Domin Chung. Zafiris Tzannatos managed the production of an earlier version of this report. The report is based on inputs and comments provided by Bahjat Achikbache, Richard Adams, Petros Aklilu, Arbi Ben-Anchour, Regina Bendokat, Judith Brandsma, Concepción Esperanza del Castillo, Daniel Dulitzky, Sophal Ear, Yasser El-Gammal, Peter Fallon, Guillermo Hakim, Sonia Hammam, Robert Holzmann, Steen Jorgensen, Qaiser Khan, Marlaine Lockheed, Rekha Menon, Mustapha Nabli, Robert Palacios, Bassam Ramadan, Elizabeth Ruppert, Jamal Saghir, Lorenzo Savorelli, Radwan Shaban, David Steel, Kutlu Somel, George Tharakan, Patrizia Tumbarello, Julia Van Domelen, Willem Van Eeghen, and Dimitri Vittas. Earlier versions of the report have been shared with government officials (including Algeria, Morocco, Tunisia, and the Republic of Yemen) and have been discussed in meetings with stakeholders. The report has also benefited from comments from and exchanges with participants in the conferences of the Economic Research Forum for the Arab Countries, the Islamic Republic of Iran and Turkey; the Mediterranean Development Forum; the Russell Sage Foundation; the Rockefeller Foundation; the International Labour Organization; the United Nations Educational, Scientific, and Cultural Organization; and the United Nations Children's Fund, especially Samir Radwan, Victor Billeh, Noha El-Mikawy, Maurice Girgis, Marsha Posusney, and Heba Handoussa. The report is part of the Bank-wide Social Protection Strategy Paper Initiative led by Robert Holzmann (Director, Human Development Network, Social Protection Group), and Steen Jorgensen (Director, Social Development Department). Jacques Baudouy (Director, Human Development Sector, Middle East and North Africa Region) facilitated and supported the team and its work. Henriette Folquet and Emma Etori assisted in the preparation of the manuscript. The team would like to thank all of those who contributed and participated in the various stages of the production of this report, including those whose names have been omitted.

# Acronyms
# and Abbreviations

| | |
|---|---|
| AGSECAL | Agricultural Sector Adjustment Loan |
| ALMP | active labor market policies |
| ANEM | *Agence Nationale de l'Emploi* |
| CMR | *Caisse Marocaine de Retraite* (Moroccan Pension Fund) |
| CNR | *Caisse Nationale de Retraite* (National Pension Fund) |
| CNAC | *Caisse Nationale d' Assurance et de Chômage* |
| CNRPS | *Caisse Nationale de Retraite et Prévoyance Sociale* (National Pension and Social Security Fund) |
| CSRO | Civil Service Retirement Organization |
| DA | Algerian dinar |
| EN | *Entraide Nationale* |
| EU | European Union |
| GDP | Gross domestic product |
| IDA | International Development Association |
| ILO | International Labour Organization |
| IMF | International Monetary Fund |
| ISSUE | Income Support Systems for the Unemployed |
| JD | Jordanian dinar |
| MENA | Middle East and North Africa |
| NGO | nongovernmental organization |
| NIS | new Israeli sheqel |
| O&M | operations and maintenance |
| OECD | Organisation for Economic Co-operation and Development |
| OPS | *Organisme de Protection Sociale* (Social Protection Organization) |
| PN | *Promotion Nationale* |
| PWP | Public Works Program |
| SAL | Structural Adjustment Loan |
| SFD | Social Fund for Development |
| SIF | social investment fund |
| SSC | Social Security Corporation |

| SSO | Social Security Organization |
|---|---|
| TFP | total factor productivity |
| TFR | total fertility rate |
| U.N. | United Nations |
| UNDP | United Nations Development Programme |
| UNESCO | United Nations Educational, Scientific, and Cultural Organization |
| UNICEF | United Nations Children's Fund |
| UNRWA | United Nations Relief and Works Agency |
| WDI | *World Development Indicators* |
| WDR | *World Development Report* |
| YR | Yemeni rial |

# Executive Summary

The economies in the Middle East and North Africa (MENA) region are diverse in many respects, making it difficult to devise a common social protection strategy. Countries differ in size, from the small state of Djibouti to the Arab Republic of Egypt and the Islamic Republic of Iran, both of which account for almost one-half of the regional population. Countries also differ by levels of per capita income, from the Republic of Yemen and Morocco to Tunisia, Lebanon, and the Gulf economies (see figures ES.1 and ES.2). Differences between urban and rural population and agricultural and nonfarm employment are also vast, as is the structure of output between oil and non-oil economies.[1]

At the same time, however, MENA countries share important socioeconomic characteristics, and their social protection systems face similar design and implementation problems. Historically, most economies have been marked by large and strong public sectors, intervening at almost all levels of the social and economic spheres. Today, the majority of economies face similar challenges in terms of promoting private-sector-led growth, reducing unemployment, and containing poverty. Another common feature is the emphasis that governments have placed on human development. Most countries have developed comprehensive social protection systems that have played a key role in promoting human capital accumulation while protecting the vulnerable and poor. These systems often follow similar design patterns and, in many cases, face analogous problems. Institutional capacity is often lacking; there are inefficiencies in the allocation of resources across competing programs and technical inefficiencies in the production and delivery of social services; targeting mechanisms for public subsidies are weak; and financing methods are not always sustainable and introduce market distortions, particularly in labor markets.

This report develops a framework for a more integrated approach to social protection and proposes general strategic lines of action to guide

*(Text continues on page 5.)*

FIGURE ES.1

## Common Characteristics of MENA Economies

### A. High Dependence on Oil

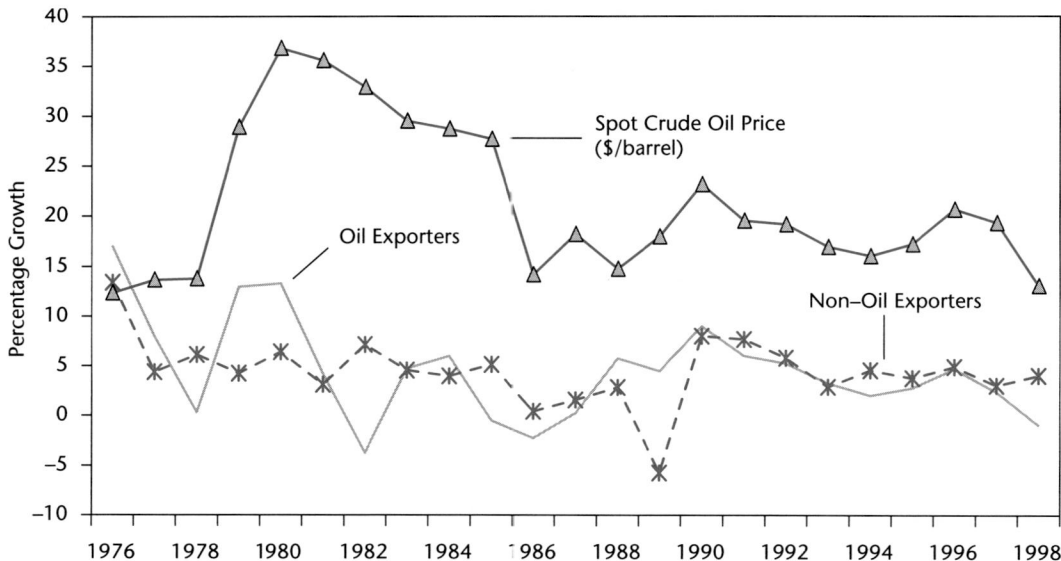

**Note:** Even non-oil exporting MENA countries are affected by oil price volatility.
**Source:** World Bank and BP Amoco.

### B. Scarce Water Resources, 1999

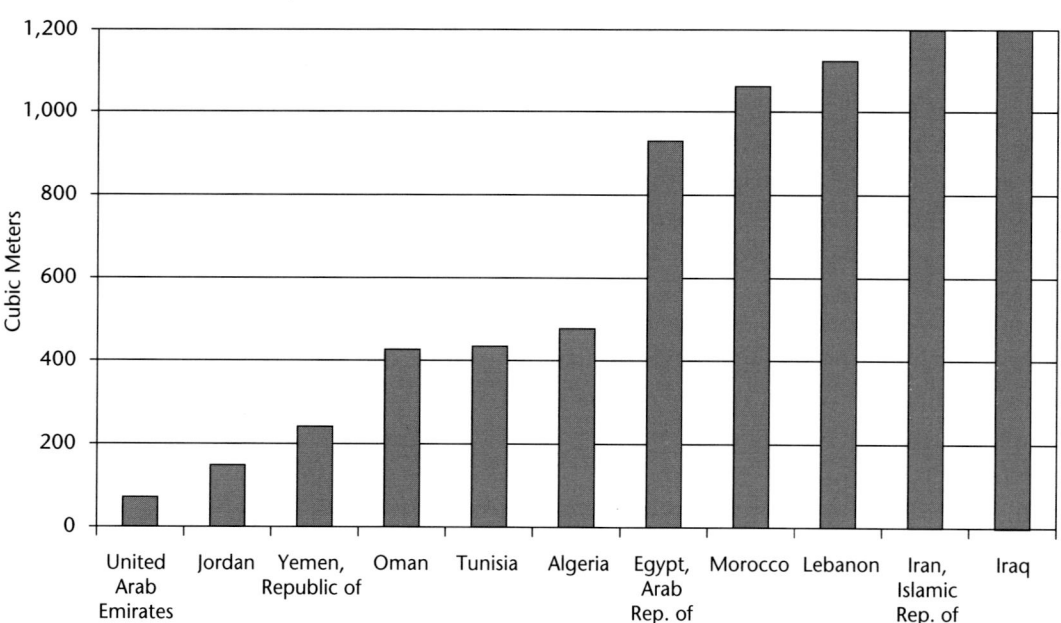

**Note:** Water availability is less than 1,700 cubic meters per person and, in some countries, substantially less. The international norm is 1,700 cubic meters per person. Below 1,700 indicates water scarcity.
**Source:** World Bank estimates; World Bank, *World Development Indicators (WDI) 2001*, 2001h.

## C. Fastest Growing Population, 1999

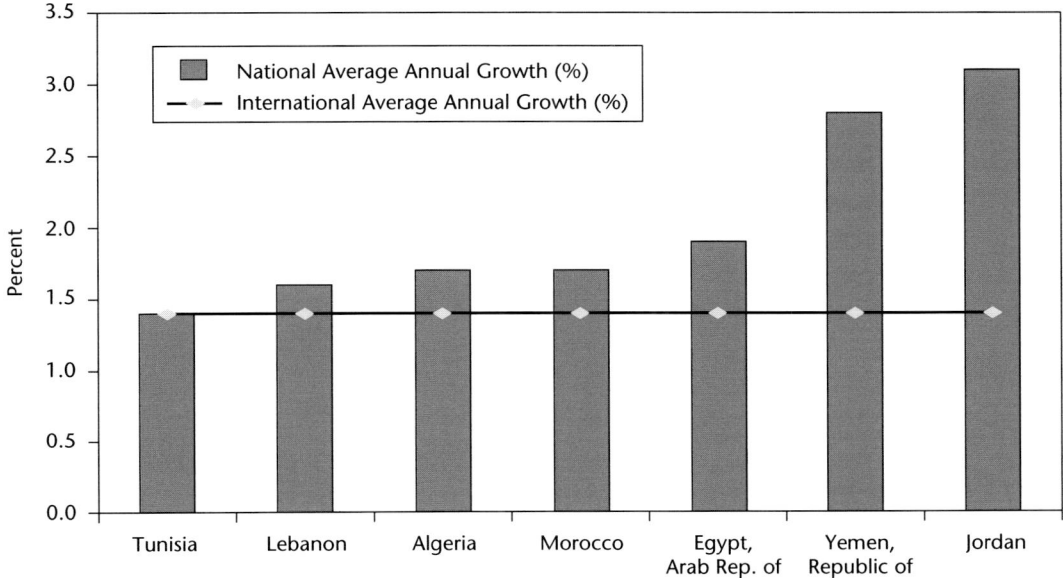

**Note:** Population is growing at a rate faster than the international average of 1.4 percent.
**Source:** World Bank, *WDI Database,* 2001g.

## D. High Unemployment, 1999–2000

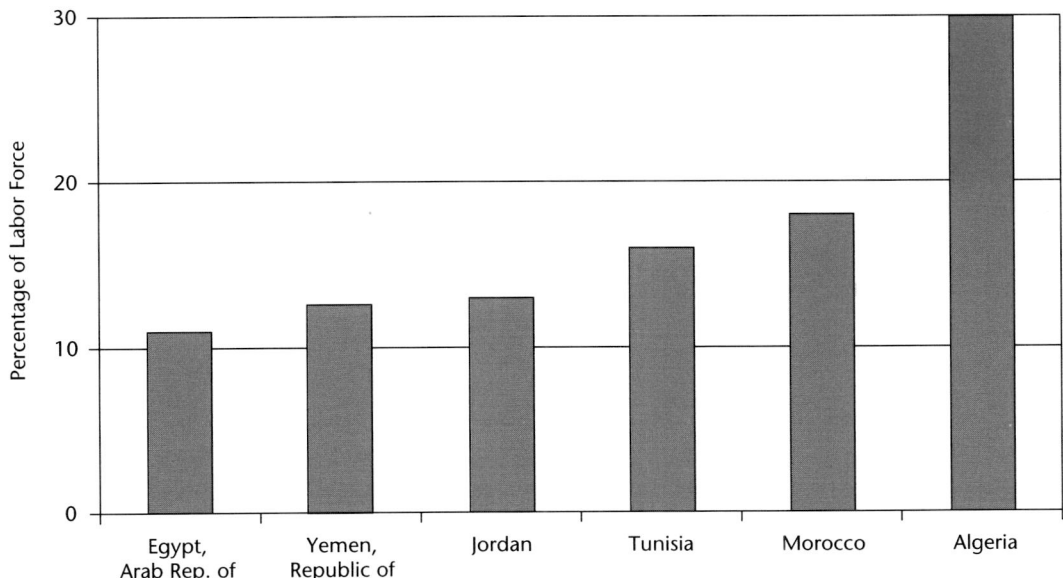

**Note:** The unemployment rate is typically greater than 10 percent.
**Source:** World Bank, *WDI 2000,* 2000b.

FIGURE ES.2

## Significant Differences among MENA Economies

### A. Population Size, 1999

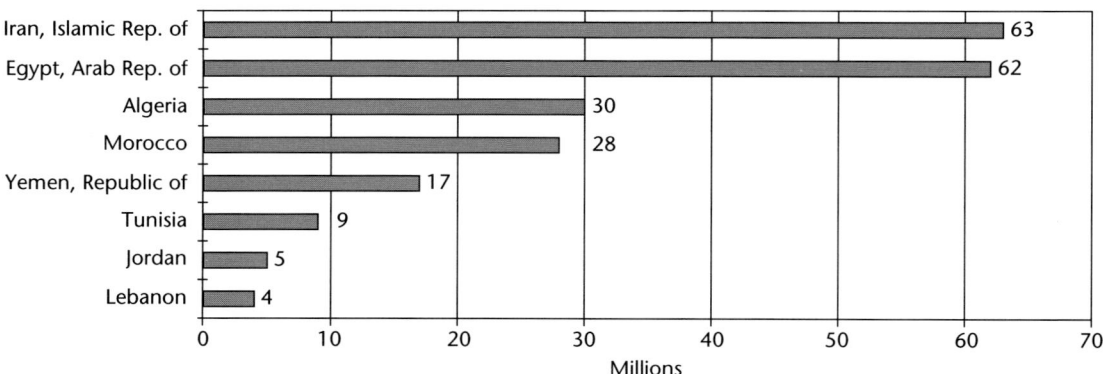

**Source:** World Bank, *WDI Database,* 2001g.

### B. Per Capita Income, 1999

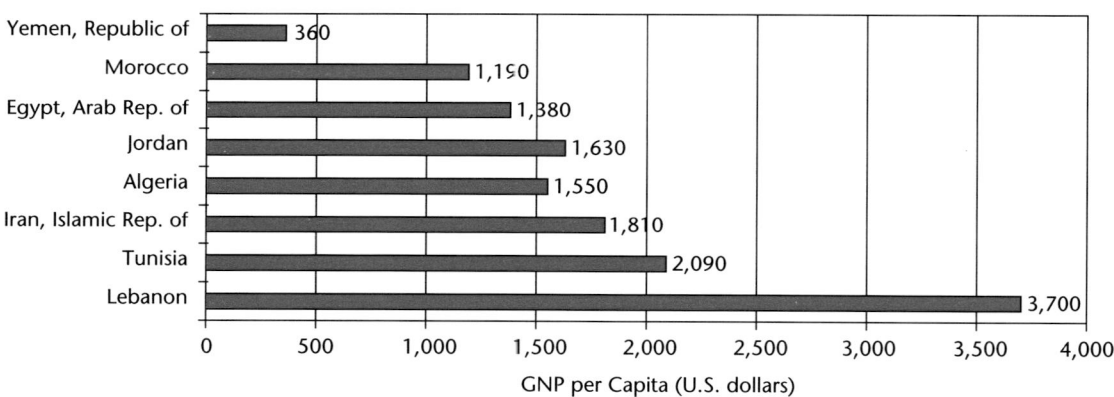

**Source:** World Bank, *WDI Database,* 2001g.

### C. Integration with the Global Economy, 2000

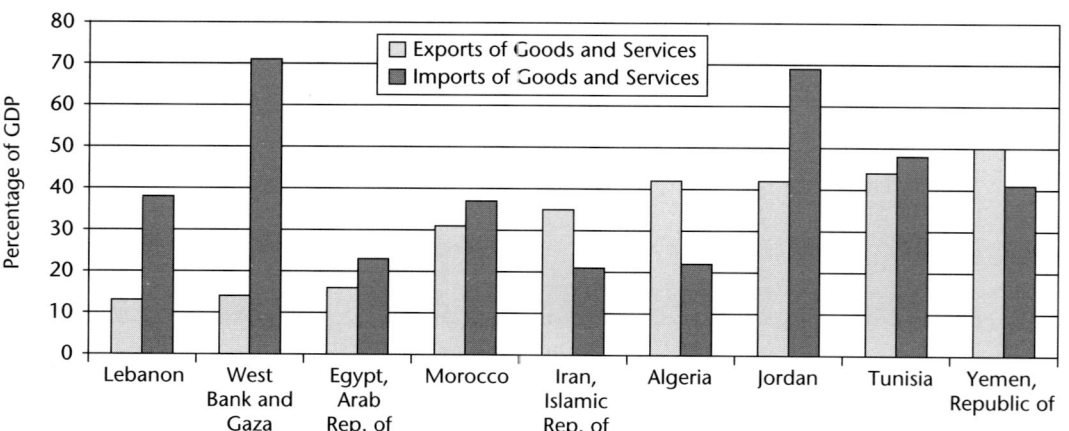

**Source:** World Bank, *WDI Database,* 2001g.

## D. Structure of Economic Activity and Output

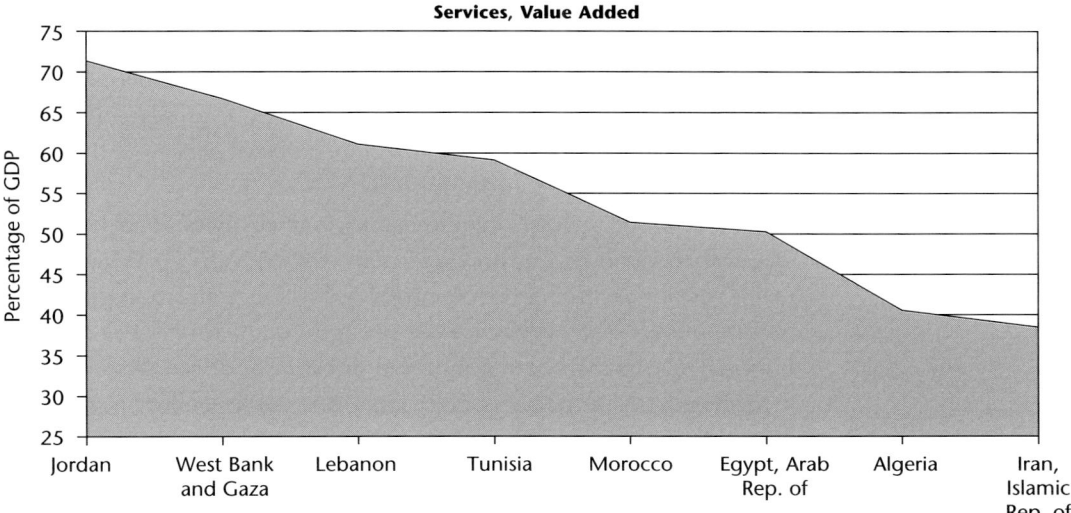

**Source:** World Bank, *WDI 2000*, 2000b.

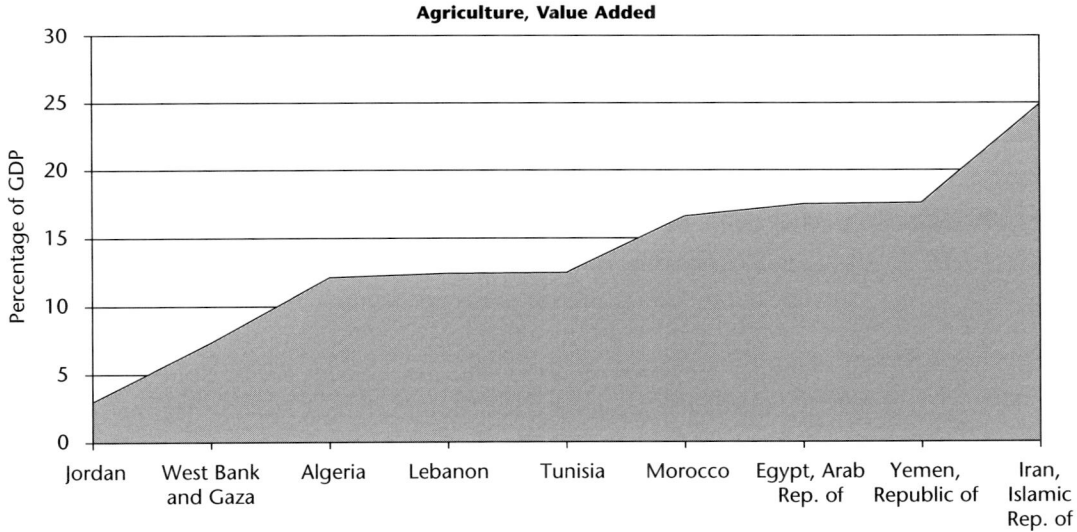

**Source:** World Bank, *WDI 2000*, 2000b.

the reform of social protection systems in the MENA region. It is meant to contribute to a better informed and more focused debate on social protection at the national, regional, and international levels. The report is sensitive to the new challenges brought about by globalization, as the ability of governments to increase budgets and pursue national policies

diminishes in tandem with a reduction in overseas developmental assistance and as social sectors become more vulnerable to swings in international financial markets. However, the report emphasizes the benefits of
globalization, which brings closer all actors from the World Trade Organization, the Bretton Woods institutions, and specialized U.N. agencies,
such as the United Nations Educational, Scientific, and Cultural Organization (UNESCO), the United Nations Children's Fund (UNICEF),
and the International Labour Organization (ILO), to bilateral donors,
regional organizations, national governments, civil society, and international nongovernmental organizations (NGOs).

The report has been organized into four chapters. The first three
chapters concentrate on three questions, respectively: (a) What are the
major social risks facing the countries and which population groups are
most vulnerable? (b) What are the strengths and weaknesses of current
informal and formal (both public and private) social protection systems
in managing these risks? and (c) How can public policy improve the
efficiency and effectiveness of these systems? Chapter 1 discusses the
rationale for governments' involvement in social protection and high-
lights common challenges of managing the risks associated with stagnant
growth, unemployment, and a rapid increase in the demand for basic infrastructure and social services. The chapter also identifies broad population groups that are likely to be more vulnerable to these risks. Chapter 2 introduces a comprehensive social risk management framework
that is then applied to the evaluation of current informal and formal
social protection systems. It delineates common institutional, operational, and financial problems facing social programs across countries.
On the basis of this assessment, chapter 3 proposes general strategic lines
of action for policy reform. It differentiates between the policies that do
not necessarily fall into the realm of the traditional social protection
system—such as improved macroeconomic management, better governance, and more efficient regulatory institutions—and those that fall
under the responsibility of the government agencies involved in social
protection. Chapter 3 also identifies priority areas where reform efforts
could concentrate. Finally, chapter 4 describes the type of support that
the World Bank could provide to governments for these reform efforts.

## Chapter 1: The Challenges of Social Protection: Identifying Risks and Vulnerable Groups in the MENA Region

Chapter 1 starts with a general review of key economic trends in MENA
countries prior and subsequent to the collapse of oil prices in the mid-

1980s. The chapter argues that while during the 1970s and early 1980s economic growth rates outweighed growth rates in other regions and social indicators improved dramatically, the model of development was not sustainable. Countries failed to introduce necessary structural reforms, partly because oil reserves provided an extra margin in which to maneuver. Today, most countries face important economic and social risks associated with stagnant growth, unemployment, and a rapid increase in the demand for basic infrastructure and social services.

Between 1973 and 1986, favorable conditions for the production of oil allowed the MENA region to outperform all other regions (except East Asia) in income growth. The rise in income was accompanied by the creation of a wide range of formal social protection mechanisms that supported investments in human capital. Public expenditures in health and education increased, thereby enhancing labor productivity and mobility. Infrastructure was expanded and improved. There was a rapid expansion in government jobs. Public works and other employment programs assisted the able-bodied poor to temporarily find work locally or engage in self-employment. Food subsidies decreased the price of most basic food products, and cash assistance helped those who could not finance basic needs. Pension schemes were expanded to provide old-age insurance. Because the economies were growing rapidly, the cost of ensuring the water supply seemed small, and high population growth rates were not perceived as a risk.

However, countries dependent on oil remained largely closed to trade and did not implement institutional reforms to promote private sector development and more competitive and diversified economies. High oil prices allowed MENA countries to delay structural reform. Economies remained largely closed to international markets, given high tariffs and nontariff barriers. The dependence on a few commodities (oil and agricultural products) rendered MENA countries vulnerable to fluctuations in international prices and weather changes. Political and social instability also contributed to high output volatility.[2] Overregulated economies and the lack of a business environment that would promote competition and innovation put a drag on total factor productivity growth.

Under these conditions, when oil prices (and the prices of other primary goods) began to fall in the mid-1980s, public expenditures became unsustainable and economic and social conditions started to deteriorate. Many economies began to experience negative growth rates. Exchange rates moved unfavorably, with adverse effects on the import bill, including food. Amid the general climate of declining revenues, informal mechanisms came under stress because of high population growth rates (the regional population in the mid-1990s was double that of 1970, just before the start of the oil boom). Formal social protection mechanisms could not keep up with growing unemployment and poverty. In fact, these social protection systems often contributed to the amplification of economic distortions and therefore hampered growth through the use of inefficient financing and delivery mechanisms such as price controls, wage subsidies, employment in stated-owned enterprises, and overhiring and underpaying teachers.

The region now faces economic and social risks that threaten investments in human capital and compromise the welfare of the population. These risks can be grouped into three categories. First, there are the risks related to the countries' inability to generate sustainable growth given poorly diversified economies, weak private sectors, and the lack of institutions to promote competitive business environments and reduce transactions costs. Second, there are the increased risks related to rigid labor markets in the face of a fast expansion of the labor force and the gradual downsizing of the public sector. Third, there are the risks associated with demographic transitions that put pressure on the supply of infrastructure and basic services such as water, as well as the finances of social insurance systems such as health insurance and pensions. While the MENA region has the lowest incidence of poverty relative to other developing regions, the risk of becoming poor, either temporarily or permanently, will continue as a result of the unfinished economic agenda; additional effects from globalization, such as the costs of sectoral adjustments in the short run; aging populations; natural disasters; and perhaps sporadic conflict situations. Particularly vulnerable population groups include the poor, who are unable to engage in high-risk, high-return activities and are likely to be marginalized from access to basic infrastructure and social services; children in low-income households, who face the risk of entering informal labor markets prematurely; small landowners, who remain exposed to unanticipated changes in weather and fluctuations in prices; first-time job seekers and low-skilled workers, who face the risk of unemployment; and the elderly, who may lack access to sustainable health insurance and pension systems.

The challenges facing traditional social protection systems therefore go beyond *poverty* reduction and include facilitating risk management mechanisms to reduce *vulnerability*, that is to reduce the likelihood that the nonpoor become poor. This idea is further developed in chapters 2 and 3.

## Chapter 2: Assessing Current Formal and Informal Mechanisms for Social Protection

Chapter 2 discusses key features and major weaknesses of the social protection systems in MENA countries. The chapter starts by defining an alternative framework for social protection. This framework differs from the traditional view of social protection as a narrow set of policies that fall under the responsibility of ministries such as labor and social affairs, manpower, social welfare, social insurance, social security, and so on. It proposes a broader approach to social protection that takes into consideration the whole set of informal and formal mechanisms that assist individuals, households, and communities to better manage risks ranging from economic crises or shocks to fluctuations in weather or longevity.

Social protection systems in MENA countries comprise a large set of formal and informal mechanisms to manage risks. For discussion purposes, it is useful to classify these mechanisms into three categories: (a) mechanisms aimed at reducing risks; (b) mechanisms aimed at mitigating risks, that is, reducing the impact of future adverse shocks; and (c) mechanisms aimed at coping with risks, that is, reversing or reducing the impact of shocks—poverty, for instance—that have occurred. Examples of risk-reducing mechanisms include hygienic practices to prevent disease (informal) or efficient macroeconomic management and labor market initiatives, such as continuous training programs, that update workers' skills and make them less vulnerable to unemployment during a downturn (formal). In terms of risk mitigation, informal mechanisms comprise multiple jobs, reciprocal gift-giving practices, and other community arrangements, while formal mechanisms include investment portfolio diversification and different types of insurance (pensions, health, unemployment), as well as interventions to provide access to capital markets to individuals with limited assets, such as microfinance programs. Risk-coping mechanisms at the informal level can be as diverse as selling real assets, migrating, borrowing from neighbors, sending children to work, or neglecting human capital (for example, reducing expenditures in food). Borrowing from a bank or introducing public works and a variety of in-kind and cash transfers, on the contrary, are examples of formal risk-coping mechanisms. A social protection strategy, therefore, is not limited to programs that help the poor (risk-coping mechanisms), but also considers mechanisms that reduce the risks of poverty for the nonpoor. Public programs ought to complement efficient informal and private formal mechanisms and replace inefficient ones, such as child labor. The costs associated with these programs should be viewed as advances on the benefits resulting from higher levels of human capital and social welfare in the future.

Among formal risk reduction mechanisms, the most popular instruments across MENA countries are active labor market policies (ALMPs). ALMPs include counseling and placement services, training or retraining of displaced workers, support for entry into self-employment, and wage subsidies. This study shows that in line with the international experience concerning ALMPs, labor market policies have had limited impacts in MENA economies. ALMPs are not panaceas for the problem of low employment creation in the region. These programs have shown that they can only marginally reduce the risks associated with structural constraints in the labor and product markets and the macroeconomy at large. If inappropriately designed, these programs can actually produce deadweight losses.

In terms of risk-mitigating mechanisms, most countries in the region have developed health insurance and pension systems, and a few have developed unemployment insurance. Common problems facing these systems are mostly related to weak institutional capacity to monitor expected revenues and expenditures and to manage reserves. In many cases, the social insurance systems have been used as a mechanism to finance and provide social assistance services. In general, benefits are not in line with contributions, leading to actuarial imbalances. The systems are often financed through high payroll taxes that contribute to the distortion of labor markets. Their financial position is expected to deteriorate in the near future as a result of the aging of the population.

Diverse social assistance programs, such as public works programs (PWPs), social funds, and cash and in-kind transfers programs, have evolved in MENA countries to help populations who have experienced adverse shocks to cope with losses. Usually, these programs yield good results in cost and effectiveness. However, there is ample room to improve efficiency. Evaluations suggest, for example, that social funds reach many of the poor but generally fail to reach the poorest or, often, women. Microcredit granted at low or even negative real interest rates is more of a transfer than a contribution to sustainable development. Public works that pay high wages or have a low labor share in their total costs are unlikely to efficiently meet poverty objectives. Food subsidies can create significant economic distortions and, if universal, are appropriated by the nonpoor. In general, targeting mechanisms are weak, leading to leakages toward middle- and high-income groups.

Outside the traditional social protection system, policies in the education and health sectors, and several schemes aimed at containing the prices of basic goods and services, have been instrumental in reducing social risks and improving opportunities. However, in the face of tight budgets and growing demands, these systems have become unsustainable. Without reforms to improve allocative and technical efficiency in the education and health sectors, as well as reviews of financing mechanisms to encourage private sector involvement, past gains in social outcomes could be reversed. Price regulations in the agricultural, transport, and basic infrastructure sectors have reduced incentives to invest in new production and delivery technologies that could reduce costs. As a result,

severe price distortions have emerged, leading to overconsumption, undersupply, and fading quality. Moreover, targeting mechanisms are generally weak, and therefore, subsidies tend to benefit mostly middle- and
high-income population groups.

While little is known about the role of informal mechanisms in MENA
countries, their importance should not be downplayed. Globally, less
than one-quarter of the population has access to formal programs, and
less than 5 percent can rely on their own assets to manage risk. Eliminating the poverty gap through public transfers is beyond the fiscal and,
particularly, administrative capacity of most developing economies. Thus,
a strategy for the social protection systems should also consider mechanisms to reinforce informal mechanisms. One of the important sources
of social assistance in MENA countries is religious charitable contributions, *Zakat* and *Waqfs*. *Zakat* is an obligation for better-off Muslims to
pay an amount to those in need. *Waqfs* are charitable foundations set up
by wealthy people to support activities such as schools for the poor. Kinship networks can also be of vital importance in spreading the risks of localized catastrophes and strengthening the economic and social capital of
a group over the long-term so that it can be accessed in times of stress.
Migration has also played an important role. International and intraregional remittances can account for between 10 and 30 percent of total household income, and therefore, the social implications of current
changes in international and intraregional migration patterns should be
carefully assessed.

In response to changes in national and international economic realities, MENA countries need to adapt their social protection systems. As
the world economies become more integrated, lax monetary and fiscal
policies cannot be used to promote growth and to finance generous, often
nontargeted, social expenditures in a sustainable way. Lower resources
combined with growing demands require new financing, production, and
delivery mechanisms for social services that promote efficiency and equity. More importantly, social protection systems need to emphasize
*ex-ante* interventions over *ex-post* interventions. This emphasis involves
strengthening risk management mechanisms to reduce poverty-related
welfare losses before they actually occur. Chapter 3 proposes strategic
lines of action in this direction.

## Chapter 3: Strengthening the Social Protection System: Setting Priorities and Reallocating Resources

Chapter 3 argues that traditional social protection schemes cannot constitute the sole mechanism to protect vulnerable population groups, help

the poor, and increase social welfare. Within a comprehensive vision of social protection, better economic management probably constitutes the main ingredient in reducing social risks and expanding the opportunities of the poor and vulnerable. Hence, prudent macroeconomic policies, better governance, and more efficient regulatory institutions are necessary elements of a global social protection strategy. Moreover, it is desirable for the private sector and civil society to have a more prominent role in developing, implementing, and managing social protection systems. A more active civil society means a different, not necessarily smaller, role for the state. The state can reduce its role as a producer (in parastatals) and provider of services, and increase its role as a regulator (enforcing competition rules and maintaining a level playing field among public and private providers), such as in the areas of social services. Here, we summarize the main recommendations for strengthening social protection systems (see also box ES.1).

## Actions outside the Traditional Social Protection System

*Promoting prudent macroeconomic management.* Most MENA countries have made considerable progress in improving macroeconomic management. The role of fiscal policy is gradually shifting from the engine of growth to guarantor of macroeconomic stability. In oil-producing countries, however, fiscal revenues remain subject to political and social pressures. Fiscal policy still needs to become countercyclical, thus accumulating savings in good times to temporarily sustain demand during bad times. Other issues to be addressed to improve long-term efficiency and stimulate productivity growth include the competitiveness of exchange rates and trade liberalization.

*Improving governance.* Good governance is a precondition for efficient economic management and social protection effectiveness. Various factors determine the quality of governance, including governments' ability to honor contracts, respect for private property and law and order, the quality of the bureaucracy, respect for civil and political liberties, and transparency in the management of public resources. These factors directly affect economic performance. The risk of expropriation and government repudiation of contracts, for instance, influences foreign direct investment. Moreover, transparency in public management, the quality of bureaucracy, and respect for civil and political rights, have a significant effect on the distribution of public resources and, therefore, the welfare of the needy. In most cases, indicators of governance have improved in MENA countries over time. Efforts to strengthen governance should continue.

**BOX ES.1**

## Regional Issues and Strategic Directions

### Context/Issues

Oil markets have had a large effect on the structure and dynamics of MENA economies. Until the mid-1980s, the MENA region benefited from fast growth, largely due to high oil prices. As a result, (a) governments increased investment in the social sectors and established a whole range of formal social protection mechanisms, (b) poverty remained lower than in other regions, (c) the state became the main employer and regulated wages, and (d) high population growth rates and high costs of providing scarce water resources were not a concern. Public expenditures became unsustainable when oil prices began to fall in the mid-1980s, and economic and social conditions started to deteriorate. Many economies began to experience negative growth rates. The situation was complicated by geopolitical conflicts—the Iran-Iraq and Gulf wars and civil wars in the Republic of Yemen, Lebanon, and Algeria.

The region now faces economic and social risks that threaten investments in human capital and compromise the welfare of the population. First, there are the risks related to the countries' inability to generate sustainable growth given poorly diversified economies, a weak private sector, and the lack of institutions to promote competitive business environments and reduce transaction costs. Second, there are the risks related to rigid labor markets that will face tremendous pressure as a result of a fast expansion of the labor force and the gradual downsizing of the public sector. Third, there are the risks associated with demographic transitions that put pressure on the supply of infrastructure and basic services such as water, as well as the finances of social insurance systems such as health and pensions.

Particularly vulnerable population groups include the poor, who are unable to engage in high-risk, high-return activities and are likely to be marginalized from access to basic infrastructure and social services; children, who face the risk of entering informal labor markets prematurely; small landowners, who remain exposed to unanticipated changes in weather and fluctuations in prices; first-time job seekers and low-skilled workers, who face the risk of unemployment; and the elderly, who may lack access to sustainable health insurance and pension systems.

### Social Protection Arrangements

*Labor markets.* Macroeconomic and trade policies implemented during the oil boom allowed the public sector to become the employer of last resort. The result is rigid labor markets that have not been able to absorb a growing labor force. As a response, almost universally, economies are employing large vocational education and training programs

*(Box continues on the following page.)*

---

**BOX ES.1    (continued)**

that attempt to reduce unemployment problems. Their impact, however, has been limited.

*Social security.* Most countries in the region have developed health insurance and pension systems, and a few have developed unemployment insurance. Common problems facing these systems are mostly related to weak institutional capacity to monitor expected revenues and expenditures. In general, benefits are not in line with contributions, leading to actuarial imbalances. These systems are often financed through high payroll taxes that contribute to the distortion of labor markets.

*Social assistance programs* (for example, public works, food subsidies, cash transfers, and social funds) have been used to provide income-earning opportunities for the unemployed and to reduce poverty and mitigate shocks and their effects on the most vulnerable groups. But the efficiency of these programs—especially those involving subsidies—can be improved.

In MENA countries, informal mechanisms have been particularly relevant in rural areas, as formal methods of social protection seldom extend to the rural population. Social organization throughout the MENA region is characterized by reliable kinship networks and stable relationships on which households rely both to offset the effects of crises and to conserve or acquire resources. These networks are of vital importance in spreading the risks of localized catastrophes and strengthening the economic and social capital of a group over the long-term so that it can be accessed in times of stress. Migration has also played an important role as a risk-coping mechanism.

**Bank Support**

Many Bank projects in the MENA region relate directly to employment or have labor market components.

*Vocational training* has been an area of emphasis for Bank operations (Algeria, Egypt, Jordan, Lebanon, Morocco, Tunisia, the Republic of Yemen).

*Pension reforms* have been limited in the region, though there is increasing awareness of the need for reform (Algeria, Djibouti, the Islamic Republic of Iran, Jordan, Egypt, Lebanon, Morocco, Tunisia, and the Republic of Yemen).

*Social investment funds* (Algeria, Egypt, the West Bank and Gaza, and the Republic of Yemen) have been used to mitigate shocks and their effects on the most vulnerable groups, and also as compensatory mechanisms to increase access to, and the quality of, basic social and infrastructure services used by the poor. However, their operations remain small compared to the magnitude of poverty in MENA.

A few adjustment loans have addressed *safety net* concerns, but the efficiency of the systems still needs to be improved.

The Bank has conducted *poverty assessments* in most economies; however, some are outdated, and data reliability may limit their usefulness.

---

**BOX ES.1    (continued)**

**Future Directions**

Traditional social protection schemes cannot constitute the sole mechanism to support vulnerable population groups and increase social welfare. Within a comprehensive vision of social protection, better economic management probably constitutes the main ingredient in reducing social risks and expanding the opportunities of the poor and vulnerable. Hence, prudent macroeconomic policies, better governance, and more efficient regulatory institutions are necessary elements of a global social protection strategy. Moreover, it is desirable for the private sector and civil society to have a more prominent role in developing, implementing, and managing social protection systems.

Improving the financial sustainability of pay-as-you-go *pension systems*, by realigning contributions and benefits, and integrating and harmonizing different schemes are important directions for reform. Countries should consider the appropriateness of multipillar systems in the medium-term.

*Labor market policies* need to facilitate efficient employment creation; in this respect, skills creation and demand-driven training are key areas of intervention. To achieve this goal, (a) employment in public enterprises needs to be rationalized and firms' adjustment costs reduced, (b) nonwage labor costs need to be better aligned with desirable objectives (for example, labor market insurance) to achieve better outcomes at lower costs, (c) ALMPs should be reconsidered on the basis of assessment of costs and benefits, and (d) vocational training reform should be a priority, considering the associated fiscal burden and the limited links to labor demand.

*Social safety nets* need to be better monitored and evaluated. *Public works* need to use self-targeting mechanisms more efficiently to attract the poor; the sustainability of *social funds* needs to be improved; *food subsidies* need to be linked to a broad poverty alleviation strategy; and the coverage of social assistance needs to be increased through savings achieved by better targeting.

The role of the government in *microfinance* could be limited to define the regulatory framework, as part of a country's financial sector development strategy.

**Source:** World Bank, various country reports.

---

*Rethinking regulatory institutions.* The challenge is to gradually eliminate distortions in product and labor markets while concentrating on building regulatory schemes that reduce transaction costs and enforce property rights. Reducing rigidities in labor markets is an issue that all MENA countries need to address in the short-term. Interventions would be required to reduce restrictions to the allocation or reallocation of labor and to minimize the burden of payroll taxes. In order to improve the quality of basic services and infrastructure and reduce shortages, it is also necessary to gradually reduce price controls. To protect producers from fluctuations in the price of agricultural products, price support systems could be replaced by insurance-based systems. To address other market failures, such as those related to excessive consumption of natural resources and environmental services, appropriate market-based regulatory instruments, such as taxes, subsidies, and permits, could be considered. Developing and enforcing property rights is another important line of action, as many low-income individuals own assets that could be an important source of collateral. The development and enforcement of these property rights would also encourage associative contracts among landowners, thus generating scale economies and promoting productive gains in otherwise overly fragmented agricultural lands.

*Reforming education and health systems.* These two systems are essential components of a sustainable social protection system, as they contribute to reducing risks and vulnerability and improving opportunities. The challenge in most countries is to shift from highly centralized systems, where financing, provision, and management functions rely on the public sector and where the allocation of resources is largely unresponsive to prices and outcomes, to systems where the private sector, outcomes, and prices play a more prominent role. This implies revisiting the role of the public sector to play down its function as a direct provider and to strengthen its function as a regulator. Governments would concentrate on implementing financing mechanisms to ensure that low-income population groups have access to education and health services, and that private providers meet appropriate quality standards and have incentives in place to control costs.

## Actions within the Traditional Social Protection System

In terms of the traditional formal social protection system (ALMPs, social security, and social assistance), a reform strategy could be developed on the basis of three principles: (a) given limited resources, governments need to prioritize the areas of intervention and avoid fighting multiple fronts at the same time; (b) there are social gains to be made by encouraging private sector participation in the financing and provision of social services; and (c) public resources should concentrate on cost-effective interventions. The following strategic actions are suggested.

*Improving the financial sustainability of social insurance systems.* Although many other areas of intervention refer to issues that are cyclical or short-term in nature—that is, they may wither away, albeit at a cost, in the absence of specific policies—social insurance is deeply embedded in the socioeconomic structures of the region. Labor insurance and pensions are already under strain, and five arguments point to the urgency of addressing them immediately: (a) the certainty that social insurance systems in all economies will require reforms sooner rather than later, since despite favorable demographics at present, pension fund reserves sink well below expected levels (some are already in deficit), and furthermore, the old-age dependency ratio is steadily deteriorating; (b) the size and (under) performance of social insurance systems have a significant adverse effect on growth, arising from poor outcomes in labor, product, insurance, and capital markets; (c) since the programs are publicly managed and yield low returns, funding them presents a sizable obstacle to a more efficient and effective use of public social spending; (d) the systems are bound to mature and expand further because of urbanization, growth, and so on, making reforms more costly over time as a result of increasing deficits; and (e) international experience suggests that reforms in this area take a long time, have heavy statistical and analytical requirements, and require substantial stakeholder consensus-building.

*Reforming training systems.* Although training cannot be blamed for much of the high (and in some cases still rising) unemployment rates in the regional economies, current training schemes tend to absorb considerable funds (often raised from payroll contributions), deprive the education and human development sector of valuable resources, and have generally poor results. Regional systems tend to be publicly dominated, supply driven, and expensive, and are often designed to act as a program of last resort for dropouts from the formal education system. But market-relevant training can help increase the employability of the young or those who lost their jobs because of economic restructuring. The way skills are created, financed, and managed, therefore, can have important implications for productivity, employability or unemployment, and poverty. National reviews of the training systems and analyses of labor market data can pave the way for meaningful reforms with far-reaching effects on economic efficiency and poverty. Reforms in the training sectors would have sizable and deep effects on product and regional markets and productivity, on the one hand, and household earnings, unemployment, and poverty, on the other hand.

*Designing safety nets as developmental and community based, not just assistance and centrally administered schemes.* An area in which the rationale for government involvement is the strongest is the implementation of risk-coping mechanisms, such as public works and safety nets. These programs can substitute for informal coping mechanisms that are welfare decreasing, such as reduced investment in human capital or child labor. This study has found that public works and safety nets usually have been the most effective, despite many being ill designed and having pervasive problems of poor targeting and lack of coordination across implementing agencies. These mechanisms could be strengthened or enhanced. This would require conducting evaluations, phasing out ineffective projects, and consolidating those with the highest potential. To increase efficiency, it is also necessary for local communities to become more involved in designing, financing, implementing, and monitoring processes. Child protection (including child labor and disability) schemes, though embryonic in most regional economies, are another area of promising developmental activities with strong participation of civil society.

*Expanding the role of the private sector in job assistance, insurance, and microcredit.* The review has suggested that the private sector could play a more prominent role in the development of risk-reducing mechanisms in labor markets. Indeed, the rationale for government control of job assistance programs and continuous training programs is weak at best. A more prominent role for the private sector in the design of risk-mitigating mechanisms such as health, pensions, and unemployment insurance systems is also desirable. Because of the imperfections in insurance markets, government involvement in the financing, management, and regulation of these systems remains important, but public-private synergies would increase efficiency. Providing access to capital markets for low-income population groups is another area in which more private and less public participation would improve efficiency. Governments could concentrate on developing and enforcing property rights and designing and enforcing an appropriate regulatory framework for microfinance programs, while the private sector would take the lead in designing, implementing, managing, and financing these programs.

## Chapter 4: The World Bank's Role

The World Bank's portfolio of social protection projects in the MENA region has increased substantially in the last eight years, as has the volume of sector work and technical assistance to governments. There are 12 active projects in the social protection portfolio: Egypt Social Fund III and Social Protection (Children) projects; Jordan Training and Employment project; Lebanon Community Development and Vocational Training projects; Morocco In-Service Training, Public Works, and Social Development projects; Yemen Vocational Training and Social Fund I and II projects; and Tunisia Employment and Training II projects. The Bank also has an active program of sector work and technical assistance designed to support governments as well as expose them to international experience.

Governments in the MENA region are placing increased emphasis on social insurance reform. Algeria, Djibouti, the Islamic Republic of Iran,

Jordan, Lebanon, Morocco, the Palestinian Authority, Tunisia, and the Republic of Yemen are undertaking or considering assessment of their pension systems with assistance from the Bank. In response to the pre-occupation of many governments with employment, the Bank also plans to expand its work in ALMPs and, in particular, education and training. In order to operationalize the newly proposed Risk Management Framework for social protection, the Bank is also expanding the set of analytical tools available to governments. Some of the new products include (a) risk and vulnerability assessments that identify vulnerable population groups and assess existing programs (have been prepared for countries in Latin America and Africa); (b) a new methodology for social sector/social protection expenditure and financing performance reviews that is now being piloted to respond to the needs of the Social Risk Management Framework; (c) an alternative template for labor market reviews that is under preparation; and (d) the new Income Support Systems for the Unemployed (ISSUE), a simulation tool to assess unemployment support programs, that is being developed and will be piloted in 2003.

# The Challenges of Social Protection: Identifying Risks and Vulnerable Groups in the MENA Region

The abundance of oil had an enormous influence on the structure and dynamics of MENA economies, and also on the ways social protection systems evolved. Large revenues allowed governments to rapidly expand investments in produced capital and infrastructure in all sectors. Governments assumed the management and financing of education and health systems and pursued goals of universal access. The public sector, both the central administration and the public enterprises, became the main source of employment for teachers, physicians, and other skilled and unskilled workers, providing generous health insurance and pension benefits. By the mid-1980s, the public sector had itself become a large safety net, and citizens had become accustomed to perceiving the government as the sole guarantor of growth, employment, and the provision of social services.

The collapse of oil prices and the advance of globalization have led governments in MENA countries to reconsider the effectiveness of the public-sector-led model of growth and social protection. Governments in the MENA region are now facing budgetary constraints, and globalization narrows the range of action of monetary and fiscal policies. Money supply and the public budget can no longer be used to promote growth and to finance generous, often nontargeted, social expenditures in a sustainable way. Fewer resources combined with growing demands require new financing, production, and delivery mechanisms that promote efficiency and equity.

This report contributes to government reform efforts by defining a framework that can be used to assess the effectiveness of alternative public social programs in order to identify areas where government could disengage, as well as areas where government participation needs to be strengthened, but that will also require better prioritization in the allocation of public resources. Within this framework, the social protection system is treated as a set of interrelated mechanisms, introduced to minimize the loss of human capital and social welfare that can result from unexpected, adverse external or internal shocks. These shocks can be man-made, such as financial crises, recessions, and unemployment, or natural, such as droughts and epidemics. Markets alone do not devise comprehensive mechanisms to manage the risks associated with these shocks, partly because of information and coordination problems, but also because individuals do not face the full social costs of the risks they take. These social costs are related to not only reduced human capital and lower growth potential, but also social instability. In addition, some segments of the population, particularly the poor, are more likely to be limited in the choice of instruments available to protect against these risks. This implies that they would remain more exposed, but also that they would be less likely to engage in high-return, high-risk activities. Governments therefore have an important role in complementing (not crowding out) formal, market-based and informal social protection mechanisms. The costs of public social protection programs incurred today are counterbalanced by the benefits resulting from higher levels of human capital and social welfare in the future. The remainder of this chapter discusses the major social risks facing countries in the MENA region and identifies the population groups that are most vulnerable to human capital and welfare loss.

## 1.1. Assessing Social Risks in the MENA Region

There are a variety of risks that can affect the welfare of the population and, consequently, human capital. While there is no rigorous methodology to set priorities, in this section we call attention to three broad categories of risk that appear to be common to most MENA countries and that are currently at the center of their development agenda. First, there are the risks related to the countries' inability to generate sustainable growth given poorly diversified economies, a weak private sector, and the lack of institutions to promote a competitive business environment. Second, there are the risks related to rigid labor markets that will face tremendous pressure as a result of a fast expansion of the labor force and the gradual downsizing of the public sector. Finally, there are the risks associated with demographic transitions that put pressure on the supply of infrastructure and basic services such as water and education, as well as the finances of social insurance systems, such as health and pensions.

### The Constraints to Sustainable Growth

Between 1973 and 1986, favorable conditions for the production of oil allowed the MENA region to outperform all other regions (except East Asia and Pacific) in income growth. The same favorable conditions, however, reduced the pressure to open markets to the world economy and introduce institutional reforms to promote private sector development and more diversified and competitive economies. Inward-looking industrialization meant that capital inflows were not actively sought, and political instability made foreign investors reluctant to expand their existing non-oil operations in the region. By the end of the oil boom of the 1980s, countries were largely closed to the international market because of high tariffs and considerable nontariff barriers. They also lacked the institutions, including financial services and export promotion strategies, necessary to penetrate the global economy.

The lack of economic diversification also brought high output volatility. The reliance on a few commodities, particularly oil, made the MENA region considerably exposed to fluctuations in international prices. In non-oil countries, volatility in the price of agricultural products combined with weather fluctuations to produce negative effects on output and unemployment. Social and political instability also contributed to higher volatility. Thus, the risks associated with output fluctuations in MENA countries have been considerably higher than in other regions of the developing world (see figure 1.1).

In the absence of mechanisms to hedge against the risks of large fluctuations in oil prices, disposable income contracted sharply when oil prices plummeted, leading to a decrease in the level of domestic and for-

FIGURE 1.1

**Output Volatility in the MENA Region Has Been Higher Than in Other Regions**

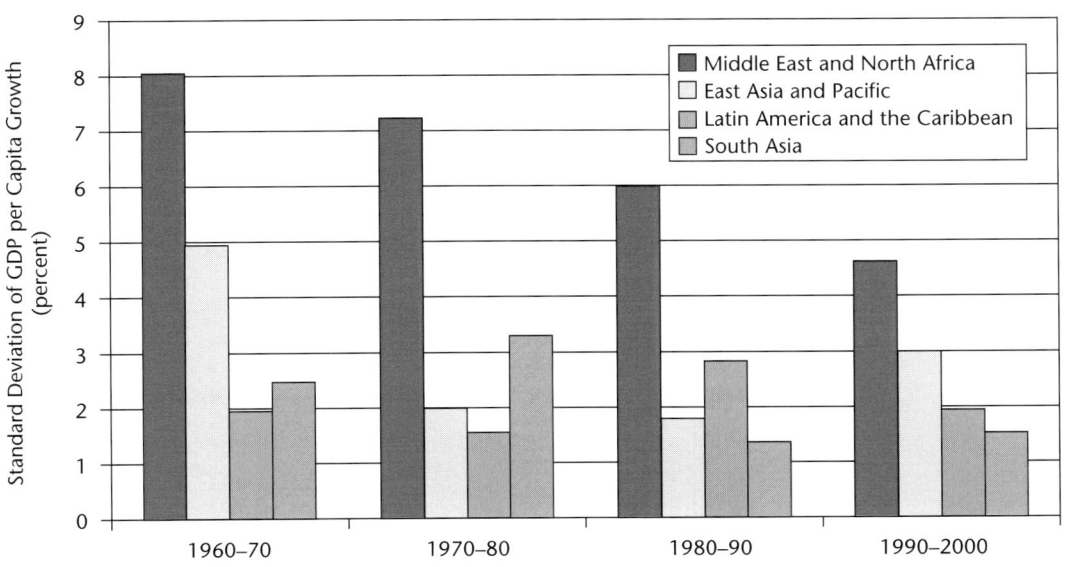

**Source:** Authors' calculations.

TABLE 1.1

**Percentage of Real GDP Annual Growth Rates for Select MENA Countries**

| Country | 1976–85 | 1986–90 | 1991–95 | 1996–98 | 1999 |
|---|---|---|---|---|---|
| Algeria | 5.8 | 0.2 | 0.2 | 3.0 | 3.3 |
| Egypt, Arab Rep. of | 8.5 | 4.2 | 3.3 | 5.6 | 6.0 |
| Jordan | 10.5 | –1.1 | 7.5 | 2.2 | 3.1 |
| Lebanon | — | — | 6.5 | 3.5 | — |
| Morocco | 4.8 | 4.4 | 1.2 | 4.2 | –0.7 |
| Tunisia | 5.3 | 3.0 | 3.9 | 5.2 | 6.2 |
| Yemen, Republic of | — | 3.3 | 3.1 | 4.6 | 3.8 |

— Not available.
**Source:** World Bank database.

eign investment. Non-oil countries in the region also felt the effects of falling oil prices through lower migrant worker remittances and reduced foreign investment. Since 1985, virtually all countries in the region have experienced lower gross domestic product (GDP) growth relative to the previous decade. In general, low growth rates observed during the 1980s continued into the 1990s, though some economies began to recover by the end of decade (see table 1.1). With high population growth, since 1986 per capita income in the region decreased by an average of 2 percent per year, the largest decline in any developing region during this period. In some oil-exporting countries, the average yearly decline was more than 4 percent.[3] Lower income also meant tighter budget constraints. Lower social expenditures were often an instrument for adjustment.

Overregulated economies and the lack of a business environment that would promote competition and innovation put a drag on total factor productivity (TFP) growth. As shown in table 1.2, TFP decreased in

TABLE 1.2

**Average Growth of TFP for Select MENA Countries**

| Country | 1980–90 | 1990–99 |
|---|---|---|
| Algeria | –2.9544 | 0.0236 |
| Egypt, Arab Rep. of | –0.8358 | 0.7906 |
| Iran, Islamic Rep. of | –1.7178 | 0.2499 |
| Jordan | –2.1723 | 0.9580 |
| Morocco | 0.5680 | 0.8383 |
| Pakistan | 1.5902 | 2.8281 |
| Tunisia | –0.2138 | 2.3129 |

**Source:** Authors' calculations using the World Bank's Poverty Reduction and Economic Management TFP tool.

FIGURE 1.2

**Share of Public Enterprises in Economic Activity**

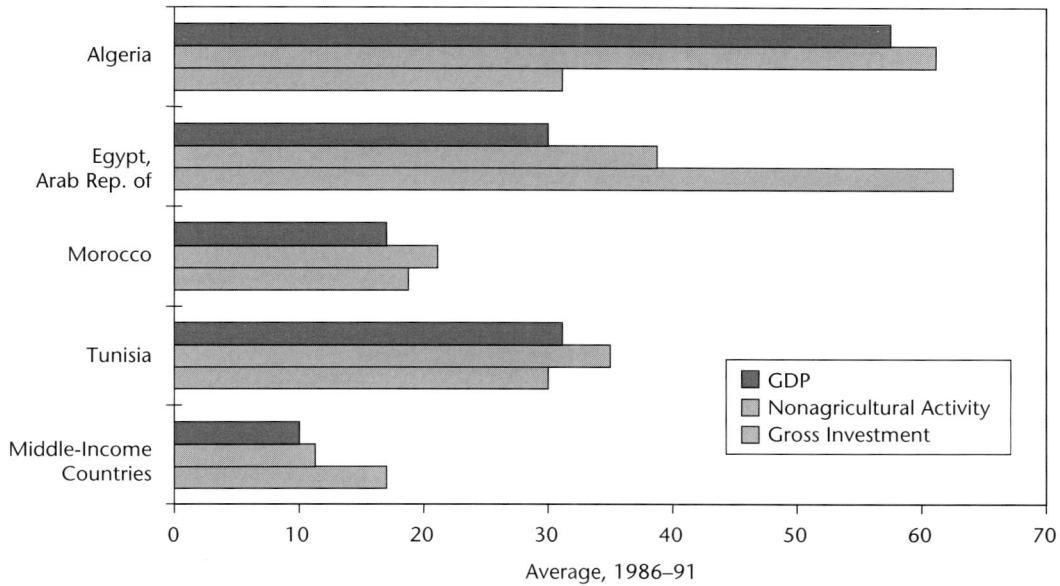

Average, 1986–91

most MENA countries during the 1980s. While the 1990s witnessed a recovery, it is unclear if it was being driven by structural reforms or simply cyclical fluctuations. Decreasing factor productivity can be explained in part by overregulated economies where distortions in the relative prices of capital and labor proliferated. Many MENA countries behaved as capital-abundant countries when, in fact, factor proportions indicated a relative abundance of labor, stemming mainly from high population growth rates. Subsidized interest rates, which became negative in real terms, and investment subsidies provided incentives for distorted choices of capital-intensive technologies. At the same time, the private sector received little boost from international markets because of too-high tariffs and an antiexport bias. Economies have been dominated by public enterprises with large-scale, capital-intensive units. The share of the government in economic production now stands out in world statistics (see figure 1.2).

The agricultural sector has also been negatively affected by poorly planned rural development strategies. Policies related to land tenure, women's access to land, water, import and export restrictions, agricultural price controls, marketing mechanisms, and restrictions on the formation of local organizations contributed to the reduction of productivity in the agricultural sector and the impoverishment of small farmers.

Weak conflict management institutions also may have contributed to the economic collapse. External shocks are only partial explanations for the economic crisis, as other regions and countries were affected by comparable or harder shocks but did not experience a collapse; in fact, some countries continued to grow quickly after a short adjustment period. Another explanation is that countries in the region lacked conflict management institutions. This made them react to the growing current account deficit by going on unsustainable, external-borrowing binges. When repayment capacity was approaching, fiscal and exchange rate adjustments were delayed. This led to increases in inflation, and when adjustment measures were finally introduced, they had huge distributional impacts brought about by changes in key relative prices (the real exchange rate, real wages, and rural and urban terms of trade). The confrontation between different socioeconomic groups trying to recover part of the wealth lost during the adjustment delayed recovery and hampered growth (see box 1.1).

In this context, globalization brings new opportunities but also new risks, and it imposes new challenges to social protection systems. As the world economies become closer, the welfare of their populations has the potential to increase as cheaper goods and services become available, new technologies and knowledge are diffused, and investors gain access to international capital markets. New opportunities and benefits, however, come hand-in-hand with new risks and costs. As local producers face increased competition and some go out of business, economies become more vulnerable to swings in capital flows, and monetary and fiscal policies can no longer be used to stimulate growth in a sustainable way and to finance the growing demands of the social sectors. Even if economies are prepared to maximize the benefits of globalization, during the transition process some individuals may become worse off. This occurs as the productive structure of the economy changes (some subsectors contract while others expand), but also as the public sector rationalizes the use of human resources. While in the medium-term the benefits of globalization can outweigh the costs, the costs are likely to be higher during the transition process. Public social protection systems then face the challenge of responding to an increasing demand for social protection with a decreasing amount of public resources (see box 1.2).

To minimize the risks and maximize opportunities, MENA countries need to accelerate institutional reforms to promote private-sector-led growth. As discussed in chapter 3, traditional social protection systems cannot substitute for structural reform. A precondition to reducing social risks is promoting private-sector-led growth. This would require establishing institutions conducive to a business environment that rewards investment and innovation. To achieve this, governments need to design

---

BOX 1.1

## Where Did All the Growth Go? External Shocks, Social Conflict, and Growth Collapses

This title describes well the situation in many MENA countries: the variability in oil prices, the instability of the peace process in some countries and internal conflict in others, and the loss of the development momentum form a significant part of the greater regional picture. Understanding the interplay of these characteristics is important for setting social insurance mechanisms with the dual objective of fostering growth (for instance, through higher and better management of savings) and offering effective and affordable protection to the population at large, both the poor and the vulnerable nonpoor. For MENA, a critical question is why so many countries in the region grew at high rates in the 1960s and 1970s but did so poorly thereafter. During that period, economic performance in MENA was not only comparable to that in East Asia, but actually superior in many respects. MENA countries had higher rates of labor and TFP than the East Asian tigers. The reputation of the East Asian miracle rests entirely on the fact that productivity growth, and hence output growth, collapsed in MENA after 1973 but not in Asia. The growth of output per worker continued at similar rates in East Asia but was sharply reduced in MENA. After 1973, the reduction in total factor productivity growth accounts for virtually all of the growth collapse in MENA.

An explanation based on external shocks is only a partial explanation for MENA, since other regions and countries were affected by comparable or harder shocks but did not experience a collapse, and in fact, some continued to grow quickly after a short adjustment period. Another explanation is that countries in the region lack conflict management institutions.

This means that, during periods of recovery that followed, social groups had two choices: to share equally the losses made during adjustment (a cooperative approach that aims to undo, in relative terms, the costs of adjustment) or to try to get back what they had before the last cycle (a noncooperative approach—albeit socially just under certain conditions). The absence of conflict management institutions gives rise to greater suspicion about others' motives and leads to a higher probability of opportunistic action by a rival group(s). When conflict management institutions are strong, distributional outcomes are less sensitive to any group's opportunistic behavior aimed at obtaining a disproportionate share of available resources.

An empirical investigation approximating the presence and strength of conflict management mechanisms by variables measuring the rule of law, bureaucratic quality, corruption, expropriation risk, government repudiation of contracts, ethnolinguistic fragmentation, and the presence of civil liberties, freedom of speech, political rights or parties, and so on, suggests that these are as important, and often more important, for explaining the diverse economic performance of countries subjected to shocks as other

*(Box continues on the following page.)*

---

**BOX 1.1    (continued)**

variables conventionally considered in comparative studies, such as outward orientation and openness of the economy, the size of the public sector, external borrowing, and so on. The shocks MENA countries will be subjected to in the future are likely to increase beyond the volatility induced by changes in oil prices as the countries become more integrated into the world economy as a result of globalization. The role of good governance and conflict management institutions can be critical in bringing MENA back to the growth rates it experienced in the 1960s and 1970s.

**Sources:** Rodrik 1999; Easterly and others 1993.

---

and enforce necessary regulations. The good news is that structural reforms seem to be gaining momentum despite a slow start in the early 1990s. Indeed, in different countries a series of adjustment and liberalization programs has been introduced that aims to enhance economic efficiency. While during the early 1990s privatization proceeds were creating negligible amounts of public revenue (less than US$25 million before 1992), by the late 1990s the amounts approximated US$2 billion (see figure 1.3). Tunisia has been the regional pioneer in this area, and Algeria, despite its stop-and-go record with privatization, has effectively sold or liquidated almost one-third of its public enterprises. The Tunisian government is privatizing half of the remaining public enterprises. Significant progress is also being observed in Egypt, Jordan, Lebanon, Morocco, and the Republic of Yemen.

### The Constraints to Full Employment

The current rigid structure of labor markets is a source of concern as the labor force continues to grow rapidly and public sector employment is reduced. During the boom years, public sector employment helped to absorb a growing labor force. As public budgets become constrained, forcing governments to reduce redundancies, the private sector is expected to take the lead. Labor markets, however, remain highly regulated, making it difficult to respond flexibly to exogenous shocks. While unemployment is generally below 10 percent for middle-income economies, it has reached high levels in MENA: more than 30 percent in Egypt and Tunisia and nearly 60 percent in Algeria (see figure 1.4).

Labor markets in MENA countries have been shaped by macroeconomic and trade policies implemented during the oil boom that are now out of step with economic reality. The oil boom years saw an expansion of the public sector, including teachers and personnel employed

---

**BOX 1.2**

---

## Globalization and Rising Demand for Social Protection

While globalization reduces the ability of governments to supply social protection, it may at the same time increase the demand for social protection. Globalization is affecting the developing countries' ability to raise taxes in several ways. At the macro and industrial level, taxes are being reduced through loss of revenue arising from reductions in tariffs in addition to the disappearance of export duties, development of common markets, pressures to reduce domestic enterprise taxes and increase international competitiveness, more generous tax incentives to foreign investors who are also increasingly using territories where taxes on profits are lower, and transfer pricing techniques, including payments for the use of trademarks.

Globalization is also affecting revenue from personal income taxes, including taxes on financial income. Often the easy availability of tax-free, foreign options implies that countries are reluctant to tax incomes from interest, dividends, and capital gains for fear capital will move abroad. This implies that the burden of taxation is progressively falling on less mobile factors, especially on labor.

But the demand for social protection may increase for many reasons. First, globalization is likely to create expectations on the part of the citizens of developing countries that the social policies of other, especially more advanced, countries should be introduced in their own countries. This demonstration effect can relate to policies on unemployment compensation, pensions, social assistance, universal education up to a certain age, and so on.

Second, globalization may shake up what have been perceived as traditional economic arrangements but are, in effect, protective walls arising from implicit or explicit government subsidies. Those benefiting from such policies would experience economic hardships, and it is likely that they would call for compensatory measures of one form or another, from monetary compensation to active measures for reemployment.

Third, the speed of technological change, the opening up of markets, and structural reforms are creating opportunities for some individuals and destroying positional rents for others (both are positive developments). But at the same time, statistics from many countries indicate that an increase in inequality is a fairly general phenomenon affecting many countries. The poor (in terms of income, wealth, and human capital endowments) cannot take advantage of the emerging opportunities, and growing inequality can lead to increasing calls on governments and international institutions to address this phenomenon.

Fourth, the combination of globalization and large capital movements, which may be induced by speculation rather than by fundamental factors, may have introduced more instability into the international financial system. Though it is not clear whether globalization makes the international financial system more unstable, financial crises generate economic hardships and highlight the need for safety nets in countries that traditionally

*(Box continues on the following page.)*

**BOX 1.2    (continued)**

had not felt the need for them. The demand for safety nets may survive the end of crises and may lead to an increased role of the government in providing social protection.

In conclusion, international developments may have reduced the countries' ability to raise the level of taxation that would be necessary to finance programs aimed at social protection. To meet the rising demand for social protection, governments need to use existing public expenditures more efficiently, try to reign in private expenditures, and develop regulations that increase the synergy between public and private and formal and informal mechanisms of social protection.

**Source:** Tanzi and Chu 2000.

FIGURE 1.3

## Privatization Revenue in the MENA Region

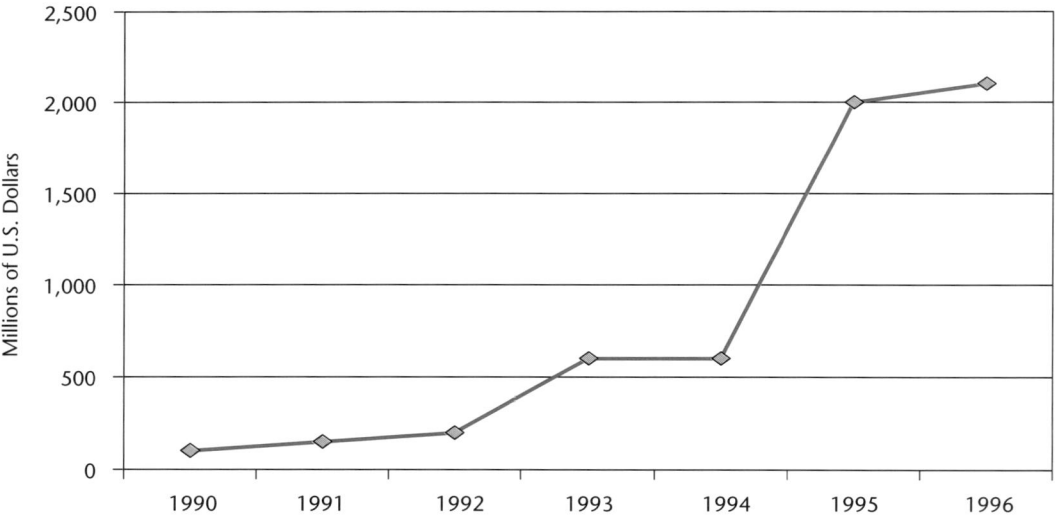

**Source:** Economic Research Forum Indicators 1998.

in state-owned enterprises and public administration. Though some of this expansion was necessary, over-recruitment also served a social protection function. In all countries, over-recruitment of teachers, workers in state-owned enterprises, and public administration personnel occurred. The share of civilian government employment worldwide accounts for about 11 percent of total employment, but for MENA countries it stands at 17.5 percent (see figure 1.5 and table 1.3). This figure is

FIGURE 1.4

## Regional Unemployment in the Early and Late 1990s

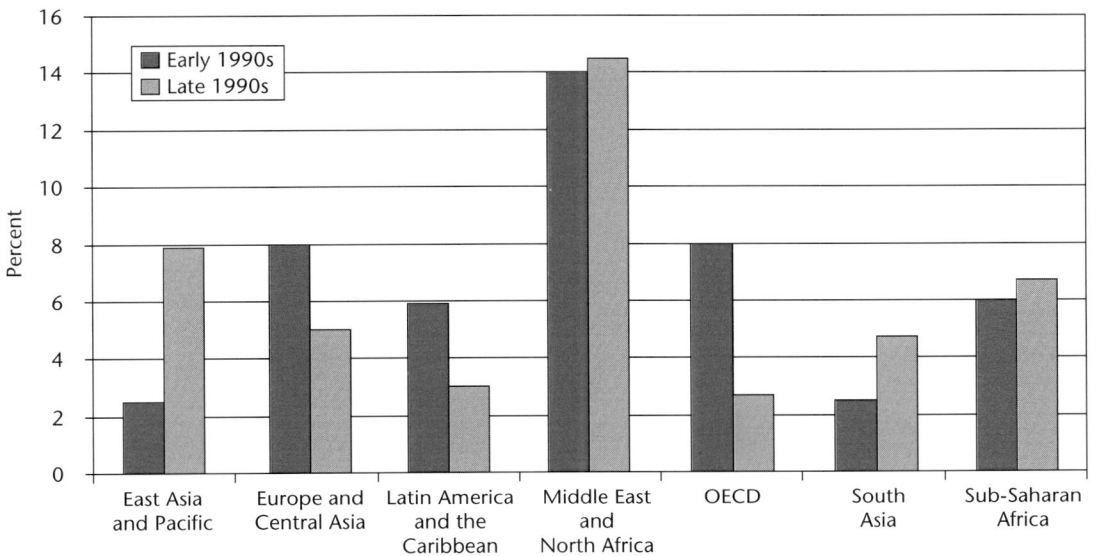

**Source:** World Bank, *World Development Report (WDR),* various years.

FIGURE 1.5

## Size of Government in the MENA Region

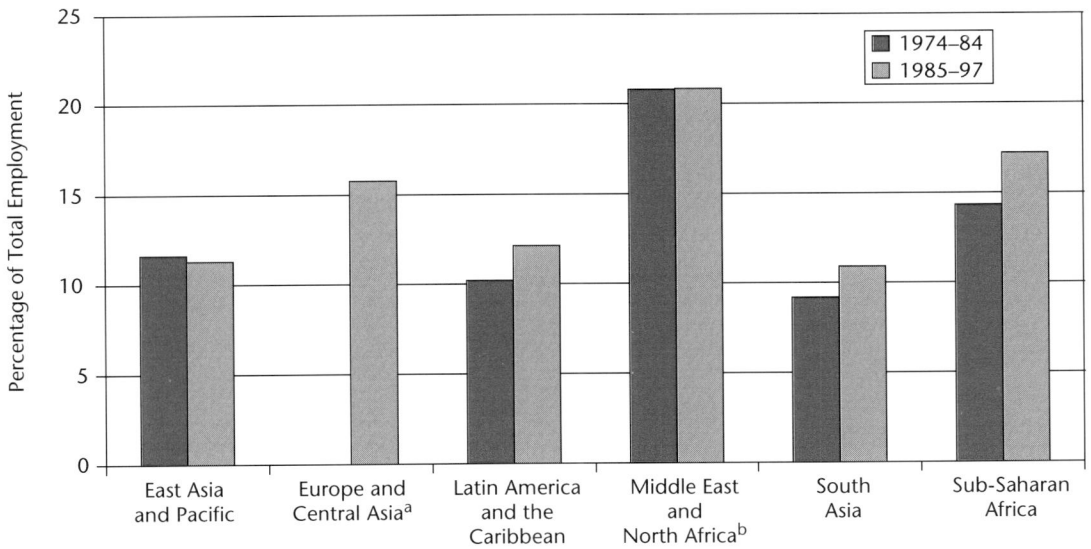

a. Data for Europe and Central Asia not available before 1989.
b. Most recent year for MENA is 1996.
**Source:** World Bank.

**TABLE 1.3**

## Government Employment As a Percentage of Total Employment in the 1990s

| Country | Total Government Employment[a] | Health and Education | Total Excluding Health and Education | Percentage of Government Employment Excluding Health and Education |
|---|---|---|---|---|
| Algeria | 27.6 | 11.3 | 16.3 | 59.1 |
| Egypt, Arab Rep. of | 28.2 | 6.8 | 21.4 | 75.9 |
| Jordan | 25.4 | 8.5 | 16.9 | 66.5 |
| Lebanon | 15.1 | 5.5 | 9.6 | 63.6 |
| Morocco | 11.0 | 3.7 | 7.3 | 66.4 |
| Tunisia | 14.9 | 7.3 | 7.6 | 51.0 |
| West Bank and Gaza | 26.2 | 9.6 | 16.6 | 63.4 |
| Yemen, Republic of | 24.0 | 3.2 | 20.8 | 86.7 |

a. This category includes the armed forces, except for the West Bank and Gaza, and it excludes parastatals.
**Source:** Schiavo-Campo, de Tommaso, and Mukherjee 1997.

much lower for other developing regions—for example, 9 percent in Latin America and the Caribbean, 7 percent in Sub-Saharan Africa, and 6 percent in Asia. Only in Lebanon and Morocco is this share lower than the world average. Figures are particularly high in the case of Egypt, where 28.2 percent of the total labor force is employed in government services. At the same time, a large part of the industrial and urban labor force became eligible for formal modes of social protection such as health benefits, retirement, and unemployment insurance. In many cases, strong unions evolved to protect the interests of public enterprise employees, gradually extending to other urban and industrial workers.

Private sector employment has remained constrained by high tariffs with an antiexport bias, as well as by significant job security provisions and costly employment benefits. These rigid institutional structures have led to the countries' inability to absorb a growing labor supply. For instance, as the labor market imbalance grew, average real wages did not fall in the formal private sector, except in Egypt, and the number of unemployed continued to increase. Given budgetary constraints, adjustments took place in the public sector. For instance, between 1988 and 1995, wages paid in the public sector in Algeria declined on average by about 1.7 percent per year. In contrast, in the private sector, between 1991 and 1994, real wages declined by only 4 percent. In Morocco, real wages stagnated between 1985 and 1995, although real increases from improved labor force composition occurred after 1990. Similarly, in Tunisia, real wages remained unchanged between 1983 and 1993 despite growing unemployment. Egypt constitutes a special case, with real wages falling considerably (close to 50 percent) between 1982 and 1985 in every sector, while employment expanded.

The decline in oil prices reduced the ability of governments to act as employers of last resort and put pressure on labor markets. First, lower revenue from oil caused investment (mostly public) as a proportion of GDP to fall across the region, with associated negative impacts on medium-term growth and employment generation. Second, public budgets came under pressure, and earlier policies of using the public sector as an employer of last resort were halted or reversed, leading to a decline in public sector employment in countries such as Algeria and Egypt. Third, countries with significant emigration, such as Egypt and Jordan, faced falling demand for their citizens abroad and substantial repatriations, particularly after the Iran-Iraq and Gulf wars.

As a consequence, countries have witnessed an increase in unemployment as well as an expansion of the informal sector. In 1995, unemployment rates in urban areas ranged from 11 percent in Egypt to 21 percent in Algeria. Generally, unemployment is worse among females and persons between the ages of 15 and 24. The incidence of unemployment in countries with major labor market imbalances, such as Morocco, seems to be worsening more quickly among older workers, changing the nature of the problem from one of unemployed dependents to one of unemployed household heads. Rising unemployment among the less educated, as seen in Algeria and Morocco, is also of great concern, particularly from a poverty perspective. Informal employment has generally grown in the region since the end of the oil boom. In Morocco, about one-half of all jobs created between 1985 and 1993 were in the informal sector. Little is known about the behavior of informal wages over time, although it is likely that these have fallen as the formal sector became increasingly less able to absorb new labor market entrants.

The challenges facing MENA countries are considerable, particularly given that the growth rate of labor supply continues to be high by international standards. This largely reflects high population growth rates (2 to 3 percent) and additional inflows to the labor force from increasing female participation rates (see table 1.4). Labor supply growth in urban areas is particularly important in countries such as Egypt and Morocco because of migration from rural to urban areas. In most cases, the growth rate of the labor force has exceeded the growth rate of employment. In Algeria, for example, private sector employment grew at nearly twice the rate of public sector employment from 1985 to 1989 (7.2 and 3.8 percent per year, respectively), but was insufficient to absorb more than 50 percent of the new labor force entrants. In Morocco, between 1986 and 1995, urban formal employment increased by 1.5 million jobs, but the urban labor force increased by nearly 2 million. In contrast, Egypt's public sector employment grew at an annual rate of 3.7 percent during the period from 1986 to 1995, while the private sector grew by only 1.9 per-

TABLE 1.4

**Percentage of Regional Population and Labor Force Growth Rates, 1990–99**

| Region | Population, 1990–99 | Population 15–64, 1990–99 | Labor Force, 1990–99 |
|---|---|---|---|
| East Asia and Pacific | 1.3 | 1.4 | 1.5 |
| Europe and Central Asia | 0.2 | 0.5 | 0.6 |
| Latin America and the Caribbean | 1.7 | 2.1 | 2.5 |
| Middle East and North Africa | 2.2 | 3.0 | 3.1 |
| South Asia | 1.9 | 2.1 | 2.5 |
| Sub-Saharan Africa | 2.6 | 2.6 | 2.6 |
| High income | 0.6 | 0.8 | 0.9 |

**Source:** World Bank, *WDR*, various years; World Bank, *WDI 2000*, 2000b.

cent. Thus, overall employment growth in Egypt was 2.6 percent per year, slightly below the 2.7 percent annual growth rate of the labor force.

The need to downsize the public sector due to high, pent-up unemployment adds additional pressure to the labor markets. In general, pent-up unemployment in the public sector is high. For example, in Egypt the initial estimate for labor redundancies in public enterprises was approximately 10 percent, but in practice this figure proved to be closer to 35 percent. In Morocco, 23 percent of public enterprises had very small returns (lower than 5 percent), 36 percent made losses, and the 14 largest public enterprises produced an annual average loss that reached more than 2 percent of GDP by 1992. In Algeria, more than 500,000 employees were retrenched during 1990–98, and the pace of adjustment has accelerated recently. Still, restructuring of the large public sector will need to take place despite the fact that the official unemployment rate has risen to 29 percent.

Most regional forecasts consider that the unemployment situation will continue to deteriorate, with potential negative impacts on poverty. On most accounts, unemployment is not expected to start declining before 2010. Given the strong linkages between unemployment and poverty, rising unemployment poses important challenges to the social protection system. First, the increased informalization of labor markets represents a relative shift from high-paying to low-paying jobs and reduces labor incomes for many households. Second, declining informal sector wages, as in Egypt, reduce household incomes further. Third, rising unemployment among older workers and among the less educated pushes nonpoor households below the poverty line and makes some poor households even poorer.

As a result, many economies have started to reform their labor laws and regulations in areas such as job security, separation compensation, and wage regulations (such as collective bargaining and minimum wages).

However, there are still issues that are hampering positive outcomes. In Algeria, compared to the old severance system (before the introduction of unemployment insurance), the new system is more expensive to firms that now pay severance (maximum of three months' salary, plus an initiating fee and a 2.5 percent payroll contribution for remaining workers). In Tunisia, modifications were made to labor legislation to revise the representation of workers and conflict resolution procedures, and to simplify layoff and recruitment procedures, but there is still government involvement in the case of retrenchments in either private or public enterprises.

## Demographic Factors and Growing Demand for Basic Services and Infrastructure

Demographic factors have important impacts on the demand for basic infrastructure such as sewerage and electricity, natural resources and environmental services such as water and clean air, and basic services such as health, education, and pensions. Today, one of the common characteristics of MENA countries is the continuing existence of high population growth rates (see section 1.2.). These demographic factors will put pressures on the supply of basic physical infrastructure and natural resources. This is particularly worrisome in the case of water, which is scarce in the region. Looking forward, as fertility rates decrease and life expectancies increase, the share of the elderly population will expand, boosting health and pension expenditures. Policymakers need to be aware of these demographic changes, since influencing them and reacting to them take considerable time. This section briefly discusses the most critical problems and risks associated with demographic trends in the MENA region.

*Water.* Water reserves in MENA are lower than in any other region and are being depleted quickly. The MENA region is the driest in the world, and its water reserves are shrinking (see figure 1.6). Although Iraq and Lebanon appear to have adequate renewable water supplies relative to their populations, the Republic of Yemen's water availability per capita per year is little more than 241 cubic meters, Jordan's is 148 cubic meters, and Kuwait's is only 11 cubic meters. International standards suggest that minimum consumption levels should approximate 1,700 cubic meters per capita per year. In 1993, annual water consumption in Libya, Saudi Arabia, the Republic of Yemen, and the Gulf states, and more recently in Jordan, exceeded renewable supplies. Each year, Jordan and the Republic of Yemen withdraw 25 to 30 percent more from their aquifers than what is being replenished.

Growing urbanization will severely constrain water consumption per capita. Urbanization increases per capita water consumption and the competition among human consumption, irrigation, and industrial use.

FIGURE 1.6

## Renewable Water Resources per Capita, by Region

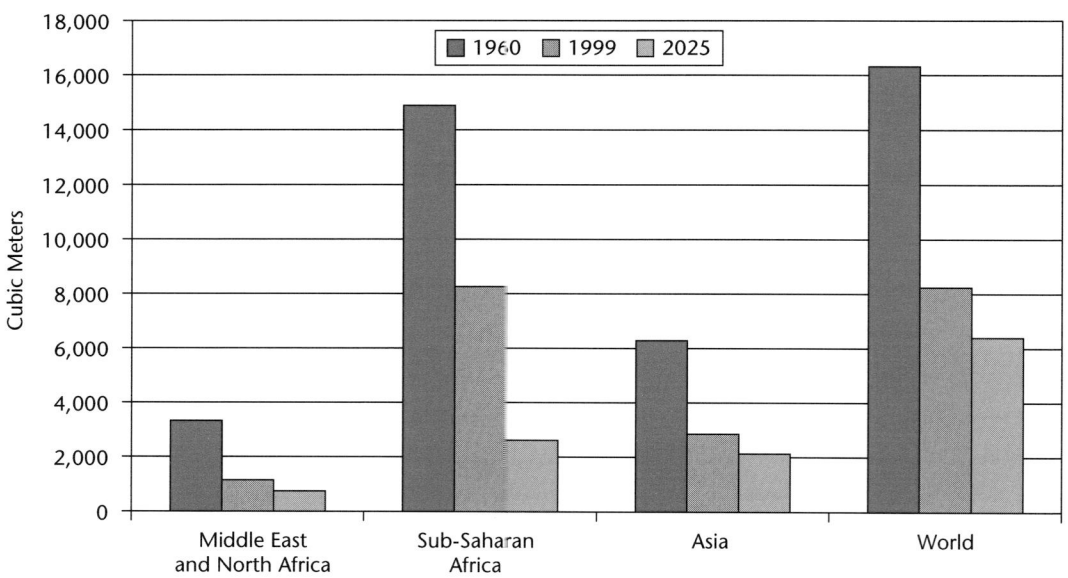

Source: World Bank, *WDI 2001*, 2001h.

Urban areas in the region are growing by more than 4 percent per year. By 2025 the share of the population living in urban areas will increase from 60 to 75 percent, and the share of renewable water supplies they absorb will rise from the current 6 percent to more than 20 percent. Overall population growth in the region will limit water consumption to only 1,250 cubic meters per person per year, on average, compared to 7,500 cubic meters in Sub-Saharan Africa and 23,000 cubic meters in Latin America and the Caribbean. The problem is aggravated by inefficient water management and high system losses. Moreover, the inadequate supply of safe water in urban areas is forcing even the poor to purchase water from private vendors at very high prices.

The scarcity of water imposes serious public health risks. About 45 million people in the region (nearly 16 percent of the population) lack access to safe water. In addition, nearly 80 million people in the region lack access to safe sanitation. Children below the age of 14 are particularly vulnerable, and they account for nearly 43 percent of the MENA region's population. Waterborne diseases, especially diarrheal diseases, are second only to respiratory diseases as a cause of mortality and morbidity among this age group.[4] According to a recent study by the United Nations Development Programme (UNDP), increasing the availability of uncontaminated water supplies can reduce the incidence of water-borne diseases in rural and urban areas by one-third (see box 1.3).

*Basic services, infrastructure, and transportation.* Population growth is rapidly increasing the demand for basic services, including education and health. In the Republic of Yemen, for example, the number of students in basic education is expected to more than double by 2020 (from 2.1 million in 1995 to 5.7 million in 2020), while health expenditures in reproductive health services are expected to double by 2020. Demands are increasing at a pace that dwarfs the Republic of Yemen's rate of economic growth. Moreover, the government is trying to meet these demands in the face of stagnant incomes.

While access to basic services, such as solid waste disposal and electricity, have expanded dramatically, some segments of the population, particularly low-income groups, remain underserved. In many cities of the region, especially in the poorer areas, the municipal solid waste disposal and sewerage are inadequate. In Jordan and Morocco, one-third of the urban population lacks adequate sewerage services. The inadequacy of basic infrastructure can lead to problems as diverse as disease, traffic congestion, environmental degradation, crime, and unemployment.

In terms of transportation, rail services represent the cheapest mode in many countries in MENA; however, low tariffs threaten the financial viability of railway companies. Road transportation lacks the government's attention to road maintenance and the needs of the rural poor. Major challenges include (a) a better understanding of the needs of the rural poor, (b) the creation and improvement of rural access infrastructure (tracks and trails) that can be used by nonmotorized transportation aids, (c) the promotion of affordable transportation aids such as bicycles, and (d) improved community involvement in the identification and management of rural access projects. Improved rural access can increase the attendance at primary schools, as has been demonstrated in a recent World Bank Operations Evaluation Department study in Morocco.

*Pensions and health expenditures.* Although the population in MENA countries remains relatively young, as fertility rates decrease and life expectancies increase, the elderly population will start to grow faster than the young population, putting pressure on the finances of the public pension and health insurance systems. Over the next 25 years, it is expected that the elderly population in the region will grow at close to 4 percent per year, while the total population will grow at 1.4 percent. Although the demographic transition is a slow process, it demands early action. Indeed, reforms to health and pension systems take time to prepare and their full impacts can only be observed after several (10 to 15) years. Therefore, it is recommended that governments not underestimate the magnitude of the problem and delay policy reforms.

**BOX 1.3**

### Transportation and Poverty in the West Bank and Gaza

Three villages, two in the West Bank and a refugee camp in the Gaza Strip, were selected to assess the importance of transportation in the lives of the Palestinian poor. These villages are located in areas that the 1998 World Bank poverty assessment identified as having high levels of poverty. The village of Tamoom near Nablus in the West Bank is primarily agricultural, while the village of Yamoun near Jenin relies principally on income from work in Israel. In the refugee camp near Deir el Balah in the Gaza Strip, about one-quarter of the working population is engaged in fishing, another one-quarter depends on work in Israel, while the rest are employed by the Palestinian Authority at various locations in the Gaza Strip. What is striking in all three cases is the degree to which incomes and living standards in these diverse economic contexts are affected by the cost of transportation.

In Tamoom (population 10,000), because of its reliance on agriculture, the primary determinant of well-being is the availability and cost of water. Water for agriculture delivered by tanker truck costs about 12 new Israeli sheqalim (NIS) per cubic meter, even though at the spring (water source) tanker trucks buy water for between 2 and 3 NIS, making transportation costs 80 to 90 percent of the delivered cost of water. For a greenhouse in Tamoom, the cost of water accounts for almost 90 percent of input costs, and when agricultural prices are low, the cost of water can exceed the value of the output. The cost of water, therefore, has a direct bearing on incomes in Tamoom, and most of this cost is determined by the cost of transportation.

The village of Yamoun, with a population of about 14,000, is located near Jenin and is about three kilometers from the northern green line separating the West Bank from Israel. About 4,000 workers from Yamoun go to Israel to work as casual unskilled and skilled workers who earn between 120 and 180 NIS per day. To get to work in Israel, these workers must spend about 10 NIS to reach the checkpoint and another 30 NIS within Israel to reach Haifa. This means that for the average worker, a third to a quarter of gross daily income could be spent on travel to and from work. When one considers that on some days the worker may fail to obtain work, the proportion of income spent on transportation becomes even larger. These costs work out to around USc7/pass-km, which is high, and reflects the lack of any form of public transportation, with workers relying on shared taxis for most of this travel.

The story in the Gaza Strip is not much different. The refugee camp of Deir el Balah is adjacent to the coastal road, and a large number of families rely on fishing. Incomes from fishing, however, are low, with reported incomes as little as 300 NIS per month, and must be supplemented with other forms of employment, typically in construction. The inability to sell independently of a middleman causes fishermen to sell their catch at less than a third of market prices. This may be due to a lack of mechanisms to transport the catch to markets rather than selling it at the dock. A large number of inhabitants in the camp work for the Palestinian Authority, earning approximately 1,200 NIS per month. For these workers, travel to and from work by shared taxi was reported to cost

> **BOX 1.3    (continued)**
>
> approximately 200 NIS per month. Shared taxis are the only available mode of transportation, since the few available buses are used to transport college students during the day and workers going to Israel in the morning and afternoon. Public transportation would reduce the cost of work trips for these workers to a third of what they now pay.
>
> **Source:** Tharakan and Wolden 2000.

## 1.2.  Identifying Vulnerable Population Groups

The focus of a social protection system ought to go beyond the poor and concentrate on individuals who face the risk of human capital loss as a result of factors as diverse as an economic slowdown, adverse weather, disease, or changes in the demand for different types of labor and capital following structural reforms. Resulting demands for some type of social protection can then be unlimited, and given scarce resources, necessary priorities can be defined. Prioritization is a challenging process from a political and technical point of view. Politically, societies need to reach a consensus about the population groups on which government assistance programs will concentrate. From a technical point of view, identifying and targeting these groups requires considerable analytical capabilities and well-developed information and management systems. Although this type of exercise is largely outside the scope of this report, this section discusses, in general terms, which groups are most likely to require government attention across MENA countries given the current economic context. The discussion is based on the analysis of recent population and poverty trends.

### Population Trends in the MENA Region

Children will continue to be an important share of the total population. MENA countries are characterized by high population growth rates. The population in the region has more than doubled between 1970 and 1999, from 132 million to 291 million. In most countries, populations are expected to double again within the next 30 years. Some MENA countries have had success with policies for controlling population growth (see box 1.4). Even if fertility continues to decline (see table 1.5) and reaches the replacement level, 40 percent of women in the region will be of childbearing age, so the number of births will continue to increase. The implication is that the share of the population younger than 15 will continue to

---

**BOX 1.4**

---

### Success with Policies for Managing Population Growth

In Tunisia, the government established the Family Planning Association in 1968. In addition to conventional measures, it has promoted the importance of birth spacing for the health of the mother and child. Legislation has also raised the legal marriage age to 17 for women and 20 for men and has limited family benefits to the first three children of a household. Basic education is provided free of charge, and girls have equal access and practically identical enrollment rates as boys, which has contributed to reducing the fertility rate. As a result of these and other measures, the total fertility rate (TFR) in Tunisia was 2.8 children per woman in 1996 compared to 6.4 children per woman in 1970.

When the population growth rate in the Islamic Republic of Iran reached 3.2 percent in 1986, the Ministry of Health and Medical Education established a Population Committee to study the implications for food, health, education, employment, and other social services. Subsequently, the government's first and second Five-Year Development Plan included a policy to reduce population growth by increasing contraceptive coverage, girls' education levels, and women's participation in society outside the family. The contraception prevalence rate (women aged 15 to 49 using some form of contraception) now stands at 55 percent, and girls' enrollment in basic education is universal. As a result, the population growth rate has been halved (1.4 percent), and the TFR has been reduced from 6.4 children per woman in 1986 to 3.8 children per woman in 1996.

Egypt has had a formal population policy since 1966, when the national family planning program was established. The first national population policy was introduced in 1973. Between 1980 and 1996, the TFR dropped from 5.1 children per woman to 3.3 children per woman, and the contraceptive prevalence rate rose from 21 to 50 percent. The population program is still a priority for the government.

**Sources:** World Bank 1995b; Government of Egypt 1995; Government of Iran 1998.

---

be important in the years to come. The major risks faced by this population group, particularly among low-income groups, are related to poverty, mortality, lack of access to health and education services, and child labor.

The share of the working-age population in the region is also expected to expand rapidly. Indeed, the share of the population aged 15 to 49 could grow one-third faster than the total population until the year 2020. While the proportion of the population engaged in the labor force is among the lowest in the world, it has been growing faster than in other regions of the world (2.3 percent between 1990 and 1997). The increase in female labor force participation (from 8 to 25 percent between 1960 and 1995) is twice the increase observed in the rest of the world. As a

TABLE 1.5

## Trends in Fertility, Mortality, and Life Expectancy in MENA, 1970–99

| Indicator | 1970 | 1980 | 1990 | 1999 |
|---|---|---|---|---|
| Total fertility rate | 6.8 | 6.1 | 4.9 | 3.0 |
| Life expectancy at birth, female (years) | 54 | 60 | 67 | 69 |
| Life expectancy at birth, male (years) | 52 | 57 | 63 | 67 |
| Infant mortality rate (per 1,000 live births) | 134 | 96 | 61 | 44 |
| Under-five mortality rate (per 1,000 live births) | 193 | 141 | 93 | 56 |
| Total population (millions) | 132 | 175 | 237 | 291 |

**Note:** The summary measures for the above indicators are weighted by population or subgroup of population, except for infant mortality and population. Infant mortality is weighted by the number of births, and population is calculated by simple addition of the populations of all MENA countries.
**Source:** World Bank, *WDI 2001*, 2001h.

consequence, today there are 7.4 million youths entering the work force every year. As discussed in section 1.1., the major risk faced by this age group is related to unemployment. Individuals younger than 25 years of age also face the risk of not having access to sustainable health and pensions systems during their old age.

Since fertility rates tend to be higher for low-income groups, the demand for food, education, health, and clothing will be higher among these groups. In Algeria, 50 percent of poor household members are under age 15, compared to about 40 percent for nonpoor households. Income per capita within low-income households could continue to deteriorate, increasing the incidence and severity of poverty. As discussed in more depth in the next section on poverty, liquidity constraints would reduce investments of the poor in the future, that is, investments in education and health, thus perpetuating their condition.

## Poverty

Compared to other regions of the world, poverty in MENA is low. Poverty estimates are often affected by a certain degree of conceptual and statistical ambiguity. Comparisons between countries are difficult and become even more spurious between regions. Nonetheless, available estimates for 1998 show that absolute income poverty in the MENA region, measured in terms of US$1 per day,[5] was the lowest in the world (only 2.1 percent of the total MENA population). If the absolute poverty is measured in terms of US$2 per day, the MENA region would still have a lower incidence of poverty when compared with the regions of East Asia and Pacific, Latin America and the Caribbean, South Asia, and Sub-Saharan Africa (see tables 1.6 and 1.7).

Poverty incidence and the absolute number of poor, however, are on the rise. Using a US$2 per day poverty line, poverty incidence has stag-

**TABLE 1.6**

## Population Living on Less Than US$1 a Day

|  | Population (%) | | Population (millions) | |
|---|---|---|---|---|
| Region | 1987 | 1998 | 1987 | 1998 |
| East Asia and Pacific | 26.6 | 14.7 | 417.5 | 267.1 |
| Europe and Central Asia | 0.2 | 3.7 | 1.1 | 17.6 |
| Latin America and the Caribbean | 15.3 | 12.1 | 63.7 | 60.7 |
| Middle East and North Africa | 4.3 | 2.1 | 9.3 | 6.0 |
| South Asia | 44.9 | 40.0 | 474.4 | 521.8 |
| Sub-Saharan Africa | 46.6 | 48.1 | 217.2 | 301.6 |
| Total | 28.3 | 23.4 | 1,183.2 | 1,174.9 |

Source: World Bank, *WDI 2001*, 2001h.

**TABLE 1.7**

## Population Living on Less Than US$2 a Day

|  | Population (%) | | Population (millions) | |
|---|---|---|---|---|
| Region | 1987 | 1998 | 1987 | 1998 |
| East Asia and Pacific | 67.0 | 48.7 | 1,052.3 | 884.9 |
| Europe and Central Asia | 3.6 | 20.7 | 16.3 | 98.2 |
| Latin America and the Caribbean | 35.5 | 31.7 | 147.6 | 159.0 |
| Middle East and North Africa | 30.0 | 29.9 | 65.1 | 85.4 |
| South Asia | 86.3 | 83.9 | 911.0 | 1,094.6 |
| Sub-Saharan Africa | 76.5 | 78.0 | 356.6 | 489.3 |
| Total | 61.0 | 56.1 | 2,549.0 | 2,811.5 |

Source: World Bank, *WDI 2001*, 2001h.

nated between 1987 and 1998 in MENA, but the number of absolute poor has increased by more than 30 percent (table 1.7). This is also confirmed by national poverty lines. With a poverty line of US$50 a month (roughly equal to the average of the various national poverty lines used in different poverty assessments), the number of poor would be much larger: about 40 million, or 20 percent, of the total MENA population.[6] Using this poverty line, in most MENA countries the percentage of population below the poverty line has increased over the period between 1987 and 1998 (see table 1.8). In Tunisia, although the poverty incidence has stagnated (7.6 percent in 1995 compared to 7.4 percent in 1990), the number of poor has increased from 600,000 in 1990 to 690,000 in 1995 as a result of population growth (see World Bank 2000a). The number of poor in Morocco is estimated to be 5.3 million in 1998–99 (or 19 percent of the total population), compared to 3.4 millions in 1990–91 (corresponding to 13.1 percent of the population). See World Bank 2001c.

Sluggish GDP growth, collapse in employment creation, and growing inequality are key forces behind the increase in poverty. In Morocco, slow

TABLE 1.8

## Percentage of Population below National Poverty Lines

| Country | Survey Year | Rural | Urban | National | Survey Year | Rural | Urban | National |
|---------|-------------|-------|-------|----------|-------------|-------|-------|----------|
| Algeria | 1988 | 16.6 | 7.3 | 12.2 | 1995 | 30.3 | 14.7 | 22.6 |
| Egypt, Arab Rep. of | 1981 | 24.2 | 22.5 | 26.0 | 1995–96 | 23.3 | 22.5 | 22.9 |
| Jordan | 1987 | 23.7 | 16.6 | 18.7 | 1997 | 18.2 | 10.0 | 11.7 |
| Morocco | 1990–91 | 18.0 | 7.6 | 13.1 | 1998–99 | 27.2 | 12.0 | 19.0 |
| Tunisia | 1990 | 13.1 | 3.5 | 7.4 | 1995 | 13.9 | 3.6 | 7.6 |
| Yemen, Republic of | 1992 | 19.2 | 18.6 | 19.1 | 1998 | 26.9 | 21.8 | 25.4 |

**Sources:** World Bank 1999a; World Bank 2001b; Yemen Household Budget Survey 1992 and 1998; World Bank 2001c; World Bank 2000a; World Bank 1991; IFPRI 1997.

economic growth during the 1990s accounted for roughly 84 percent of the increase in poverty at the national level. The remaining 16 percent of the increase is explained by a more unequal income distribution. Inequality patterns are roughly the same in both urban and rural areas (see World Bank 2001c).[7] The richest 50 percent of the Moroccan population makes almost 75 percent of the total expenditure, while the top 10 percent accounts for more than 30 percent of the total expenditure on consumption (see table 1.9). A better understanding of the determinants of the income distribution in the region demands further research. Important factors to consider include growing urbanization, lack of education, and increasing unemployment. In general, the distribution of income has had a tendency to deteriorate, but for the region as a whole, inequality is less pronounced than in other regions. In Tunisia, despite the increase in average income, poverty has stagnated between 1990 and 1995. This can

TABLE 1.9

## Income Inequality in MENA, 1990s

| Country | Survey Year | Gini Index[a] | Percentage Share of Consumption | | | | | | |
|---------|-------------|---------------|--------|--------|--------|--------|--------|---------|---------|
| | | | Lowest 10% | Lowest 20% | Second 20% | Third 20% | Fourth 20% | Highest 20% | Highest 10% |
| Algeria | 1995 | 35.3 | 2.8 | 7.0 | 11.6 | 16.1 | 22.7 | 42.6 | 26.8 |
| Egypt, Arab Rep. of | 1995 | 28.9 | 4.4 | 9.8 | 13.2 | 16.6 | 21.4 | 39.0 | 25.0 |
| Jordan | 1997 | 36.4 | 3.3 | 7.6 | 11.4 | 15.5 | 21.1 | 44.4 | 29.8 |
| Morocco | 1990–91 | 39.3 | 2.7 | 6.6 | 10.5 | 15.0 | 21.5 | 46.2 | 30.5 |
| | 1998–99 | 39.5 | 2.6 | 6.5 | 10.6 | 14.8 | 21.3 | 46.8 | 31.2 |
| Tunisia | 1990 | 40.2 | 2.3 | 5.9 | 10.4 | 15.3 | 22.1 | 46.3 | 30.7 |
| Yemen, Republic of | 1992 | 39.5 | 2.3 | 6.1 | 10.9 | 15.3 | 21.6 | 46.1 | 30.8 |

a. See World Bank 2000.
**Note:** Gini Index indicates income inequality. The lower the ratio, the less severe the income equality. Income inequality is derived from the distribution of expenditures across the population in the absence of income surveys. This is not largely different from total expenditures on consumption.
**Sources:** World Bank, *WDR 2000/2001,* 2001i; World Bank 2001c; World Bank 2000a; World Bank 1999a.

only be explained by the deterioration of income distribution.[8] The story is different in the case of Algeria where, between 1988 and 1995, the share of income going to the poorest deciles did not change, while the share going to the wealthiest decile declined from 33 to 27 percent.

Although poverty is still more pronounced in rural areas, urban poverty in MENA is on the rise due to rural-urban migration. In Algeria, in 1988 and 1995, almost 70 percent of the poor lived in rural areas. The head count index in rural areas (close to 19 percent) was twice as high as in urban regions. In Egypt, Morocco, and Tunisia, poverty also remains largely a rural phenomenon. Nonetheless, there is some evidence that poverty incidence is growing faster in urban areas than in rural areas, in part as a result of migration from the fields to the cities, particularly among small landowners and their families, given a stagnant agricultural sector.

## Vulnerable Population Groups

Given the types of risks facing the MENA region and current population and poverty trends, governments may need to concentrate on five non-mutually exclusive population groups: (a) the poor; (b) children, particularly low-income children; (c) small landowners; (d) first-time job seekers and low-skilled workers; and (e) the elderly.

*The poor.* We have seen that poverty is likely to continue on an upward trend both in absolute and relative terms. At the same time, population growth will increase the demand for basic services. Many of the poor, who tend to have larger families, face the risk of being excluded. The poor are also more limited in the types of instruments that they can use to hedge against various risks. They also lack access to capital markets and may be unable to invest in human capital or engage in high-risk, high-return activities.

*Children.* Children are a particularly vulnerable group among low-income populations. The MENA region has the lowest participation of children in the labor force compared to other developing regions, but child labor, though often hard to capture in conventional statistics, remains high in the Republic of Yemen, Morocco, and Egypt. Children are among those with the highest poverty rates. For example, in Morocco children (below the age of 15) have higher poverty rates (24 percent) than adults (16 percent). This is also true for Jordan (see figure 1.7). Regarding health issues, in countries such as Djibouti, Morocco, and the Republic of Yemen, child and infant mortality rates remain considerably high. In terms of education, while enrollment rates in primary education have increased dramatically in all MENA countries, repetition and drop-

FIGURE 1.7

**Poverty Rates by Age in Jordan, 1997**

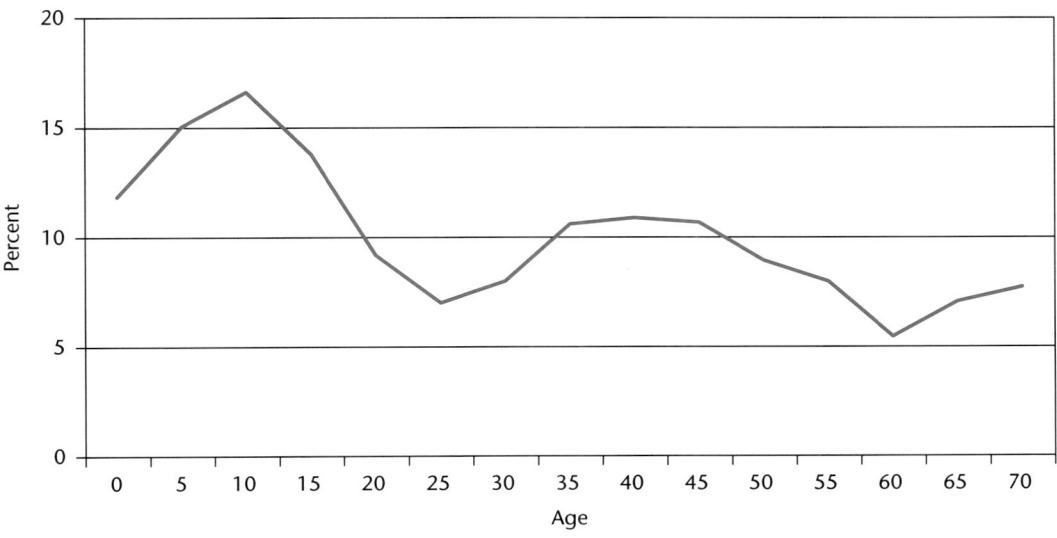

**Source:** Shaban and Ghaida 2000.

out rates remain considerably high, particularly among low-income girls. In the case of Algeria, for instance, of every 100 children who enter the first grade, only 12 will graduate from high school.

*Small landowners.* The data reviewed in the previous section suggest that poverty remains a rural phenomenon, often concerning small landowners. Indeed, land tenure in the region suffers from inefficient and inequitable distribution, lack of property rights, and inappropriate pricing mechanisms. Land tenure has the following characteristics: (a) Landholders are mainly small and, for many, farm size is economically inadequate; (b) there is extreme fragmentation of holdings and prevalence of joint ownership resulting from Islamic inheritance law; (c) insecurity of tenure and lack of land titles also cause inefficient and unsustainable exploitation, as well as constraints in access to official credit (collateral issue); (d) common lands, that is, those without titles, are exploited through customary rights; (e) small landholders and peasant agriculture coexist with a structure of tenancy and sharecropping; and (f) land markets are virtually nonexistent and are encumbered by costly and time-consuming bureaucratic processes. In Morocco, 69 percent of the rural farmers have less than 5 hectares and own only 23 percent of the land, while less than 1 percent of farmers have 50 hectares or more and own 15 percent of the land. In rural Tunisia, 43 percent of farm families own less than 5 hectares and control only 6 percent of the arable land. In Jordan, land tenure is characterized by a large number of small holdings. Three-quarters of farmers either have no land or have landholdings of less than 5 hectares.

*First-time job seekers and low-skilled workers.* The challenge of generating employment given a fast growing labor force is considerable. The number of young first-time job seekers with no practical skills and highly academically oriented high school or university diplomas is expected to increase, and many of them face the risk of unemployment. As the economies reshape institutions in the quest for diversification, competitiveness, and innovation, there will be winners and losers. Low-skilled workers currently employed in public enterprises will have to compete for scarce jobs. The means of support for them and their families are therefore threatened.

*The elderly.* The previous section showed that as the demographic transition takes place, old-age dependency ratios will increase pressure on pension systems. At the same time, the demand for health, social services, pensions, and associated expenditures is likely to increase. These problems still may be many years down the road, but policymakers need to start addressing them today to protect current generations, particularly low-income workers, from the risk of not having access to health services and adequate pensions during old age.

# CHAPTER 2

# Assessing Current Formal and Informal Mechanisms for Social Protection

## 2.1. Managing Social Risks

As previously discussed, societies develop a series of informal and formal mechanisms to manage risks related to phenomena ranging from fluctuations in output to disease and longevity. Through these mechanisms, individuals attempt to reduce risks; mitigate risks, that is, decrease the impact of future adverse shocks; and cope with risks by reversing or reducing the impact of shocks that have already occurred. Examples of risk-reducing mechanisms include hygienic practices to prevent disease (informal) or company-based and market-driven labor standards (formal). In terms of risk mitigation, informal mechanisms include multiple jobs, reciprocal gift-giving practices, and other community arrangements, while formal mechanisms include investment portfolio diversification and damage insurance for crops or fire, for example. Risk-coping mechanisms at the informal level can be as diverse as selling real assets, migrating, borrowing from neighbors, sending children to work, or neglecting human capital. Borrowing from a bank, however, is an example of a formal risk-coping mechanism.

For a variety of reasons, private formal and informal systems[9] are not comprehensive or fully efficient from a social point of view, and governments are called to intervene. Given market failures resulting from information and coordination problems and the fact that individuals do not capture the full social costs of the risk they take, and because low-income groups may lack access to appropriate risk management instruments, governments have a role in providing formal social protection mechanisms and regulating privately managed ones. Governments' interventions in the area of social protection can reduce private incentives to invest in insurance or risk-reducing activities. Establishing the proper balance between private and public mechanisms is therefore an important, although not easily achievable, goal of social protection policy.

Governments have several instruments at their disposal that serve risk reduction, risk mitigation, and risk-coping functions. Most MENA countries have programs and instruments operating at these three levels. For instance, within the category of risk reduction, countries have usually implemented labor market initiatives and continual training programs that update workers' skills and make them less vulnerable to unemployment during a downturn. In terms of risk mitigation, the most common instruments are different types of insurance (pensions, health, and unemployment) as well as interventions to provide access to capital markets to individuals with limited assets (microcredit programs). The majority of social protection programs, however, serve a coping function. These include public works and a variety of in-kind and cash transfers. These programs provide income support to individuals in distress so that their human capital and social welfare are not compromised. Other policy instruments, usually outside the scope of the traditional social protection system, can influence risks at various levels. Macroeconomic stability and financial transparency, for instance, reduce the risk of inflation and swings in capital flows that would affect output. Efficient public health programs, such as vaccination campaigns and public infrastructure programs that expand access to safe water, reduce the risks of disease. Appropriate environmental policies reduce the risks associated with the depletion of natural resources.

The objective of this chapter is to assess the scope of informal and formal mechanisms (both public and private) in the MENA region and to evaluate the effectiveness and efficiency of the resulting social protection system in the context of the risks and vulnerabilities identified in chapter 1. An inventory of the complete list of informal and formal risk management instruments is outside the scope of this chapter. The focus is on broad categories of systems that are common to most MENA countries. In terms of informal systems, this chapter concentrates on the management of portfolios of crops, livestock, and off-farm labor; kinship networks and family support; religious charitable contributions; and migration. The chapter also looks at three formal instruments that lie outside the traditional social protection system but that are key in influencing risks and vulnerability: the education and health systems and the wide array of price controls that MENA countries have adopted to protect consumers and producers. Finally, we assess programs within the traditional social protection system that encompass ALMPs, social assistance programs, and social insurance programs. Given data constraints, private formal mechanisms are discussed only indirectly when analyzing public mechanisms. Hence, in most cases the discussion is limited to an assessment of the degree of private participation in the provision or financing of a given risk reduction, mitigation, or coping service.

## 2.2. Informal Mechanisms

Despite a large part of the poor in the MENA region being in rural areas and the agricultural sector, formal methods of social protection rarely extend to the rural population. The effects of rural unemployment, invariably at higher rates of incidence than national averages, are compounded by the structural underemployment that characterizes agricultural production, with its elements of seasonality. Rural populations also have lower access, in quality and quantity, to public services such as education and health systems, as well as to basic services such as potable water, sanitation, power, and so forth.

### Managing Portfolios of Crops, Livestock, and Off-Farm Employment

A typical farm family manages a portfolio of crops, livestock, and off-farm employment as the main coping mechanism against the effects of factors such as drought, pestilence, and natural disasters that cause disruptions in income and consumption flows. The farm family manages a portfolio comprising three main elements: (a) crop production, (b) livestock production, and (c) farm-family labor resources. They try to maintain the stability of income and consumption streams through managing the stability of this portfolio. For example, livestock are effectively stores of wealth in which the outputs of crop production are accumulated. This will allow livestock to be converted back into food through livestock sales and food purchases when crop production becomes inadequate, which is not infrequent under the highly variable rainfall conditions in the MENA region. The most critical element in the portfolio is the farm labor resources. Part of these labor resources are used on the farm, and a significant part of the farm-family resources are employed off the farm in temporary, seasonal, or permanent jobs in the agricultural sector or rural or urban areas both in the region and abroad. Such off-farm employment is different from models of part-time employment or part-time farming seen in typical industrialized economies. The most important aspect of such off-farm employment is that income transfers from those employed off the farm to the farm, invariably in a regular manner, are an essential component of farm-family income. In Tunisia, the incidence of such off-farm income is inversely related to farm size and, for smaller farms, this off-farm income is a more important source for farm investments than farm-generated income. In the Syrian Arab Republic, such income totaled an average of 35 to 40 percent of farm income.

### Kinship Networks and Families

Social organization throughout the MENA region is characterized by kinship networks, which are stable relationships on which households rely both to offset the effects of crises and to conserve or acquire resources. These networks are of vital importance in (a) spreading the risks of localized catastrophes and (b) strengthening the economic and social capital of a group over the long-term, so that it can be accessed in times of shock or stress. Studies conducted in the West Bank and Gaza illustrate that the closer the kinship and community ties, the higher the incidence of informal support, which helps to cushion the effect of economic shocks on poorer families. Conversely, informal support is lowest in the refugee camps, where dispersion and dispossession have weakened kinship relations (see box 2.1).

To cope with short-term crisis, individuals also turn to relatives. Short-term crises are often related to unexpected death or to illness requiring a doctor or hospital care. In both rural and urban areas, households living at the subsistence level rarely have savings to meet such crises, except perhaps in the form of livestock, jewelry, or rugs. If additional resources are needed, the household has limited options and often turns to close relatives for a loan or in-kind services. Relatives may render assistance back and forth, depending on who is in need. The tacit understanding is that the value of the loan or service will be repaid when

---

**BOX 2.1**

### Informal Social Support Systems in the West Bank and Gaza

Strategies adopted by poor households tend to be formed mostly within the framework of kinship, local community, and the workplace. In a study of informal support systems in the West Bank and Gaza, nearly one-half of the households reported giving assistance, mostly in the form of gifts for religious and social occasions. Only 10 percent, however, reported providing regular informal support to other individuals or their families within their kinship group, and less than 4 percent gave regular assistance to individuals or families outside their kinship group.

While most households tend to rely almost exclusively on such informal means of social support, those who are structurally denied access to the labor market, such as refugees, or those who have no access to it for a prolonged length of time, may eventually seek assistance from formal support institutions such as the Ministry of Social Affairs, the United Nations Relief and Works Agency (UNRWA) in the case of refugees, and the various charitable organizations, such as *Zakat*[10] committees.

---

**BOX 2.2**

### Coping Strategies of Poor Communities in the Republic of Yemen

To assess the coping mechanisms of poor communities in the Republic of Yemen, a 1998 social protection field study targeted communities identified as very poor by their very low levels of household income—fewer than 5,000 riyals per month (the food poverty line estimated by the statistical office of the Republic of Yemen in 1998 was approximately 2,500 riyals per month per capita, or 20,000 riyals for a household of three adults and five children). To verify that the poorest have been covered, the study asked the participants to prioritize how they would spend an additional 5,000 riyals per month. More than 85 percent said they would spend the entire amount on food; 4 percent would spend some on clothing; 4 percent on repaying loans; and fewer than 1 percent would spend some money on medicine or medical treatment. How do these families survive? It appears that informal lines of credit were their major coping strategy. More than one-half of the participants indicated that they were in debt, predominantly to relatives or neighbors (47 percent) and local retailers and traders (42 percent). The debt ranged from approximately 20,000 riyals (60 percent of participants) to 40,000 riyals (15 percent), up to 100,000 riyals (9 percent). In such poor communities, the capacity to repay is extremely low: approximately 65 percent have not paid back their debts, 15 percent have partially repaid them, and only 20 percent have fully repaid them. The study revealed that the unpaid or partly paid debt, especially to retailers and traders, was essentially a running line of credit, with the debtors paying off what they could when they were able. Debts to family and neighbors were usually much smaller and tended to be repaid quickly (or "borrowed back"). The participants did not mention public assistance programs (cash or in-kind) as regular—or even irregular—sources of urgently needed income. Indeed, very few programs of public provision had reached into these communities, and none of the participants was aware of assistance available from the Social Development Fund.

**Source:** Mitchell 1999.

---

the crisis is over (see box 2.2). However, this type of mechanism is often insufficient to manage medium-term risks or seasonal risks.

## Religious Charitable Contributions

Religious charitable contributions are an important component of MENA countries' safety nets. Islam instructs better-off Muslims to contribute to the well-being of the poor by paying *Zakat* and *Waqfs*. *Zakat* is an obligation to pay an amount to those in need. The exact amount of the *Zakat* obligation is based on a family's wealth. *Waqfs* are charitable foundations set up by wealthy people to support activities such as schools for the poor. Unlike *Zakat*, this is not an obligation, but it is highly recommended for practicing Muslims. Some countries enforce *Zakat*, while in others it is private and sporadic. The growth of *Waqfs* (except in the Islamic Republic of Iran) has become limited as a result of a combination of economic constraints and the development of formal safety nets that have reduced the community obligations. In some countries, *Zakat* funds have been organized by the state, but the administration of the resources is not always efficient. For instance, there are cases where *Zakat* funds have been collected by the state and not used. Many funds were not invested either, and inflation eroded the real value of the assets. Nevertheless, in counties such as the Republic of Yemen, the inflow of *Zakat* funds, especially during Ramadan, provides a major source of social protection. In areas where some traditional systems persist, the tribal leader may be asked for help. However, a recent study in the Republic of Yemen, where traditional systems are most widespread, shows that tribal leaders are becoming less of a source of support than in the past. In the areas under the Palestinian Authority, the dominant model for delivery of social services is through NGOs and charities using resources collected from *Zakat* and *Waqfs*. This is changing as the Palestinian Authority assumes more responsibility. Despite the recent growth in state-sponsored social protection, *Zakat* continues to be the most important source of social assistance for most of the region's poor. A problem with *Zakat* is that flows are not smooth over the year, but tend to concentrate during Ramadan. Local businessmen, however, are aware of this and are therefore willing to extend credit to the poor on the expectation of receiving repayment during Ramadan. In the case of the postrevolutionary Islamic Republic of Iran, the system of *Waqfs* has been developed very strongly. Private foundations (called *Bonyads*) assume the bulk of social protection responsibilities.

## Migration

Poverty and the need to diversify risks have had a strong impact on regional migration. During the 1970s and 1980s, intraregional migration was driven by higher wages in the oil-rich countries. The greater financial returns from working abroad, as well as the common language shared by the MENA countries, led to increased regional migration during the years of the oil boom. Expected wages in the oil-rich Arab Gulf were often four to five times higher than those earned in the urban areas of most non-oil countries. In 1985, there were more than 5 million migrant workers in the oil-exporting countries of the region, about 3.5 million of whom came from Egypt, Jordan, and the Republic of Yemen. Two mil-

## TABLE 2.1

### Worker Remittances in Select MENA Countries, 1970–99

(millions of U.S. dollars)

| Country | 1970 | 1980 | 1985 | 1990 | 1995 | 1999 |
|---|---|---|---|---|---|---|
| Algeria | 206 | 243 | 1,358 | 1,530 | 1,120 | 790 |
| Egypt, Arab Rep. of | 29 | 2,696 | 3,212 | 4,284 | 3,003 | 3,196 |
| Jordan | 16 | — | 1,022 | 429 | 1,137 | 1,460 |
| Morocco | 63 | 989 | 967 | 1,995 | 1,955 | 1,918 |
| Tunisia | 89 | 207 | 351 | 545 | 659 | 754 |
| Yemen, Republic of | 60 | — | 1,391 | 1,498 | 1,080 | — |
| Total | 463 | 5,004 | 8,301 | 10,281 | 8,954 | 9,008 |

— Not available.
**Note:** Official international remittances include both monetary transfers to banks and exchange imports.
**Source:** World Bank, *WDR,* various years.

lion of these were from rural areas. By 1990, however, the decline in oil prices, and the expulsion of Yemeni and Jordanian workers from Saudi Arabia and Kuwait as a result of the Gulf War, caused the Arab share in nonnational employment in the oil-exporting countries to be more than halved.

International migration was also driven by higher wages in the industrialized European countries, although lately the demand has shifted away from unskilled workers from the Maghreb. Migration patterns and remittance flows in MENA countries have also been affected by economic and political changes in the European countries, particularly those related to the formation of the European Union (EU). During the 1960s and until the oil crisis in 1973, only males migrated to European countries, following the traditional pattern, to send remittances home. However, when EU countries reduced the importation of labor in the 1970s because of insufficient employment creation for their own labor, three types of migration emerged. The first, family reunion migration, which already existed, became more significant. As a result, an increasing number of young people (men and women) began to migrate to Europe. The second, seasonal migration, workers employed under short-term contracts, represented a small fraction of migrants. The third, illegal migration, has risen since the adoption of the Schengen Agreement[11] in 1990 (see table 2.1). In addition to these forms of migration, there has been continued legal migration from the Maghreb to Europe (more than 2 million workers in 1993), although the decrease in employment in traditional industrial sectors (automotive, steel, textile, and chemical) has reduced the demand for unskilled workers from the Maghreb in favor of more skilled and educated Asian immigrants. These changes have resulted not only in the return of expatriates, but also in a reduced flow of hard currency remittances (see table 2.1).

TABLE 2.2

### Distribution of International Migrants in Rural Egypt, 1986–87

| Income Quintile Group[a] | Percentage of International Migrants |
| --- | --- |
| Lowest | 22.9 |
| Second | 18.5 |
| Third | 22.9 |
| Fourth | 18.4 |
| Highest | 17.4 |

**Note:** There was a total of 353 international migrants in the sample of 1,000 rural households.
a. Based on per capita income, excluding remittances.
**Source:** Adams 1991.

Remittances have often been critical to the economic survival of poor households. International and intraregional remittances can account for between 10 and 30 percent of total household income; thus they represent an important means for lifting poor households out of poverty. When remittances are included in total household income in rural Egypt, for example, the number of poor households declines by 10 percent. This may account for the fact that the poorest income quintile group in rural Egypt produced more than its proportionate share of international (including intraregional) migrants in 1986–87 (see table 2.2). Most of the labor flows between MENA countries have consisted of unskilled labor, and most migrants to European countries also appear to be unskilled.

Rural-urban migration has generally not helped to alleviate poverty. The declining share of employment in the agricultural sector (from 50 percent of the region's labor force in 1970 to 35 percent in 1996) and income fluctuations in agriculture and livestock have led many rural households to attempt to reduce their vulnerability by sending one or more members to work in urban areas. But rural-urban migration has often resulted in migration from rural to urban poverty. The migrants face inferior employment opportunities and have limited access to social services, even as they lose the safety nets provided by kinship networks in their areas of origin. This may directly affect the incidence of poverty. Migration patterns over the next few decades will depend on (a) how governments harness remittance flows with growing formal global production networks and (b) liberalization in regimes regulating trade and foreign direct investment.

### Neglect of Human Capital

Despite the wide array of informal social protection mechanisms, these mechanisms fall short of protecting the human capital of the vulnerable and poor, and call for public intervention. Other risk-coping mechanisms, such as changes in consumption patterns, male absenteeism, and child labor, complement the portfolio of choices. Unfortunately, these mechanisms are welfare-decreasing because they contribute to a deterioration of human capital. Indeed, changes in consumption patterns usually involve reducing food consumption as well as health expenditures that result in child malnutrition. The social opportunity cost of child labor has also been extensively documented. In addition, male absenteeism has negative consequences for the household and higher risks of disease (for example, HIV/AIDS) for the husband leaving the household (see box 2.3). Public policy has a role in substituting this type of risk-coping mecha-

---

**BOX 2.3**

### Coping with Liberalization: Egypt's Small Farmers

Recent liberalization measures in Egypt have linked agricultural reform to broader social and economic reforms. However, this approach—designed to increase the productivity and market orientation of larger farmers—has resulted in the elimination of a range of social security benefits for the poorer, very small farmers, thus creating a social and economic crisis for the majority of rural households. Three major impacts of the crisis are shifting consumption patterns, resulting in poorer nutrition; increased male absenteeism, resulting in intensification of women's efforts to acquire food, health care, and income; and a loss of economic opportunities in rural areas, resulting in reduced social cohesion and rising crime, including the theft of farm tools.

*Shifting household consumption patterns.* Initial evaluations of the effects of the reforms show that poor farm households are shifting their consumption patterns in an attempt to preserve assets needed for survival. This has caused a decline in food consumption and a change in dietary patterns, with households purchasing cheaper commodities with lower nutritional value.

*Male absenteeism.* Men are increasingly migrating outside rural areas or to other countries in search of employment, leaving women to maintain the survival of households with diminished revenues. Women thus spend their time in search of cheaper foodstuffs, in waiting for health services at rural health centers (which are operating with reduced budgets and personnel), in agricultural activities, and in the production and sale of handicrafts. These income-generating activities have become a pivotal part of rural households' survival strategies.

*Loss of economic opportunities.* With increasing prices and diminished opportunities for employment in rural ventures, the reforms have resulted in a decline of village social life. The cost of festive occasions has become prohibitive for many households. There has also been a decline in the number of village associations and an increase in crime, including the theft of tools, hand pumps, and crops.

**Source:** World Bank 1997a.

nism. At the same time policymakers ought to be careful not to over-shadow other informal initiatives, such as *Zakat* and *Waqfs*, which appear to be efficient.

## 2.3. Formal Mechanisms outside the Traditional Social Protection System

With the objectives of reducing poverty and vulnerability, achieving greater equality, and promoting broad-based growth, governments in the region have pursued a wide range of social policies in education and health while putting in place diverse regulatory schemes to control the prices of basic services, infrastructure, and food.

### Education and Training

Most MENA countries have achieved universal primary school enroll-ment and significant increases in secondary school enrollment, but public education systems are now facing major difficulties as budgets are re-duced, demand increases, and efficiency lags behind. While expenditures on education in MENA countries still average 5 to 6 percent of GDP, a considerable share of these expenditures, compared to international stan-dards, has been significantly reduced in real terms during the last 10 years (see table 2.3). Lower expenditures have not been absorbed by higher ef-ficiency but rather through lower quality. In Algeria, for instance, a recent study shows that 90 percent of the reduction in expenditures per student is explained by lower real wages for teachers and lower expenditures on services and materials. Efficiency gains in terms of higher student-teacher ratios and lower administrative staff-teacher ratios have been minimal. Thus, 90 percent of expenditures continue to be concentrated on wages.

TABLE 2.3

## Total Education Expenditures as a Percentage of GDP

| Country | 1990 | 1993 | 1995 | 1999 |
|---|---|---|---|---|
| Algeria | 6.9 | 7.0 | 7.0 | 6.0 |
| Egypt, Arab Rep. of | 4.2[a] | 4.5 | 5.7 | 5.9 |
| Iran, Islamic Rep. of | 4.1 | 5.3 | 4.5 | 5.0 |
| Jordan | — | 4.1 | 6.0 | 6.7 |
| Morocco | 5.3 | 5.9 | 5.5 | 5.9 |
| Tunisia | 6.0 | 6.1 | 6.5 | 6.9 |
| Yemen, Republic of | 7.6[a] | 6.2 | 5.1 | 7.7 |

— Not available.
a. Data are from 1991.
**Sources:** World Bank 1998a; UNESCO 2000.

Inefficiency is partly explained by the lack of appropriate delivery, financing, and management mechanisms that are almost entirely in public hands. Governments finance the majority of expenditures in education at all levels. While social spillovers related to investments in education justify the use of public funds, the share of current subsidies in total costs appears excessive in most countries, particularly in the case of higher education and vocational training. Moreover, subsidies are poorly targeted and tend to benefit all students independently of their level of income. In Algeria, for instance, the so-called *Oeuvres Universitaires* consume 40 percent of total expenditures in total education and are used to finance close to 95 percent of subsistence expenditures (food, transportation, and housing) for the majority of students. Inefficiency also results from centralized management practices, with poor coordination channels across ministries and little participation of the private sector. Private involvement in the supply of education services remains highly constrained in most countries, and there is little or no involvement from families, students, and communities in the management of schools and training centers. Under these conditions, there are few incentives to improve efficiency and the quality of education.

The quality of education is compromised as the system fails to maintain and improve the standards for teaching staff, infrastructure deteriorates, and curricula become obsolete. Motivation and the quality of the teaching staff have deteriorated over time, in part as a result of falling wages and the lack of incentives to invest in training. Teachers are often ill prepared, particularly in primary education. Quality is also affected by the severe deterioration of the physical infrastructure. The situation is complicated by the lack of coherent education policies and curricula. Diverse studies suggest that education systems in the MENA region are not designed to effectively impart the higher order cognitive skills such as flexibility and problem solving needed to compete in the global economy.

As quality declines, dropout and repetition rates tend to increase; the number of out-of-school children is now expected to grow by more than 40 percent within the next 10 years, with disproportionate shares among girls and the rural poor. Nearly 5 million children aged 6 to 10 and another 4 million children aged 11 to 15 in the region were out of school in 1995; by 2015 these numbers are expected to increase to 7.5 million and 5.6 million, respectively. Many of the dropouts are children from poor families who are likely to join informal labor markets during times of economic hardship. In Egypt, the enrollment rate for children in the top quintile remains above 80 percent, whereas enrollments in the poorest one-fifth of households are around 50 percent. In Morocco, net primary enrollments in rural areas are 58 percent, compared to 85 percent in urban areas. In Tunisia, secondary enrollments in rural governorates are as low as 19 percent, while in Tunisia they are 78 percent. Lower quality is driving upper-middle income households to complement children's education through private tutoring. In Egypt, for instance, expenditures in private tutoring represent 20 percent of total expenditures.

Vocational training programs tend to target those who have dropped out of the education system for academic reasons; thus graduates of such programs are often ill prepared for the job market and remain unemployed for long periods. In Egypt, for example, out of the 52,000 students who graduated from vocational programs in 1996, fewer than 10 percent have been absorbed by the labor markets each year. The rest engage mostly in low-paying jobs in informal markets or seek assistance from government programs.

The vocational system is expanding with no analysis of market requirements, no coherent national strategy, and weak linkages to the private sector. In Tunisia, there are 26,000 students in 411 private training centers that offer training in more than 50 different specialties with little relevance to the job market. Algeria has the largest training system, with 290,000 training posts, of which 260,000 are provided by public training centers and 15,000 by public enterprises. Procedures to certify private centers remain lengthy and cumbersome. In Egypt, there are 36,000 students in 120 publicly managed training centers with weak links to the private sector. In the West Bank and Gaza, there are 29 centers outside of the Ministry of Education and Ministry of Higher Education, with around 3,000 trainees and 24 specializations, again with little coordination with the job market. In the Republic of Yemen, there are 5,000 students in 15 public training centers that focus primarily on industry and commerce. In most countries, the system is fragmented, with too many training programs with the same purpose but lacking coordination. Moreover, training programs focus on preemployment services, while there are few incentives for lifelong, in-service training. In Tunisia, however, in-service training is encouraged through tax rebates. The overall result is a supply-driven vocational training system with publicly funded programs that do not correspond to labor market realities. With little interaction with the private sector, the system does not meet the evolving needs of the economy. Morocco is an important exception. In Morocco, reform programs are being introduced to develop in-service training and create a closer link between the needs of enterprises and training centers.

## Health

Living standards and health status in the region have improved significantly over the past 30 years, but some countries are lagging behind. In 1998, except in Djibouti, Morocco, and the Republic of Yemen, more than

TABLE 2.4

## Health Expenditures by Region

| Region | GDP per Capita, 1990–98 (US$) | Per Capita Health Expenditure, 1990–98 (US$) | Total Health Expenditure as Percentage of GDP | Public Share of Health Expenditures (% total) |
|---|---|---|---|---|
| East Asia and Pacific | 3,023 | 106 | 3.6 | 50.7 |
| Europe and Central Asia | 4,331 | 315 | 5.4 | 72.8 |
| Latin America and the Caribbean | 6,153 | 425 | 6.7 | 49.0 |
| Middle East and North Africa | 5,818 | 262 | 5.8 | 56.0 |
| South Asia | 1,348 | 64 | 5.0 | 38.5 |
| Sub-Saharan Africa | 1,729 | 87 | 2.9 | 55.4 |
| Low income | 1,893 | 78 | 4.2 | 36.8 |
| Middle income | 5,198 | 264 | 5.1 | 52.3 |
| Low and middle income | 3,027 | 139 | 5.0 | 42.3 |
| High income | 21,788 | 2,227 | 9.6 | 62.0 |

**Note:** Regional averages do not add up due to incomplete data on private health expenditures. Averages in columns may not correspond due to differences in coverage of data.
**Sources:** World Bank estimates; World Bank, *WDI 2000,* 2000b.

90 percent of the population had access to health services. While mortality and morbidity rates in the region have declined, countries are at substantially different stages of the epidemiological and demographic transformations. Djibouti, for example, has the highest infant mortality rate (106 per 1,000 live births, compared to a 35 per 1,000 live births regional average rate in 1999) and has an epidemiological profile comparable to the least developed countries of the world. Djibouti, the Republic of Yemen, and parts of rural Egypt and Morocco continue to have high mortality from infectious diseases, especially among children and mothers. The low health status of the population is a consequence of poverty (low income, poor sanitation, lack of safe drinking water, poor nutrition, and low educational attainment), as well as a lack of access to health services.

The MENA region spends, on average, 5.8 percent of GDP on health care, with a significant share of private outlays. The private share ranges from just above 70 percent in Morocco to less than 30 percent in Algeria and less than 20 percent in Saudi Arabia and Kuwait. This wide variation reflects differences in government provision of health financing, as well as in the size of the public sector relative to national income (see table 2.4).

Health insurance is prevalent in all countries in the region, to varying degrees, to pool population health risks and mitigate the consequences of catastrophic health care expenditures. Public systems generally cover public sector employees, the military, and in some countries, formal sector workers through social security systems. The Gulf countries provide universal coverage for their nationals and expatriate workers through national health service approaches, but are increasingly adopting employer mandates to provide private health insurance for expatriate populations. There are still significant gaps in coverage in most countries in the region. Public spending on health accounts for only a little more than one-half of all health spending. There are generally significant gaps in coverage for workers in the informal sector, and in some countries, formal sector employees. The ministry of health's facilities are generally the social safety net for the poor and disadvantaged populations. For these groups, coverage is often far from complete, particularly in rural areas and where the ministry's budgets are severely constrained. Many of the public systems are not equitable, actuarially sound, or sustainable in light of the epidemiological and demographic transitions.

Private insurance generally accounts for only a small fraction of private spending. The reliance on out-of-pocket spending signifies that most individuals and households have little or no financial protection (insurance) in the event of a catastrophic illness or injury. Low-income households in particular allocate a higher share of their budget to health care services. In Algeria, for instance, the share of household health expenditure for the poorest 10 percent of the urban population is three times higher than for the richest 10 percent; for the rural population it is twice as large. In Tunisia, health expenditures as a share of total household expenditures for the poorest 5 percent of the urban population account for about 1.2 percent of total expenditures, while for the corresponding rural population, which has less access to basic services, the expenditure share increases to about 2.1 percent. In the future, as the share of the population aged 65 or more increases to more than 10 percent, health expenditures are expected to increase considerably.

## Price Regulations and Subsidies

Diverse arrangements to manage and price agricultural products, basic infrastructure, and resources such as water have proliferated in MENA countries in order to protect consumers and producers. Unfortunately, these systems, in most cases, have brought more harm than good, as severe price distortions emerged, leading to overconsumption and undersupply. Moreover, targeting mechanisms are generally weak, and therefore, subsidies tend to benefit mostly middle- and high-income population groups. In this section, we briefly discuss these issues. Since consumer food subsidies are generally considered part of formal social assistance programs, their discussion is deferred to the next section.

*Price controls in agriculture.* Agricultural production, particularly cereals, is subject to high variability due to climatic changes. To protect farmers, countries have often misused producer and input subsidies. The production of cereals is characterized by high climatic variability due to rainfall conditions and associated risks that diminish the incentive for investments in technology (fertilizers and improved seeds, for instance) to increase yields. To deal with these risks, governments have provided support in the form of guaranteed minimum prices, obligatory delivery and collection prices given by state monopolies, or floor prices with a premium over reference prices based on production costs or international or import prices. These producer support prices are essentially transfers because, especially in less favorable areas with low rainfall, they have had a small impact, if any, as incentives to raise production and productivity. Input subsidies aim, in part, at the diffusion of new technologies. Diffusion, however, has been slow, and the end results are distorted markets where prices no longer reflect marginal costs.

The effects of these subsidies as instruments of social protection are diluted because they are not targeted to the more needy and poorer segments of the rural society.[12] In fact, larger farms benefit disproportionately more than smaller farms. Smaller farmers who produce cereals essentially for family consumption, or who do not have access to markets or state purchases (because of, for instance, distance or volume restrictions), do not benefit from price supports. Such interventions to support and stabilize prices can actually have adverse effects. Indeed, if the commodity price that is being stabilized is negatively correlated with the other elements of the portfolio, the stabilization policy would have negative impacts on the overall portfolio (Newberry and Stiglitz 1981).

*Subsidies for water.* Natural water scarcity is aggravated by inappropriate pricing mechanisms that lead to inappropriate delivery systems and inefficient use. The majority of MENA countries lack mechanisms to internalize the social costs associated with the private consumption of water (usually water extraction by a given individual increases the extraction costs for everyone else). As a consequence, reserves are quickly being depleted while production costs for farmers are increasing. Today, farmers have difficulties making a living from farming alone (World Bank 1997b). For example, a typical farmer near the capital of Sana'a has deepened his well by 50 meters over the last 12 years—increasing his costs—while the amount of water he can extract has dropped by nearly two-thirds (see box 2.4). Government interventions such as subsidies for water consumed in export-related crops have aggravated the problem, and now important inefficiencies can be observed in delivery systems. For instance, while only one-quarter of the cultivated land is under irrigation, 87 percent of the water withdrawn goes to irrigation, and only 13 percent to industrial and municipal uses, compared with 69 percent and 31 percent, respectively, worldwide. Irrigation is extremely inefficient in

---

**BOX 2.4**

## Costs of Inadequate Water Supplies for Domestic Use and a Community's Response

*Economic costs.* The Republic of Yemen's total annually renewed water resources are estimated at 4.1 billion cubic meters. With a population of around 17 million, available resources amount to about 241 cubic meters per capita each year. The urban poor often have to buy water from private vendors at a price 10 to 25 times higher than the price of water from the National Water and Sanitation Authority. Jordan's per capita availability of water resources amounts to around 148 cubic meters per year and is expected to be reduced to about 88 cubic meters per year by 2025. Increasing population, inefficient water distribution, and inadequate infrastructure have led to a shortage of water resources available for household use. This has had an adverse impact, especially on the urban and rural poor. Water consumption in urban areas is rationed and is generally available only two times a week in summer, and less in some communities. To meet household demand, even the urban poor are compelled to purchase water from tankers supplied by the Water Authority of Jordan at a price of 1.5 to 1.7 Jordan dinars per cubic meter, or from private tankers at a wider range of prices.

*A community's response.* In an Egyptian village in the Nile delta, village women helped facilitate water, sanitation, and environmental health improvements by working with an action research team. The village had a population of 5,000 and had no sewage, solid waste, or sewage-disposal system. It had access to three water sources: piped water through public standpipes, shallow wells with hand pumps, and canal water. The women identified two problems: a malfunctioning standpipe (forcing them to walk miles everyday to fetch water) and a highly polluted canal. The lack of clean water caused widespread gastrointestinal and eye diseases among the children. The women organized the village to repair the standpipe and formed two women's committees, one to maintain the repaired standpipe and another to monitor the cleanliness of the canal.

**Sources:** World Bank 1997a, 1997b.

---

most countries. For example, in flood irrigation, only 30 percent of the water reaches the crops. The long-run marginal cost of irrigated water in Jordan, for example, is an estimated US$0.32 per cubic meter, higher than the estimated value added from most agricultural production. In the Republic of Yemen, agriculture supports nearly 81 percent of the population but produces only 18 percent of GDP. Wheat production using nonrenewable fossil groundwater in Saudi Arabia is an example of inefficiency and waste. This problem is also observed in countries such as Jordan and Algeria. In general there are high system losses.[13]

*Subsidies for infrastructure and transport.* Countries in the MENA region have different schemes for providing basic physical infrastructure (electricity and housing) and transportation services to the poor. In most cases the schemes involve keeping the prices of these services low to make them affordable. The downside of this strategy is that revenues are not sufficient to cover maintenance expenditures and new investments. Over time, infrastructures and the quality of services deteriorate, and the supply cannot keep up with a growing demand. Shortages of basic services often concentrate on poor rural areas, in part because poor population groups have less capacity to finance these services and less political clout to lobby for subsidized investments. In the meantime, urban areas, usually with higher levels of income, enjoy generous subsidies for services such as water, electricity, and transportation.

## 2.4. Formal Public Mechanisms within the Traditional Social Protection System

This final section assesses programs within the traditional social protection system. These include labor market programs that contribute to reducing the risks of unemployment, social insurance programs that have a role in reducing the impact of future adverse shocks (risk mitigation), and social assistance programs mainly designed to reverse or reduce the negative impact of shocks that have already occurred (coping function), particularly among low-income population groups. In the majority of countries, these programs consume sizable resources ranging between 6 and 20 percent of GDP (see table 2.5).

### ALMPs: Job Search Assistance, Vocational Training, Wage Subsidy Programs, and Microfinance

Governments often offer a wide range of employment programs that are conventionally lumped together under the heading of ALMPs. ALMPs include counseling and placement services, training or retraining of displaced workers, support for entry into self-employment, and wage subsidies. These programs attract budgetary expenditures ranging from 0.3 percent of GDP in Algeria in 1998 to 0.7 percent in Morocco in 1997. In line with the international experience on ALMPs (see box 2.5), labor market policies have had limited impacts in MENA economies. ALMPs are not panaceas for the problem of low employment creation in the region. These programs can only marginally reduce the risks associated with structural constraints in the labor and product markets and the macroeconomy at large. If inappropriately designed, these programs can

**TABLE 2.5**

## Social Sector Expenditures in the 1990s

(percentage of GDP)

| Country | Food Subsidies (1) | Cash and In-Kind Transfers (2) | Public Works (3) | Public Pension (4) | Total (1+2+3+4) (5) | Housing (6) | Public Health (7) | Education (8) | Total (6+7+8) (9) | Grand Total (5+9) |
|---|---|---|---|---|---|---|---|---|---|---|
| Algeria | 0.0 | 0.4 | 0.2 | 4.6 | 5.2 | 5.5 | 2.6 | 6.1 | 14.2 | 19.4 |
| Egypt, Arab Rep. of | 1.3 | 0.2 | 0.3 | 2.5 | 4.3 | 2.0 | 1.8 | 4.8 | 8.6 | 12.9 |
| Iran, Islamic Rep. of | 2.7 | 1.2 | — | 1.5 | 5.4 | 1.5 | 2.4 | 4.0 | 7.9 | 13.3 |
| Jordan | 0.0 | 0.9 | — | 4.2 | 5.1 | 0.7 | 5.3 | 6.8 | 12.8 | 17.9 |
| Lebanon | 0.1 | 0.9 | — | — | 1.0 | — | 2.2 | 2.5 | 4.7 | 5.7 |
| Morocco | 1.6 | 0.1 | 0.2 | 1.8 | 3.7 | 0.1 | 1.2 | 5.9 | 7.2 | 10.9 |
| Tunisia | 1.7 | 0.5 | 0.1 | 2.6 | 4.9 | 1.7 | 3.0 | 6.9 | 11.6 | 16.5 |
| Yemen, Republic of | 0.0 | 1.0 | 0.2 | 0.1 | 1.3 | 0.7 | 2.2 | 7.0 | 9.9 | 11.2 |

— Not available.
**Note:** Social assistance includes cash and transfers but excludes public works.
**Sources:** Various World Bank reports and recent Social Safety Net Updates 1995–2000; World Bank, *WDI 2000*, 2000b.

actually produce deadweight losses (for example, social costs of subsidies that exceed productivity gains).

*Job search assistance.* Job search assistance is generally less costly than other programs but does not seem to significantly improve either the employment prospects or wages of the youth. Job search assistance programs usually reach a small fraction of the labor force. In Morocco, labor intermediation services, currently the monopoly of the state, account for only a small fraction of the labor force. In Algeria, only 7 percent of the 2.2 million unemployed registered with *Agence Nationale de l'Emploi* (ANEM) in 1998. Usually, the organization managing job search assistance lacks appropriate information systems and technologies as well as qualified personnel to support the task. Thus, the programs are not very effective. In Algeria, the 730 staff of ANEM place an average of only three demands per month each. In many countries the operation of private employment services is prohibited by law, without clear justification.

*Vocational training.* Vocational training for the long-term unemployed or retraining programs for retrenched workers have not been cost-effective; real rates of return, on average, have been negative. These programs are no more successful than job search assistance programs in terms of post-program placement and wages. In Morocco, low insertion rates have prevailed in public preemployment vocational training. Results are better in the case of programs operated through the formal business sector, but these represent only a small portion of in-service

**BOX 2.5**

## International Experience

Many interventions in the labor market are clustered under the title of ALMPs. Such programs may lead to direct job creation (through additional jobs offered by a new public works scheme), help the unemployed fill existing vacancies (through retraining to meet new job requirements), or improve the functioning of the labor market (through employment information and labor offices). Expenditures on ALMPs vary, as do the analytics of these programs. For example, public works is very much a demand-side intervention and training is a supply-side one, while labor market intermediation can be seen as an attempt to bridge these two sides of the labor market.

In almost all Organisation for Economic Co-operation and Development (OECD) countries, training for the unemployed is "the largest category of active programs and is often perceived as the principal alternative to regular unemployment benefits." In many countries, in fact, training—for those laid off en masse, for the long-term unemployed, and for youth—accounts for more than 50 percent of the expenditure on ALMPs. This is followed by expenditures on employment services and PWPs. Countries generally spend less than 10 percent of expenditures on microenterprise development or wage subsidies.

The results of evaluations of ALMPs from OECD countries are summarized programmatically:

- *Public works* can help the more disadvantaged groups (older workers, the long-term unemployed, those in distressed regions) as a poverty or safety net program. They are ineffective instruments as an escape route from permanent unemployment. Program participants are less likely to be employed in an unsubsidized job, and they earn less than individuals in a control group.
- *Job search assistance* has a positive impact and is usually cost-effective relative to other ALMPs. Programs that have yielded positive results have generally been implemented under favorable macroeconomic conditions. However, job search assistance does not seem to significantly improve either the employment prospects or wages of youth.
- *Training for the long-term unemployed* can help when the economy is improving. Small-scale, tightly targeted, on-the-job training programs, often aimed at women and older groups, offer the best returns. However, the cost-effectiveness of these programs is generally disappointing. The real rate of return is rarely positive, and they are no more successful than job search assistance programs in terms of post-program placement and wages. A caveat here is that job search assistance may not be a direct substitute for training, as it may cater to different groups of the unemployed.
- *Retraining for those laid off en masse* usually has little positive impact and, as in the case for the long-term unemployed, is more expensive and no more effective than job search assistance. Again, job search assistance may not be a direct substitute for retraining, as the target groups may be somewhat different.

**BOX 2.5   (continued)**

- *Training for youth* generally has no positive impact on employment prospects or post-training earnings. It clearly cannot make up for the failures of the education system. Taking costs into account, the real rate of return of these programs in both the short and long run is usually negative.
- *Microenterprise development* programs are usually taken up by only a small fraction of the unemployed and are associated with high deadweight and displacement effects. The failure rate of these businesses is quite high. As in the case of training for the long-term unemployed, assistance targeted at particular groups—in this case, women and older individuals—seems to have a greater likelihood of success.
- *Wage subsidy* programs are unlikely to have a positive impact. They have substantial deadweight and substitution effects. The wage and employment outcomes of participants are also generally negative as compared with a control group. Careful targeting can reduce but not eliminate substitution and deadweight effects, and further controls may be necessary to ensure that firms do not misuse this program as a permanent subsidy program.

**Sources:** OECD 1994; Dar and Tzannatos 1999.

training. Algeria has the largest vocational and technical training system in the Maghreb region. It includes preservice training, provided mainly by public training institutions, and in-service training, provided by public enterprises. Unit costs per student are high (roughly six times the unit cost in secondary education), and training has weak linkages to the labor market. Coordination among various agencies and programs is almost nonexistent, and each one operates without the guidance of a coherent national strategy.

*Wage subsidy programs.* Wage subsidy programs are usually welfare-decreasing; the wage and employment outcomes of participants are generally inferior to those observed in the case of a control group. All MENA countries use this scheme to help first-time job seekers. Wage subsidies can be justified if used temporarily as a mechanism to increase workers' productivity, leading to permanent employment. This result, however, is seldom observed. Usually subsidies constitute direct transfers to workers and firms, with little or no value added. Since financing the subsidy has costs, the net change in welfare is often negative. Indeed, substitution effects tend to neutralize the subsidies, as firms do not expand the demand for labor but rather the demand for other inputs.

While careful targeting and regulation can reduce, although not eliminate, substitution and welfare losses, implementation and monitoring costs can be high. In Algeria, job subsidy schemes for low-skilled workers provide amounts lower than the minimum wage and are used to give firms incentives to hire the unemployed. Though the program has not been properly evaluated, there is some evidence that employers utilize the subsidy schemes to hire workers they would have hired anyway. The net job creation effect is negligible: between 1990 and 1998 over a million jobs have been financed in this way, but the retention rate at the end of the subsidy is very low (about 2 percent of the beneficiaries have stayed in the job as permanent workers at the end of the subsidized period).

## Social Insurance: Pensions and Unemployment Insurance

*Microfinance.* There are more than 60 microfinance programs operating in Algeria, Egypt, Morocco, and Tunisia; the majority are run by NGOs. The rationale behind these programs is strong, as fewer than 2 percent of the 7.5 million poor households in MENA (more than 60 million poor people) have access to formal financial services.[14] The outreach gap (people needing and willing to pay for financial services but who nevertheless lack access) is estimated at 2 to 4 million households, while the funding gap (funds needed for lending) is estimated between US$750 million and US$1.4 billion, or less than 1 percent of total lending of the formal financial sector in the region. Together, these programs serve more than 112,000 active borrowers, 75,000 of whom are in Egypt. Fourteen percent of active borrowers live in rural areas, and 36 percent are female (see box 2.6).

Of the 60 programs, however, only 17 are fully sustainable[15] or have the potential to become sustainable.[16] These 17 best-practice programs together serve the majority (70 percent) of current active borrowers. Most of the remaining 43 programs are funded by the government, charge subsidized interest rates, and are financially unsustainable.

While banks could represent the most effective means of addressing the funding and outreach gap because they have wide branch networks, financial systems that are in place, and a business orientation, current practices are not generally exploiting this comparative advantage. Subsidized lending programs channeled through banks—and often imposed on the banks under political pressure—have proven largely unworkable. In Egypt, Morocco, and Tunisia, for example, borrowers are often selected based on their poverty or unemployment status and not their entrepreneurial capacity. Banks do not receive technical support to develop the loan screening and monitoring capabilities required for successful micro- and small-business lending. As a result, repayment rates remain low and banks incur high losses.

*Pensions.* Most countries in the region have moved to defined benefits, unfunded (pay-as-you-go) pension systems that are, in general, facing

---

**BOX 2.6**

### Community-Driven Development and Microfinance for the Poor in the Republic of Yemen

The Republic of Yemen is the poorest country in the MENA region, yet with World Bank support the Republic of Yemen has developed a successful approach to community-driven development and financially sustainable microfinance. Even in the most remote corners of this mountainous country, small community projects financed by the Bank are being implemented in partnership with the community. The process started with the Public Works Project (fiscal 1996) and was strengthened with the Social Fund for Development (SFD). SFD not only finances community-demand-driven subprojects, but also works with members of the community to ensure that the subproject is a priority. Special care is taken to ensure that the more marginal members of a community are consulted. Community ownership is ensured by upfront contributions, and SFD finances the subproject after ensuring that a system of user charges (including cross-subsidies for the poor) is in place to ensure operations and maintenance. SFD also supports community capacity building so that communities are better able to plan and execute development projects. In microfinance, SFD provides technical assistance, training, and loan funds to support the development of sustainable microfinance entities using best-practice approaches. To avoid local prejudices against interest-based lending, SFD has developed loan products using Islamic banking principles that have been very successful financially. SFD microfinance intermediaries have also provided savings services to the poor.

The success of these activities is apparent all over the Republic of Yemen. In remote mountaintop villages, SFD has worked with the communities to restore a traditional water-harvesting system and increased girls' school enrollment by providing facilities. In some communities SFD has supported new health facilities and, in others, helped improve access by supporting a road. SFD-supported clients have moved on to their third-generation loan, moving from selling fruits out of a wheelbarrow to a small store. One woman beneficiary of an SFD microfinance program reports dropping out of school before she was 10 years of age, but she returned to school many years later after SFD's microfinance programs helped stabilize the family income.

**Sources:** Social Fund for Development Project Mid-Term Review 1999; Project Appraisal Document 2000.

---

financial difficulties. Pension systems in the region were usually created as defined benefits systems with some degree of prefunding. This implies that while the contributions of workers were not actuarially linked to their benefits—that is, benefits depend on years of contributions and accrual rates, not on the level of savings that individuals accumulate during their working lives—the systems were supposed to accumulate reserves to smooth future adjustments to the contribution rates in response to increasing dependency ratios. However, these reserves usually have been poorly managed, often covering deficits from the central government, financing investments in real estate or projects with low internal rates of return, or financing subsidized loans for workers.[17] Today, in most countries, the largest share of fund reserves is invested in illiquid assets and government debt (often without formal financial arrangements and repayment plans), and real rates of return are low or negative. In the Islamic Republic of Iran, assets of the Social Security Organization (SSO) account for 4.3 percent of GDP, and 95 percent are invested in companies operating in a large number of economic sectors. Real rates of return during the last decade have been below 2 percent and often negative. In Algeria and Egypt, assets represent 1.2 percent and 33 percent of GDP, respectively, and 100 percent of these are invested in the public sector, where rates of return are highly negative. In Morocco, total reserve funds represent about 9 percent of GDP and are yielding negative rates of return. In Djibouti, 100 percent of assets are in real estate and government debt and also generate negative real rates of return. There are also systems such as the civil service and military pension systems in Jordan where reserves have been depleted. However, there are exceptions, such as the Social Security Corporation (SSC) in Jordan, in which funding levels are high and only 4.5 percent of assets are in the form of real estate, while bank deposits, shares, and bonds capture more than 70 percent of the portfolio. During the last decade, real rates of return have fluctuated around 5 percent.

Although, for most systems, the contributions that cover the revenues of private sector workers still exceed pension expenditures, the majority of systems covering civil servants and the military are already running deficits. Dependency ratios tend to be higher in systems for private sector workers, and benefits are usually less generous. This has contributed to a better financial position for private sector pension funds. In Djibouti's *Organisme de Protection Sociale* (OPS; Social Protection Organization), pension payments represent 48 percent of revenues; in the Islamic Republic of Iran's SSO, payments represent 57 percent; and in Jordan's SSC, payments represent 50 percent. In these same countries, however, the systems for the civil servants and the military are generating large deficits. In the Islamic Republic of Iran, total expenditures for the Civil Service Retirement Organization (CSRO) exceed revenues by 18 percent. In the Jordanian pension fund for the military, the deficit approximates 3.5 percent of GDP. Over the long run, the financial position of the systems for workers in the private sector is also expected to deteriorate. Even in systems such as Jordan's SSC, with a high level of funding, the present value of expected liabilities for the next 30 to 40 years surpasses the present value of total assets.

FIGURE 2.1

## Formal Pension Cost and Population Older Than 60 in MENA

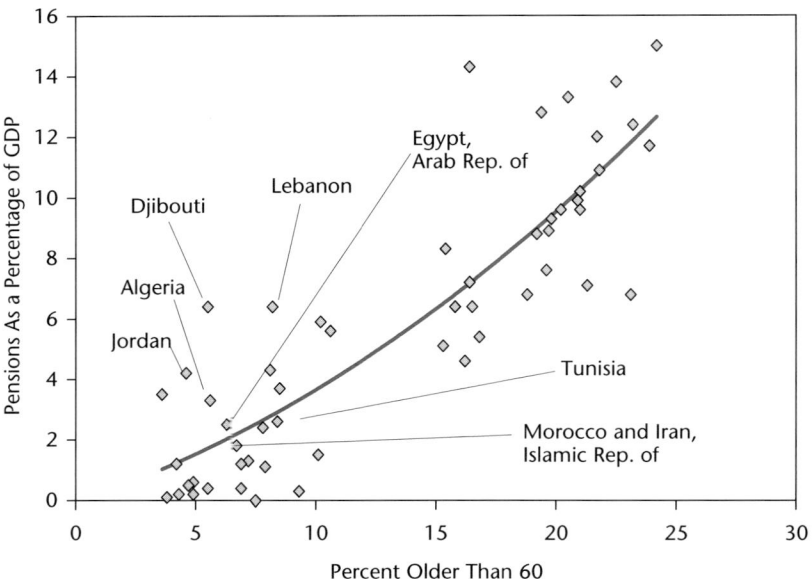

**Source:** International Labour Organization 2000.

Pension systems in the region are relatively generous, but at the same time not designed to protect retirees from increases in prices. Pension expenditures in the region are large relative to other countries with similar demographic structures. For example, in countries with a demographic structure similar to Jordan's, where the population aged 60 and older represents 4.6 percent of the total population, pension expenditures are below 2 percent of GDP. But in Jordan these expenditures are approximately 4.2 percent of GDP. Similar statistics apply to Algeria, Djibouti, and Lebanon (see figure 2.1). In most cases, higher expenditures are not explained by higher levels of coverage (since coverage rates are similar to other countries at the same level of income), but rather by openhanded provisions. Indeed, replacement rates are rarely below 50 to 60 percent. In Algeria, the *Caisse Nationale de Retraite* (CNR; National Pension Fund) has an average replacement rate of 80 percent; in the Islamic Republic of Iran's CSRO, this rate is 75 percent; and in Tunisia's *Caisse Nationale de Retraite et Prévoyance Social* (CNRPS; National Pension and Social Security Fund), the replacement rate is 90 percent. In general, systems for civil servants and the military are more generous than systems for private workers, and these systems often include special provisions. In the Jordanian military system, for instance, the "four-year rule" allows officers with four or more years of service at a given rank to retire with a pension based on the salary of the next higher rank. In Djibouti, ministers and parliamentarians contribute to their own regime, but also to the regime of regular functionaries, thus receiving two pensions that are equivalent to an average replacement rate of 120 percent. At the same time, none of the countries has a formal indexation mechanism, and therefore, real benefits are affected by inflation and discretionary adjustments. This increases the level of uncertainty about the real value of future pensions and induces workers to view contributions as an additional tax rather than savings, thus promoting evasion.

Coverage is usually limited to the formal sector of the economy, and workers in the informal sector and rural areas remain largely unprotected. Available data suggest that there are more than 10 persons between the ages of 20 and 59 for every person over age 60. Yet system dependency ratios in the region range between 18 and 36 percent (three to five workers per pensioner). High dependency ratios are explained by low coverage, which ranges from 42 percent of the labor force in the Islamic Republic of Iran[18] to about one-half in Egypt, or between 18 and 34 percent of the working-age population in the region. One reason for low coverage rates is the large informal sector. Indeed, a very large part of the agricultural sector is informal (ranging from 50 percent of total male employment in the Republic of Yemen to 18 percent in Algeria), and informal jobs among nonagricultural workers represent approximately 57 percent of the total in Morocco, 47 percent in Tunisia, and 40 percent in Egypt.[19] A second reason for low coverage is evasion of pension payments because of high contribution rates and pessimistic expectations about future benefits. Evasion is also fueled by the lack of appropriate information systems to monitor and track contributions. Finally, low vesting periods and retirement ages, and weak penalties on early retirement, contribute to increased dependency ratios.

The systems in the region are sustained by high payroll taxes that introduce distortions in labor markets. Payroll taxes for pensions as a share of total labor costs[20] range from 8 to 14 percent in the main schemes of Algeria, Libya, Morocco, and Tunisia, to more than 23 percent in Egypt and the Islamic Republic of Iran. If other social insurance contributions (health, family allowances, and so forth) are taken into account, the range is between 13 and 40 percent of total labor costs.[21] High labor costs affect the competitiveness of firms and reduce labor demand. Moreover, they encourage evasion and expansion of the informal sector.

Beyond financial and economic problems, there are inter- and intra-generational equity issues. For young workers, given high contribution rates, current rates of return for contributions are low or negative. In the Islamic Republic of Iran's SSO, for instance, workers younger than 30 are currently being offered pension benefits that in present value are 10 percent below their contributions. Forced adjustments to keep the systems afloat usually exacerbate the problem as benefits for future retirees (today's younger workers) are cut and contributions increase. Thus, to finance high replacement rates for the current generation, future generations are likely to be penalized. There are also equity problems within the current generations. Since benefits received are partly related to life expectancy, healthier individuals, who are usually middle- and high-income individuals, tend to receive more benefits in proportion to their contributions. Finally, since all the systems are unfunded (the present value of future pension liabilities is higher than the present value of accumulated assets), there is an implicit government liability targeted at a minority of the population, which is covered by the systems, composed predominantly of workers in the formal sector of the economy.

The problems facing the pension funds can be explained partly by weak governance structures. With very few exceptions, such as Saudi Arabia's and Jordan's SSCs after the issue of the new royal decree on investments, governance structures and incentives are not conducive to prudent management of the funds' resources, or to preventing discretionary changes to contributions and benefits. In terms of the management of reserves, most pension systems have established investment committees. But there is often a lack of investment policies, investment plans, and monitoring of these plans, as is the case in the civil service pension funds of Algeria, Djibouti, Egypt, the Islamic Republic of Iran, Morocco, and Tunisia. Representation on the boards of these committees tends to be biased toward the public sector, with a lack of participation from workers and the private sector. Managers are usually appointed by line ministries and are not accountable for investment decisions (in none of the countries studied can the board replace the manager of the pension fund), and thus the funds are rarely free from political pressure. Investment policies are seldom subject to external reviews, and managers tend to be subject to institutional constraints. In the Islamic Republic of Iran, for example, fund managers cannot freely sell the stock owned in public companies. Inappropriate governance structures also lead to discretionary adjustments of contributions and benefits, which are often arbitrary and driven by political pressures that compromise the financial sustainability of the systems. In Algeria, for instance, the value of the minimum pension was recently increased without appropriate sources of financing. Pension benefits were also extended, without new financial resources, to vulnerable individuals who cannot pay contributions. In the Islamic Republic of Iran's CSRO, during the 1990s, the retirement age and the penalties for early retirement were reduced as part of a policy to rationalize the size of the civil service. This policy is largely responsible for the current financial crisis.

Weak institutional capacity has also contributed to the current problems. Visits to pension funds in the regions and discussions with managers and technical staff have enabled partial assessments of institutional capacity. In general, administrative processes such as registration of new contributions, follow-up of life events, collections of contributions, and liquidations and payments of benefits are inefficient and lead to duplication of effort and high administrative costs (7 percent in Tunisia and the Islamic Republic of Iran and 10 percent in Djibouti). While basic information technologies are generally available, these do not operate in the context of an integrated information system that could streamline administrative processes. For example, the CNR in Algeria, the SSO in the Islamic Republic of Iran, and the OPS in Djibouti still lack a system to routinely collect information about contributors and beneficiaries. Administrative inefficiencies are then reflected in the quality of services. Problems are particularly severe in local offices. In Jordan, workers outside Amman need to wait an average of two months to process their liquidation. However, some of the funds are making important progress in this area. The OPS in Djibouti has just contracted for the development and implementation of a new information system. Jordan's SSC has integrated all branches into a central information system and is currently developing a project that will allow contributors and beneficiaries to access their records via the Internet. The Iranian CSRO has developed in-house, state-of-the-art software to manage contributions and pensions. The new system has doubled productivity per employee, as measured by the number of liquidations processed by an employee during a given period of time. In Tunisia, the Center for Social Security Research is currently evaluating options to develop a comprehensive social security database.

In the absence of reforms, the financial situation of the pension funds will continue to deteriorate as the share of the elderly population increases in MENA countries. As previously discussed, over the next 25 years the elderly population is expected to grow nearly 4 percent per year while the total population grows at 1.4 percent. This demographic transition will increase dependency ratios and put considerable strain on the finances of the pay-as-you-go systems. Given that contribution rates are already high, solutions will need to come from a better use of reserves, a rationalization of current provisions, and the introduction of alternative financing mechanisms that reduce labor distortions and evasion. The reform options are discussed in the next chapter.

*Unemployment insurance.* Unemployment insurance schemes are still relatively new mechanisms in the region. The major problems associated with these systems are related to inefficient financing arrangements. Given high uncertainty about the future dynamics of labor markets, determining the level of contributions, the length of benefits, and replacement rates are delicate issues. Benefit periods are often too long and generate negative incentives for job search. Costs to firms tend to be high, thus discouraging hiring. Most pension systems are funded and therefore require that reserves be managed with prudence. This is not always the case. In Algeria, reserves accumulated in the newly created unemployment insurance system are being allocated to a series of interventions (training, credit support to the private sector), many of which are known not to be cost-effective. This compromises the financial sustainability of the system.

## Social Assistance Programs: Public Works and Safety Net Programs

*Public works.* PWPs create temporary jobs for the unemployed and underemployed while providing poor communities with basic infrastructure (table 2.6). They can also become a more permanent feature of a community by including triggers for additional hiring when poverty increases, as in the case of crop failure (see Ravallion 1998). Morocco and Tunisia both have a long tradition of PWPs (see box 2.7). In other cases, public works have been introduced as needed, as in Algeria and Egypt in the 1990s, following structural adjustment measures.

Unfortunately, PWPs are often supply driven, are not always designed to address the specific needs of the poor, and create only limited value-added. The share of wages out of the total cost of a PWP is about 60 percent in Tunisia, 50 percent in Morocco, and 40 to 60 percent in Algeria. In Egypt, where most program activities are capital intensive (water supply and sewerage), the wage share is 30 percent of total cost. Worldwide experience has shown that the most cost-effective and well-

TABLE 2.6

### Job Creation as a Result of Public Works

| Country | Programs | Workers As a Percentage of Labor Force |
|---|---|---|
| Algeria | IAIG/TUP/Rural Employment | 2.3 |
| Egypt, Arab Rep. of | Public Works (part of SFD) | 0.4 |
| Morocco | *Promotion Nationale* | 0.6 |
| Tunisia | *Chantiers Nationaux/Regionaux* | 2.7 |
| Yemen, Republic of | Public Works | 0.1 |

**Source:** Various World Bank country and poverty reports.

---

**BOX 2.7**

### Public Works Programs in Morocco and Tunisia

In Morocco, the 30-year-old *Promotion Nationale* (PN) manages projects located mostly in disadvantaged rural areas, including reforestation, the capture of well water, dam and road construction, and road paving. During 1990–99, the program has created about 40,000 personyears of employment through labor-intensive activities. Moreover, a large share of resources goes to assist local governments in paying the wages of administrators instead of reaching low-income groups in poor communities.

In Tunisia, PWPs (*chantier public*) are an important source of employment for the poor. In urban areas, activities include road maintenance, sewer cleaning and installation, removal of wastewater, and cleaning of public roads. Rural activities include road work, soil conservation, and forestry. These programs, which provide short-term jobs for unskilled workers in an attempt to reduce underemployment and unemployment, are a key vehicle for transferring income to the poor. Participants are primarily from agriculture (66 percent) and construction (28 percent). During 1987–91, all programs employed an average of 75,000 workers per year, one-third in urban areas and two-thirds in rural areas.

**Source:** Social Safety Net Updates 1999.

---

targeted PWPs entail a high wage share in total cost while providing highly labor-intensive work for wages at or below the market rate for unskilled labor.[22] However, PWPs in the region are generally not very successful when measured in terms of productivity and the economic value of assets created and have paid little attention to the quality of assets created and the costs of maintaining those assets.[23] In addition, programs often could be more carefully designed, monitored, or evaluated. Thus, little is known about the cost and managerial requirements of the programs, the number of jobs created, and the impact of these programs on long-term unemployment and poverty reduction. Recently, however, governments have tended to decentralize and increase private sector participation in the management of the programs, and to make programs more responsive to community demands (see box 2.7).

*Social funds.* Government- and donor-financed social funds have been used to mitigate the effects of shocks on the most vulnerable groups, and also as compensatory mechanisms to increase access to, and improve the quality of, basic services used by the poor. Traditional public expenditures in the social sectors have recently been supplemented with social funds (or social investment funds [SIFs]),[24] an increasingly common feature of the region's social protection portfolio. Social funds cover a range of programs, including infrastructure (health and education infrastructure), community development, and microfinance, many of which had previously been undertaken as stand-alone programs.

Social funds have been instrumental in transferring resources to target groups, but current resources are limited relative to the need. Poor communities and beneficiaries have received a far greater degree of government support through social funds than would have been the case if the funds did not exist. However, the operations are small compared with the magnitude of poverty in MENA. In terms of total resource transfers, Egypt's social fund is the most important, but its annual expenditures amounted to only 0.2 percent of GDP in 1993–96. Egypt also has the largest per capita transfers, as well as the largest total transfers per poor person—an estimated US$83 to US$125 per year. However, if every poor person received an equal share of social fund transfers, the annual amount transferred by the MENA social funds would represent less than 4 percent of their average income (see table 2.7).

Social funds in the region use a variety of intermediaries. In the financing of community infrastructure projects, for example, Egypt works mainly with governorates, the Republic of Yemen with NGOs and community groups, and the West Bank and Gaza with a combination of the three (governorates, NGOs, and community groups) (see box 2.8). Within the project cycle, social funds differ widely in the extent to which projects are demand driven, and participation is built into operating procedures. In general, few build beneficiary participation into the identification and supervision of investments,[25] except where local project committees are eligible as sponsors—even though coordination and collaboration with beneficiary communities, as well as with intermediary organizations, are central to the impact and effectiveness of social fund investments. Gaps in coordination have, as a result, hurt the sustainability of certain social fund investments (see box 2.8).

TABLE 2.7

## MENA Social Fund Spending on Target Population

| Social Fund Spending | West Bank and Gaza – CDP[a] | West Bank and Gaza – NGO | Yemen, Republic of | Egypt, Arab Rep. of[b] | Algeria |
|---|---|---|---|---|---|
| Total US$ per capita | $11.11 | $6.30 | $5.23 | $25.03 | $2.91 |
| Total US$ per poor person | $46.30 | $26.23 | $27.52 | $83.45–$125.17 | $17.96 |
| Average annual US$ per poor person | $15.43 | $4.37 | $5.50 | $11.92–$17.88 | $4.49 |
| Average annual US$ as % of poverty line | 2.4% | 0.7% | 3.4% | — | 1.2% |

— Not available.
a. CDP is defined as community development project.
b. Includes SFD Phase I and Phase II. Poverty headcount index information varies from 20 to 30 percent.

---

**BOX 2.8**

### Social Fund Operations in MENA

The main social funds in the MENA region are the Algerian Social Development Agency, the Egyptian SFD, the Yemeni SFD, and the West Bank and Gaza Community Development and NGO Projects. Morocco has a proposed social fund, and the MENA region has several World Bank projects, such as the Community Infrastructure Project in Jordan, that are similar to social funds in their approach to job creation if not in their operational mechanisms. The importance of social funds in the overall social protection system, and in terms of job creation, varies from one country to another: the SFD is of moderate importance in Egypt, while the Social Development Agency in Algeria has had much less impact. Most funds in the region have been successful in terms of outputs. Egypt's SFD, for its size and number of years of operation (about 10 years), has generated the largest level of outputs. As of June 30, 1998, its small-business support program had assisted more than 63,000 small businesses, with loans averaging US$5,000; and its community development program had assisted more than 40,000 microentrepreneurs, with loans averaging US$500. About 30 percent of small-business loans have gone to women. More than 1 million adults have benefited from the SFD's literacy programs, and communities have been given greater access to better-quality infrastructure and services. Even in countries with newer and smaller social funds, the delivery of significant benefits has been notable.

The social fund in the Republic of Yemen has surpassed most of its targets. By the end of 1998, it had provided support to 269 communities, compared with an expected 25, and to 2,168 microentrepreneurs, compared with a target of 2,000.

In the West Bank and Gaza, the community development project is a follow-up to the first-phase pilot project, and it will continue to improve infrastructure services. Nevertheless, the strategy will be redefined to target marginal and poor communities, with an emphasis on identifying poor areas, focusing on labor-intensive microprojects, which will preserve capital assets as well as promote local job opportunities.

**Source:** Various World Bank project appraisal reports.

---

Social funds have been able to absorb foreign assistance in a number of ways. With their emphasis on locally driven investments, such funds have offered an innovative approach to building modern civil society and promoting self-help mechanisms. In MENA, social funds have successfully contributed to mitigating risks and reducing income variability in the case of shocks through support for social and economic infrastructure improvements, asset accumulation by households and communities, and microenterprise development. Key factors in the efficiency of the

funds are legal and operational autonomy and the presence of highly mo-
tivated and efficient managers.

Although social funds have created jobs, little is known about their effect on permanent employment and on the living conditions of beneficiaries. In Algeria, the West Bank and Gaza, and the Republic of Yemen,
social funds have generated permanent and temporary employment for
far less than 1 percent of the total labor force. The Egyptian social fund
has been more successful. It accounted for an estimated 25 percent of
permanent nonagricultural jobs generated in the nation between 1993
and 1996—equivalent to about 10 percent of the estimated 2.2 million
unemployed—as well as temporary jobs for an additional 2 percent of the
unemployed.[26] Little is known, however, about the impact of the region's
social funds on the income, skills development, health, and education
level of beneficiaries. Although anecdotal evidence suggests positive effects, there have been no systematic evaluations.

Efficiency in generating jobs is difficult to estimate. Since social funds
are concerned as much with the type of infrastructure created as with
generating employment, most projects have had medium rather than
high labor intensity For instance, improving access to services has often
meant new construction, usually far more capital intensive than routine
repair and maintenance. In addition, wage rates are administratively set
at levels comparable to those prevailing in the labor market. Therefore,
labor unit costs appear to be higher than in other national job creation
programs, as in Algeria, which follows minimum wage regulations.

Sustainability depends heavily on donor money. Given their concerns
about addressing urgent community needs, most social funds are more
concerned with outputs than with their financial sustainability, at least
during their early years of operation. Thus, there has been little provision in the region for maintaining social funds from domestic finance
should international donor money be exhausted. In some countries,
however, community and local resources are already playing a significant
role in the sustainability of social funds. In the West Bank and Gaza, for
example, such resources account for 25 percent of the community development project, which is higher than initial estimates. In Egypt and
the Republic of Yemen, local and community resources account for an
average of 10 percent in the PWP.

*Cash and in-kind transfers.* Many governments provide cash and in-
kind transfer programs in their direct efforts to reduce poverty. The
amounts spent on transfer programs range between 0.2 percent and 1
percent of GDP. These programs include (a) in-kind transfers such as
food aid through schools (Tunisia), food aid to the elderly and handicapped (Morocco), nutritional programs for mothers and children (Morocco and Tunisia), training centers for poor, illiterate or dropout girls,

and shelters for school-age children and orphans (Morocco); (b) financial aid to hardcore poor who cannot support themselves, such as the elderly and handicapped (Algeria, Egypt, and Tunisia); and (c) means-tested cash transfers to poor families who need income support (Jordan, Tunisia, and the Republic of Yemen). These programs are usually publicly administered, but in some cases they take the form of partnerships with local charities, such as the *Entraide Nationale* (EN) in Morocco (see box 2.9).

The efficiency of the resources allocated to transfer programs is compromised, as monitoring mechanisms and coordination channels with other social programs are lacking. Though transfers are targeted to the "categorically" poor—that is, those who cannot help themselves (children) or those who cannot work because of physical, age, or other reasons—they are often paid to the nonpoor, as there are no mechanisms in place for assessing whether an individual is working or determining his or her income level. In Jordan and Tunisia, a recent cleanup operation eliminated about one-third of the beneficiaries of cash transfers who were receiving benefits without being eligible. Finally, transfer programs are not coordinated with other social programs, leading to overlaps among programs; their administration is hampered by weak management, and they are characterized by high administrative costs for each beneficiary they assist.

*Consumer food subsidies.* The design and objectives of consumer food subsidies vary across countries, ranging from universal subsidies to self-targeted systems, and from rationed schemes to targeted safety nets. In Morocco, subsidy programs were introduced to stabilize prices of strategic basic goods, with no explicit focus on the poor. This was achieved through subsidies, taxation, and a reallocation of resources among commodities to adjust for international price fluctuations. In Tunisia, the system aims at stabilizing prices of basic food staples, protecting the purchasing power of the poor, redistributing income to the poor, and improving the nutritional status of the poor as well as that of the population at large. This has required multiple interventions along the supply chain, from importers to refiners to distributors. Since the early 1990s, self-targeting mechanisms have been introduced to improve system effectiveness. In Egypt, a ration scheme was initially introduced to ensure the supply of essential goods to the population at large, but over the course of the 1980s, policy objectives were reoriented toward poverty alleviation, and measures were adopted to reduce the number of goods subsidized and to improve targeting through emphasis on inferior goods. In the Republic of Yemen, subsidy schemes were introduced through the application of preferential exchange rates for imports, but since 1999 they have been eliminated. In the Islamic Republic of Iran they were carried out through maintenance of multiple official, overvalued exchange

### BOX 2.9

## Direct Transfer Programs in Morocco and Tunisia

*Morocco. Entraide Nationale* (EN) is a public establishment under the authority of Morocco's Ministry of Social Development and Social Solidarity. Since its creation in 1957, its mission has been to support the poor. It manages a number of different programs, often working in partnership with local charities. It also has the authority to raise its own funds. But of an estimated 5 million poor, EN reaches only 80,000 (1.6 percent of the poor). Lack of coordination with other agencies (such as the ministries of health and education, and vocational training agencies) often results in duplication, while thinly stretched EN activities tend to be scattered and unfocused. EN's recurrent expenditures are high compared with the number of beneficiaries. The budget allocated to EN's activities is small (about 0.1 percent of GDP in 1996), and most is spent on salaries for its 6,300 employees (1,900 permanent staff and 4,400 temporary staff are paid near the minimum wage). The share of EN's budget allocated to wages increased from 69 percent in 1993 to 81 percent in 1996, while the share allocated to programs dropped from 27 to 14 percent. On average, there is one staff member for nine assisted poor. About 24 percent of EN staff are illiterate. These problems are also found in other government agencies, since public sector employment is used as a form of social protection. EN's administration is highly centralized, allowing little room for local decisionmaking. The *délégués* (regional coordinators for EN programs) have no power to make decisions about personnel or their activities. There is no system for monitoring the cost of each program, the performance of the centers, or their impact on the poor.

*Tunisia.* In Tunisia, the Ministry of Social Affairs provides direct transfer programs to the hardcore poor unable to support themselves. Direct transfers provide cash assistance to poor families who need income support (about 101,000 *familles nécessiteuses* in 1992). Although the number of households benefiting from direct cash transfers has been increasing, coverage is still inadequate, including in the poorest regions—the northwest and center-west. In its first year, 1986, the program covered about 65,000 families, about 81 percent of the eligible population. In 1994, coverage had reached 107,000 families, about 72 percent of the eligible population. If the program had attained full coverage, providing transfers to all those meeting its eligibility criteria, it would have reached almost 700,000 people, nearly 100,000 more than the 1990 household survey estimated to be below the poverty line. Partial comparison of the number of households benefiting from cash transfers and the number of households below the poverty line (as defined at the national level by the 1990 Household Consumption Survey) confirms that coverage under the cash transfer program is not fully satisfactory. In addition, the administration of transfer programs is complex, and eligibility lists are rarely updated. Even when they are, coverage is not always extended to those newly identified as eligible. Furthermore, because of lack of information on the characteristics and determinants of poverty, the eligibility criteria are very general, and entitlement to benefits is not always fully defined.

---

**BOX 2.9    (continued)**

As a result, some of the truly needy do not benefit from the program, while others re-ceive multiple benefits from various social assistance and insurance programs. The lack of distinction between group-based and need-based approaches also leads to overlap among programs. Finally, financial constraints have also kept cash transfers to needy families consistently below subsistence.

---

rates and controlled prices. Algeria and Jordan used to have food subsidy schemes, but abandoned them in the first half of the 1990s and have re-inforced transfer mechanisms instead.

In the MENA region, government spending on consumer food sub-sidies can reach levels comparable to public spending on education and health (up to 5 percent of GDP). While there are positive impacts on the poor, the nonpoor tend to absorb most public funds distributed in this way. Although much progress has been made in controlling the cost of subsidy programs, these remain expensive and subject to fluctuations in international prices and exchange rates (see table 2.8). Their effective-ness is questioned, as leakages toward middle- and high-income groups are pervasive (see table 2.9). Food commands a larger share of total spending for lower-income than for well-off households. For the poor, subsidized foods contribute an important share of protein consumption and about 40 percent of total caloric intake. In Tunisia, for example, the share of subsidized food per capita expenditure in 1990 was five times higher in the lowest quintile than in the highest. In Jordan, a 1987 household survey showed that subsidies represented about 14 percent of expenditures for the lowest quintile compared with 8 percent for the top

TABLE 2.8

**Food Subsidy Expenditure in MENA during 1990–99**
(percentage of GDP)

| Country | 1990 | 1995 | 1999 |
|---|---|---|---|
| Algeria | 4.3 | 0.9 | 0.0 |
| Egypt, Arab Rep. of | 4.4 | 1.3 | — |
| Iran, Islamic Rep. of | — | 2.9 | — |
| Jordan | 3.4 | 1.4 | 0.3 |
| Morocco | 1.3 | 1.7 | 1.7 |
| Tunisia | 2.4 | 2.1 | 1.2 |
| Yemen, Republic of | 3.7 | 2.6 | 0.3 |

— Not available.
**Source:** World Bank 1999b.

TABLE 2.9

## Incidence of Food Subsidies by Quintile
(percentage of total subsidies)

| Country | Targeting | 1 | 2 | 3 | 4 | 5 |
|---|---|---|---|---|---|---|
| Algeria (1991) | Universal subsidies | 13 | 17 | 19 | 22 | 29 |
| Egypt, Arab Rep. of (1994) | Self-selection | 21 | 21 | 22 | 19 | 17 |
| Morocco (1996) | Universal subsidies self-selection | 15 | 19 | 20 | 21 | 25 |
|  | Extraction rate flour | 23 | 24 | 22 | 18 | 13 |
| Tunisia (1993) | Self-selection | 21 | 20 | 21 | 20 | 18 |

**Source:** World Bank 1999b; other World Bank reports.

quintile. However, higher-income groups benefit more in absolute terms than do the poor because they consume greater quantities of subsidized goods (see World Bank 1999b). In Morocco, for example, people in the top quintile consume twice the value of subsidized food as do those in the lowest quintile. In the Republic of Yemen, the wealthiest 10 percent of the population spends 10 times more than the poor spend on subsidized wheat and flour, that is, the wealthy benefit 10 times as much.

# Strengthening the Social Protection System: Setting Priorities and Reallocating Resources

This chapter outlines the key elements of a comprehensive strategy to reform social security systems in the MENA region in order to improve their reach and effectiveness. The central message of the chapter is that a large set of policy interventions to reduce social risks and improve welfare exists outside the social protection system and basically involves more efficient economic management. These include stable macroeconomic policies, nondistorting pricing mechanisms, institutional reforms to promote competitiveness, and good governance. The implementation of these policies is essential to resolving social risks related to unemployment and poverty. Social protection programs such as active labor markets and social transfers are not viable substitutes. Improving the efficiency of financing and spending mechanisms in the education and health sectors is also a precondition for a sustainable social protection system. Within a comprehensive strategy, traditional social protection programs could focus on a few well-designed and integrated interventions that aim mostly at mitigating and coping with risks, particularly among vulnerable population groups. These can be classified within two major categories: (a) sustainable social insurance programs and (b) streamlined public works and safety net programs.

This chapter is organized into three sections. The first section briefly discusses necessary reforms to improve economic management. The second section outlines necessary reforms in the education and health sector. The third section presents a plausible reform strategy for the traditional social protection system that identifies areas where governments could consider disengaging and areas where public resources and reform efforts could be concentrated.

## 3.1. The Key to Lower Risks: Improving Efficiency in Economic Management

Higher social welfare will ultimately depend on the ability of MENA countries to create and distribute wealth. Above all, this will require stable macroeconomic policies, institutional reforms to promote a more diversified and competitive economy (including interventions to eliminate price distortions), and better governance.

## Macroeconomic Management

Prudent macroeconomic management will continue to be a precondition for sustainable growth in MENA. Most MENA countries have made considerable progress in improving macroeconomic management. The role of fiscal policy is gradually shifting from engine of growth to guarantor of macroeconomic stability. In oil-producing countries, however, fiscal revenues remain subject to political and social pressures. Improved governance is necessary for a better management of these resources. Fiscal policy needs to be countercyclical, as opposed to procyclical, in order to accumulate savings in good times to temporarily sustain demand during bad times.

## Good Governance

Governance is an important condition for efficient economic management and social protection effectiveness. Various factors determine the quality of governance, including governments' ability to honor contracts, the respect of private property, law and order, the quality of the bureaucracy, the respect of civil and political liberties, and transparency in the management of public resources. These factors directly affect economic performance. The risk of expropriation and government repudiation of contracts, for instance, influences foreign direct investment. Transparency in public management, the quality of bureaucracy, and the respect of civil and political rights, however, have a significant effect on the distribution of public resources, and therefore the welfare of the needy. In most cases, indicators of governance have improved over time in MENA countries (see "Institutional Country Risk Guide" indicators; Economic Research Forum 1996). It is desirable that these trends continue.

## Labor Market Reforms

Reducing rigidities in labor markets is an issue that all MENA countries need to address in the short-term. Interventions would be required to reduce restrictions to the allocation and reallocation of labor, and to minimize the burden of payroll taxes. Reforming labor markets does not imply eliminating workers' protection mechanisms, but rethinking them to improve efficiency. Three areas would need to receive particular attention. First, given that labor is often poor people's only asset, governments would need to ensure that access to labor markets is not restricted and sanction firms that practice some form of discrimination. Second, basic standards in labor markets need to be preserved and enforced. These include the prohibition of forced labor, the freedom of association, and the right to collective bargaining. A complement to public labor standards is market-based standards established by stakeholders (for example, consumer associations), including corporate benchmarking, codes of conduct, and voluntary enforcement of industry standards. Third, sustainable unemployment insurance systems are required to minimize the negative impacts that labor market adjustments can have on workers. These will also be necessary to mitigate the impacts of civil service reform.

## Eliminating Price Distortions

In order to improve the quality of basic services and infrastructure and reduce shortages, it is necessary to gradually reduce price controls in water, basic infrastructure and transportation, food, and other agricultural products. To ensure that low-income groups have access to basic services, governments could use direct transfers instead (see section 3.3.). To address other market failures, such as those related to an excessive consumption of natural resources and environmental services, appropriate market-based regulatory instruments (taxes, subsidies, and permits) could be considered. In the case of the Islamic Republic of Iran, for instance, a recent study finds that eliminating price distortions (tariffs, exchange rates, and food subsidies) would increase aggregate welfare by an equivalent of 4 to 7 percent of total income (World Bank 2001a).

In the case of water, governments need to review current policies on subsidies and implement appropriate pricing mechanisms while improving the regulatory framework. To eliminate price distortions, willingness-to-pay studies can be conducted with users' participation. While subsidies are desirable to ensure that low-income groups have access to clean water, thus reducing morbidity and mortality, these should be appropriately targeted.[27] In terms of institutional capacity, governments could enhance cost recovery systems, strengthen local capacity in water resource management and planning through the formation of water organizations, and promote awareness of water issues and programs. Mechanisms could also be identified to improve water quality, promote innovative approaches in the management of water resources, and induce the adoption of low-cost technologies and the use of alternative or nonconventional sources of water (treated wastewater, river cleanup, desalination, and water imports).

To protect producers from fluctuations in the price of agricultural products, it is desirable to switch from price control systems to insurance-based systems. Price floors can be costly to implement, difficult to manage, and not necessarily welfare-increasing for the poor. A more promising alternative would be to move to insurance-based systems, financed directly by producers. The degree of sophistication of this type of system is, of course, constrained by the degree of sophistication of the financial sector and the availability of financial instruments. In East Asia and Pacific, where financial markets are more developed, price support programs for crops such as rice are being replaced by option-based systems. Producers *buy* the option to sell their product at a minimum price if the market price drops below this minimum. While the ability to hedge against risks through insurance is not always available to low-income producers, usually because of liquidity constraints, governments could devise mechanisms to pool their risks and subsidize their insurance. The costs of these targeted subsidies would be considerably lower than the costs of indiscriminate price floors.

## Strengthening Regulatory Institutions

*Streamline and strengthen regulatory frameworks.* Markets are usually efficient in allocating scarce resources to their best use, but there are several imperfections that need to be dealt with—for instance, monopolies, imperfect information in capital markets, and the excessive depletion of natural resources. Governments need to develop and enforce efficient regulatory frameworks to cope with these imperfections. Laws to enforce competition, improve transparency in the financial sector, and protect natural resources and reduce pollution, and institutions that can efficiently enforce these laws, are necessary. Adopting this type of regulatory framework, however, is far from a simple task. Nonetheless, governments in the MENA region can benefit from international experience in these areas.

*Develop and enforce property rights.* A recent study shows that in developing countries, the market value of land owned by low-income population groups, but not legally registered, exceeds current transfers of foreign aid (de Soto 2000). This implies that many low-income individuals own assets that, if enforced by property rights, could be an important source of collateral. The development and enforcement of these property rights would also encourage associative contracts among landowners, generating scale economies and promoting productivity gains in otherwise overly fragmented agricultural lands.

## 3.2. Reducing Vulnerability: Improving Efficiency in Education and Health Expenditures

Education and health systems are essential components of a sustainable social security system, as they contribute to reducing risks and vulnerability. The challenge in most countries is to shift from highly centralized systems where financing, provision, and management functions rely on the public sector, and where the allocation of resources is largely unresponsive to prices and outputs, to systems where the private sector, outputs, and prices have a more prominent role. This implies revisiting the role of the public sector to play down its functions as a direct provider and to strengthen its functions as a regulator. Governments would concentrate on implementing financing mechanisms to ensure that low-income population groups had access to education and health services, and that private providers met appropriate quality standards and had incentives in place to control costs.

## Education and Training

Improving the quality of education and training will reduce the vulnerability of the poor by enabling them to participate more effectively in the labor market and thereby share the benefits of economic development. This can be accomplished by:

- Reviewing current financing mechanisms to ensure that households finance part of the cost of their education. While it is difficult to determine the appropriate level of the public and private shares, it is recommended to have a higher share of public funding in primary and secondary education than in higher education and vocational training.

- Providing sources of financing to students, such as student loans, to address liquidity constraints. Direct subsidies for the poor are also desirable, but their efficient use requires appropriate targeting mechanisms to minimize leakages.

- Reviewing management and delivery mechanisms. The private sector could have a more important role in the provision of education services. Communities could be more involved in the management of public schools. Decentralizing management can help improve budget allocations.

- Improving continuous training programs while developing incentive systems that encourage teachers to invest in their training.

- Reviewing current curricula at all levels, making them better suited for a knowledge-based economy.

- Improving efficiency by identifying incentives for institutions and teachers, leading to lower unit costs and higher quality.

## Health

To help eliminate disparities and inefficiencies in health care coverage, thereby improving the health of the poor and reducing their vulnerability to financial catastrophe from injury or illness, it will be necessary to implement coherent, systematic restructuring and reform of the region's health systems. This will entail the following:

- Changing the role of the state. Governments could reduce their role as direct service providers, while encouraging the expansion of private providers, by becoming purchasers of private health services. This will require an expansion of their role as a regulator of the health sector, including regulation of private health insurance.

- Improving the performance of the public delivery system through better intersectoral coordination of policies that affect health.

- Addressing the consequences of epidemiological and demographic transitions by strengthening maternal and child health services and health education programs, focusing on the large, impending non-communicable disease burden, and increasing support for women's organizations and other community-based efforts.

- Improving risk pooling for the entire population through the expansion of formal health insurance coverage to all groups, particularly vulnerable populations such as the poor.

- Improving public and private sector equity, quality, efficiency, and sustainability through appropriate financing, management, regulatory, and cost containment policies.

## 3.3. Mitigating and Coping with Risks: Redefining Priorities for the Social Protection System

The review of traditional social protection programs in the MENA region suggested that risk-reducing mechanisms such as labor market policies (job search assistance, wage subsidies, and continuous training programs, for instance) often have not achieved desired objectives. In general, risk-coping mechanisms such as public works and safety net programs have been more effective. The review also identified major constraints affecting risk-mitigating mechanisms, such as pensions and unemployment insurance systems.

In terms of the traditional formal social protection system (ALMPs, social security, and social assistance), a reform strategy could be developed on the basis of three principles: (a) given limited resources, governments need to prioritize the areas of intervention and avoid fighting on multiple fronts at the same time; (b) there are social gains to be made by encouraging private sector participation in the financing and provision of social services; and (c) public resources should concentrate on cost-effective interventions. The following strategic actions are suggested.

*Improving the financial sustainability of social insurance systems.* Though many other areas of intervention refer to issues that are cyclical or short-term in nature—that is, they may wither away, albeit at a cost, in the absence of specific policies—social insurance is deeply embedded in the socioeconomic structures of the region. Labor insurance and pensions are already under a strain, and five arguments point to the urgency of addressing them immediately:

- The certainty that social insurance systems in all economies will require reforms sooner rather than later, since despite favorable demographics at present, pension funds have reserves well below expected levels, and some are already in deficit. Moreover, there is steady deterioration in the old-age dependency ratio.

- Their size and underperformance have a significant adverse effect on growth arising from poor outcomes in labor, product, insurance, and capital markets.

- Since the programs are publicly managed and yield low returns, funding them presents a sizable obstacle to a more efficient and effective use of public social spending.

- The systems are bound to mature and expand further (due to urbanization, growth, and so on), making reforms more costly over time because of increasing deficits.

- International experience suggests that reforms in this area take a long time, have heavy statistical and analytical requirements, and require substantial stakeholder consensus building.

*Improving training systems.* Though training cannot be blamed for much of the high (and in some cases, still rising) unemployment rates in the regional economies, current training schemes tend to absorb considerable funds (often raised from payroll contributions), deprive the education and human development sector of valuable resources, and have generally poor results. Regional systems tend to be publicly dominated, supply driven, and expensive. They are often designed to act as a program of last resort for dropouts from the formal education system. However, market-relevant training can help increase the employability of the young or those who lost their jobs because of economic restructuring. The way skills are created, financed, and managed can, therefore, have important implications for productivity, employability and unemployment, and poverty. National reviews of the training systems and analyses of labor market data can pave the way for meaningful reforms with far-reaching effects on economic efficiency and poverty. Reforms in the training sectors would have sizable and deep effects on product and regional markets and productivity, on the one hand, and household earnings, unemployment, and poverty, on the other hand.

*Designing safety nets as developmental and community based, not just as assistance and centrally administered schemes.* An area where the rationale for governments' involvement is the strongest is the implementation of risk-coping mechanisms, such as public works and safety nets. These programs can substitute for those informal coping mechanisms that are welfare-decreasing, such as reduced investment in human capital or child labor. This study has found that public works and safety nets usually have been the most effective, despite the fact that many are ill designed and problems related to poor targeting and lack of coordination across implementing agencies are pervasive. These mechanisms could be strengthened. This would require conducting evaluations, phasing out ineffective projects, and consolidating those with the highest potential. To increase efficiency, it is also necessary for local communities to become more involved in the design, financing, implementation, and monitoring processes. Child protection (including child labor and disability) schemes, though embryonic in most regional economies, represent another area of potentially promising developmental activities with strong participation of the civil society.

*Expanding the role of the private sector in job assistance, insurance, and microcredit.* The review has suggested that the private sector could play a more prominent role in the development of risk-reducing mechanisms in labor markets. Indeed, the rationale for government control of job assistance programs and continuous training programs is weak at best. The private sector could also be more involved in the management and financing of risk-mitigating mechanisms such as health, pensions, and unemployment insurance systems. Providing access to capital markets to low-income population groups is another area where more private and less public participation would improve efficiency. Governments could concentrate on developing and enforcing property rights and designing and enforcing an appropriate regulatory framework for microfinance programs, while the private sector would take the lead in designing, implementing, managing, and financing these programs.

## Reforming Pension Systems

The fact that pension systems in the region are relatively young creates the perfect setting to initiate a reform process. Indeed, the social costs of reforming pension systems increase as the population ages and unfunded pension liabilities accumulate. Over the last 10 years, knowledge about pension reform has accumulated rapidly as diverse countries have been faced with the crisis of their traditional pay-as-you-go systems. The debate about which is the appropriate system design continues to evolve, but consensus has been reached at different levels. Thus, on the basis of lessons from international experience, a three-staged approach for pension reform is proposed.

*Stage 1.* Consolidate the short-term and medium-term financial situation of current funded or unfunded defined-benefit systems by strengthening institutional capacity (for example, administrative process, information systems, and reserves management practices), and introducing, when necessary, gradual parametric reforms to realign contributions and benefits. The main purposes of the defined-benefit schemes would be to address equity issues by, for instance, guaranteeing a minimum pension for low-income workers.

*Stage 2.* Develop an institutional framework in order to increase savings and future replacement rates to stimulate the expansion of personal and occupational savings. The development of contractual savings will also contribute to the development of capital markets, paving the way for a third stage.

*Stage 3.* Introduce a mandatory, publicly or privately managed, defined-contribution system with individual accounts. This system can contribute to addressing the problem of an aging population (as the link between financial stability and dependency ratios is broken) and would eventually generate the largest share of the total replacement rate.

*Improving institutional capacity.* A first step toward pension reform is to streamline current administrative processes and update information and management systems. While this may appear to be a simple task, it usually consumes considerable amounts of resources and time. The goal is to get pension funds to review basic administrative processes, such as registration, contributions tracking, follow-up of life events, and pension payment, to improve efficiency. It is also crucial to modernize information systems (databases on contributions and beneficiaries, for instance), accounting systems, and reporting and auditing practices. Usually, achieving these goals requires contracting with specialized firms to assess the current situation and preparing recommendations and an implementation plan.

*Improving the financial situation of the pensions funds by adjusting the parameters used to calculate contributions and benefits while protecting the poor with a minimum pension and appropriate indexation mechanisms.* There are different options that governments could consider to realign contributions and benefits. These include changing contribution rates, vesting periods, retirement ages, accrual rates, and the rules governing early retirement. Choices need to be guided by appropriate actuarial analysis and also by the political viability of alternative reform proposals. In general, parametric reforms should respond to four principles: (a) adjustments should be gradual, (b) acquired rights should be honored, (c) changes in contribution rates should not harm the competitiveness of firms, and (d) mechanisms should be adopted to protect low-income groups. It is also necessary to separate the accounts of the pension system from other social assistance or insurance programs. When special pension programs exist (such as noncontributory programs for low-income groups), the costs and sources of financing should be clearly specified. Reforms to improve the financial sustainability of these programs often need to be considered.

*Reserves management.* In the case of partially funded systems that have accumulated reserves, management practices need to be reviewed in order to increase rates of return. With the support from experts, regulations and appropriate incentives systems need to be designed and put in place. Even when funds choose to outsource the management of reserves, the appropriate regulatory infrastructure needs to be in place. Areas that need to receive attention include the selection and evaluation of fund managers, as well as the development of guidelines to limit the range of possible investments as a function of their expected return and risk.

*Refinancing the government debt.* Most governments have accumulated arrears with pension funds. It is desirable that these arrears be properly audited and then refinanced. Often, this implies registering arrears as a formal debt with the pension system and agreeing to a schedule of payments. The refinancing plan needs to be consistent with macroeconomic and fiscal objectives. The goal is not to clear governments' debt and increase pension reserves that would then be allocated to alternative investments, but rather to ensure that the short-term deficits of the pension fund, if observed, are covered.

*Voluntary savings.* Both occupational and personal savings schemes enable workers who earn more during their active years to accumulate larger pension rights for their retirement. Even though promoting long-term personal savings and occupational plans will require structural reforms to create a more dynamic and diversified economy, along with an efficient and properly regulated financial sector, in the short-term, different types of incentives can be considered. For instance, countries such as the Republic of Korea, Malaysia, and Singapore have established postal savings systems that offer greater security and accessibility, higher interest rates (often tax free), and lower transaction costs, especially in rural areas. The development of occupational plans can also be encouraged by making contributions tax deductible and deferring taxes on investment income. These types of incentives have been common to most countries and have made occupational programs suitable substitutes for higher wages, thus encouraging their diffusion. In the developing world, occupational pension programs have been growing in countries such as Brazil,

India, Indonesia, Mexico, and Zimbabwe. While there is a gradual tendency to make these programs mandatory, particularly in the case of OECD countries, countries should initially adopt a flexible stance, given the still frail situation of the economy. Nonetheless, a minimum regulatory framework should be in place to require that the programs are appropriately funded and of sufficient portability. Incentives would need to be carefully designed to ensure that benefits do not concentrate on high-income households that would have been saved in any event.

*Introducing a defined-contribution system with individual accounts when necessary conditions (capital markets, regulatory framework) are in place.* There is by now considerable international experience to guide MENA countries contemplating pension reform (see Palacios and Whitehouse 1998). An important message is that the necessary regulatory framework for this type of system is highly complex. Countries should not consider introducing defined contributions if this framework is not in place. The costs of a funded system with individual accounts are also considerable. Indeed, most countries that have introduced this system have given current workers the choice between the standard pay-as-you-go and the two types of schemes. This involves making explicit a much larger liability than is currently the case. However, the window of opportunity to introduce a fully funded system closes further as each new cohort of workers acquires pension rights under the increasingly unfunded pay-as-you-go system. Nonetheless, potential fiscal benefits justify these short-term costs. Besides addressing the problem of an aging population, a defined-contribution system may provide incentives for a more efficient use of capital. There are also labor market efficiency gains as workers perceive pension contributions as true savings, not as an additional tax. Indeed, under the defined contribution system, workers can monitor the management of their contributions and link them to future earnings.

The key to success of any reform is to keep a fluid dialogue with different stakeholders. The financial implications of any policy interventions should be assessed within a long-term framework. This would reduce the likelihood of adopting reform packages that focus solely on short-term problems and leave future financial problems to the new generations.

## Reducing Government Involvement in ALMPs and Microfinance

*ALMPs.* The present strategy recommends a gradual disengagement of public resources from labor market interventions such as wage subsidies, job search assistance programs, and continual training programs. For current programs, the following recommendations are given:

- If a country is going to institute labor market programs, a good practice is to start with modest programs.

- Sound impact evaluation techniques should be used to evaluate the instituted programs. Relying only on nonscientific evaluations may lead to incorrect policy conclusions. A good microevaluation will involve comparing labor market outcomes for individuals who have gone through a particular program with those of a control group of their peers, and will also use data on program costs. These will help to answer three important questions: What is the impact of the program? Is the impact large enough and are the costs low enough to yield net social gains? Is the observed outcome the best outcome that could have been achieved for the public resources spent?

- Based on these evaluations, the programs should be tightly targeted at those for whom they are found to be the most cost-effective, or if the evaluations point toward these programs being ineffective, the programs should be amended or discarded.

- A national labor market information system should be established in order to monitor employment trends and to assess the cost-effectiveness and the impact of the various public interventions in this area.

- Private employment services should be allowed to operate and complement the publicly provided services.

*Microfinance.* Microcredit programs can be important mechanisms to mitigate the risks facing the poor. In general, however, international experience suggests that governments' involvement should be limited to the design and enforcement of an appropriate regulatory framework. Moreover, this framework should be part of a wider strategy for the financial sector. As previously discussed, the major contribution that government could make to provide access to capital markets to low-income population groups is to design and enforce property rights.

In terms of current public programs, governments could consider the following:

- Gradually transferring management of programs to NGOs.

- For those programs remaining temporarily under government control, adopting newly developed evaluation standards (see Micro-Banking Bulletin) to assess management and financial performance.

- On the basis of this assessment, evaluating whether the programs are realistically sustainable, given targeted population groups and cultural and religious constraints (Islamic banking principles, for example).

- Incorporating banks as part of the delivery mechanism. As shown by emerging developments in Morocco and Lebanon, banks or financing companies with a retail focus, if operating in a competitive environment, can be the most effective mechanism to deliver microcredit programs.

## Selectively Strengthening Risk-Coping Mechanisms

*Improving institutional capacity for better targeting and delivery.* The main challenge to improving the effectiveness of current risk-coping mechanisms across MENA countries is to clearly define priorities in terms of which groups ought to benefit from subsidies and transfers and for how long, while improving institutional capacity (such as information systems and targeting methodologies) to reach these groups at minimum cost (by minimizing leakages to individuals who are not eligible).

*Defining priorities.* Social assistance programs can be classified into three groups: (a) those that define *ex ante* the vulnerable population groups that need to be targeted *and* have appropriate targeting mechanisms, (b) those that define *ex ante* target population groups but do not have proper targeting mechanisms, and (c) those programs that do not target vulnerable population groups *ex ante*. Very few programs in the MENA region fall into the first category. Often, social assistance programs do not focus on vulnerable groups from the outset. An example is the family allowance program in Algeria that benefits middle- to high-income households. Countries need to clearly establish priorities in terms of coverage for social assistance programs. As previously discussed, this is a challenging task both politically and technically. However, countries can benefit from a large body of research in the area and from the lessons of international experience.

*Information and monitoring systems.* Once priorities have been defined, updated regional maps of vulnerable population groups are required. To be developed, these maps require sound household and labor force surveys, as well as a recent census. Computerized monitoring systems are also essential. These systems allow policymakers to evaluate the performance of the programs by following up on beneficiaries and implementation costs. On the basis of this information, programs can be corrected or eliminated. Information systems are also required to improve targeting mechanisms.

*Targeting.* Poor targeting is pervasive among MENA social assistance programs. Different types of targeting mechanisms are necessary at different levels. While self-targeting methods are desirable to distribute resources at the local level (community level), centralized mechanisms are necessary to distribute resources across regions. Usually, shares are proportional to the weighted shares of the different targeted population groups living in each region. Weights reflect the relative importance given to each of these groups. Defining these weights necessarily involves using subjective criteria. A suggested approach implies working with representatives from different segments of the civil society, engaging them in a guided dialogue, and helping them to reach a consensus. Targeting methods can also be reinforced by introducing regular audit and control systems based on statistical analysis. These are similar to the methods used in OECD countries to monitor tax evasion. The method consists of using household surveys to predict the probabilities of being eligible for subsidies and transfers on the basis of demographic, social and economic, and geographic characteristics. Randomly selected beneficiaries, with low probabilities given their known characteristics, can then be audited.

*Coordination.* Coordination across implementing agencies is indispensable to reducing the duplication of effort and improving efficiency. Coordination needs to be managed by a selected agency that monitors the inventory of programs and assesses the appropriateness of new programs.

*PWPs.* To enhance the ability of PWPs to protect vulnerable populations against both long-term unemployment and sudden loss of income while creating the infrastructure needed to improve rural and urban living conditions, the programs need to achieve the following:

- Improve self-targeting. PWPs can attract the poor through self-targeting mechanisms such as payments below market wages, labor-intensive activities, and regional distribution of worksites based on poverty measures.

- Improve monitoring and evaluation. PWPs should include mechanisms to monitor the medium- and long-term effects of the programs on the populations they are intended to benefit.

- Encourage greater participation among women. PWPs in MENA countries have created employment predominantly for men, but international experience has shown that women can be employed through piecework or task-based payment, and through the provision of work close to their homes and flexible work schedules.

- Increase economic returns by taking into account the level of development of basic infrastructure in poor regions of the country. It is desirable to estimate economic rates of return to different projects in different regions prior to project selection. Maintenance costs should also be taken into account in the selection process.

- Increase participation of the private sector. Involving private operators, managers, and small contractors can increase the effectiveness of PWPs.

*Social funds.* To increase their contribution to the protection of vulnerable populations by channeling resources to small and locally initiated infrastructure, microfinance, and community development projects, social funds need to take the following into account:

- Improving sustainability. This will depend on the evolution of national policies in terms of fiscal decentralization, sectoral cost recovery, and greater participation of communities in decisionmaking and cost sharing.

- Measuring and enhancing impacts, especially for the poorest. Social funds need to improve their methodologies for identifying and enumerating beneficiaries and evaluating program benefits.

- Seeking an optimal portfolio mix. In all cases, social funds will need to experiment with the composition of the services they offer (for example, community development, public works, and microfinance) in order to identify which vulnerable groups are not reached and which programs have the greatest impact.

- Promoting learning across organizations. The experience of social funds in managing demand-driven portfolios; working with NGOs, community groups, and small-scale contractors; encouraging community participation and cost sharing; and using beneficiary assessments and other participatory evaluation methodologies can add to the knowledge base of local governments and line ministries.

*Food subsidies.* To improve the nutritional status and food security of vulnerable populations, food subsidy systems need to be gradually eliminated while transfer programs are strengthened. More targeted food programs, including direct transfers, would enhance the likelihood that the poor would benefit while reducing the total cost of the programs. To this end, governments could consider the following:

- Improving institutional capacity to assess the magnitude of current food subsidy systems policy and its economic and social impact.

- Preparing a strategy for gradually phasing out untargeted subsidy systems while designing appropriate compensatory measures (cash transfers and targeted food programs) for the poor.

- Reducing producer protection simultaneously with consumer food subsidy reform to promote efficient domestic food production and lower effective prices. The transition should be gradual and may require extensive rural development measures targeted at small farmers.

*Transfers.* To improve the impact of transfers on poverty and contain their costs, governments could consider the following:

- Improving targeting and delivery mechanisms (see page 95)

- Promoting partnerships and complementary relationships with other agencies and civil society

- Undertaking regular monitoring and evaluation of the impact of transfer programs.

# CHAPTER 4

# The World Bank's Role

## 4.1. World Bank Involvement in Social Protection

The World Bank's involvement in the broadly defined social sectors includes substantial support for educational, health, water, agricultural, urban and rural, infrastructure, environmental, transportation, and so on, lending and nonlending services. In the more conventional area of social protection, the Bank has addressed consumer food subsidies, labor markets and vocational training, social funds, pensions, and more recently, children's issues through a mix of investment and adjustment projects and analytical and advisory services. The Bank's lending on social protection has increased substantially in the last eight years (see figure 4.1).

Similarly, the regional social protection program has grown during the 1990s. There were two social protection projects at the beginning of the 1990s (two vocational training projects—one in Algeria and one in Tunisia) to which three credits for the Egyptian social fund, one credit for the Yemeni social fund, and one loan for the Algerian social safety net were added.

These were followed by a training and employment project in Jordan, an in-service training project in Morocco, and a skills development project in the Republic of Yemen. The region also made initial steps in other areas of social protection—for example, some initial work on pensions and a pioneering project for child protection in Egypt. There are currently 12 projects in the social protection portfolio (see table 4.1).

Economic and sector work has been the cornerstone of the Bank's development agenda. The analytical work on social protection in the region is driven by country priorities, and the current plans are indicated in table 4.2. Much of this work is undertaken jointly with other sectors within the Bank—for example, poverty assessments with the Poverty Reduction and Economic Management Network and pensions and microfinance with the Financial Sector Development Department. The recent emphasis of the Bank on more comprehensive approaches to development (such as the Comprehensive Development Framework and

FIGURE 4.1

## Increase in World Bank Lending for Social Protection

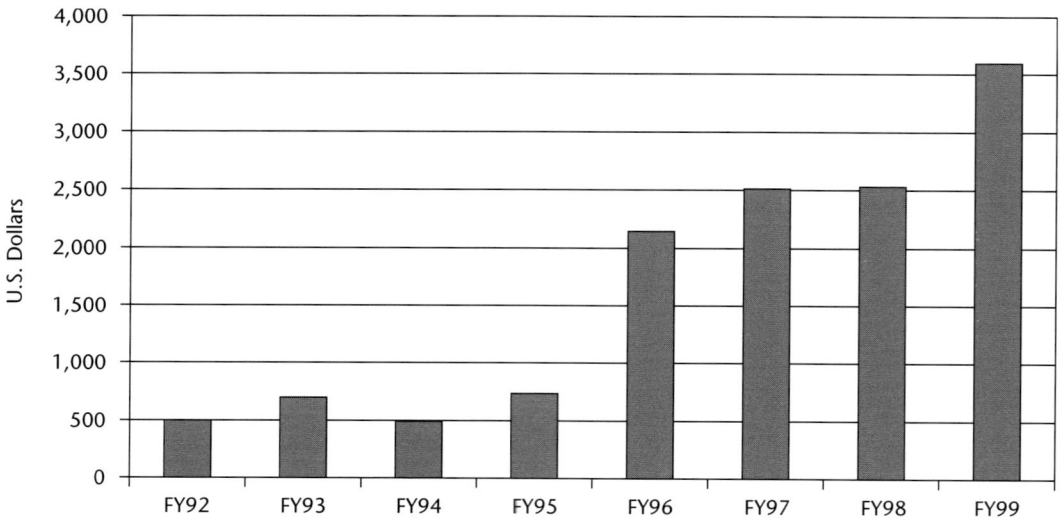

Source: World Bank, Social Protection Network.

TABLE 4.1

## Social Protection Projects, 1996–2000

| Country | Project Name | Start Year | Loan/Credit Amount (US$ millions) |
|---|---|---|---|
| Algeria | Social Safety I | 1996 | 50 |
| Egypt, Arab Rep. of | Social Fund II | 1997 | 120 |
|  | Social Fund III | 2000 | 50 |
|  | Social Protection (Children) | 2000 | 5 |
| Jordan | Training and Employment | 1998 | 5 |
| Lebanon | Vocational Training | 1999 | 63 |
| Morocco | In-Service Training | 1996 | 23 |
|  | Social Priorities | 1996 | 28 |
| Tunisia | 2nd Employment and Training | 1996 | 60 |
| Yemen, Republic of | Vocational Training | 1996 | 24 |
|  | Social Fund Dev. I | 1997 | 30 |
|  | Social Fund Dev. II | 2000 | 70 |
| Total Social Protection Projects = 12 |  |  | 528 |
| *Memorandum Items* |  |  |  |
| Total Health Projects = 12 |  |  | 645 |
| Total Education Projects = 20 |  |  | 1002 |

Source: World Bank, Human Development Sector, MENA Region.

the Poverty Reduction Strategy Paper) may imply fewer direct operations in each sector (not just social protection), but at the same time, it
may also create greater opportunities for mainstreaming social protection. The MENA social protection team has been active in the Bank's activities on the community-driven development approach and works in a

**TABLE 4.2**

## Current and Planned Economic and Sector Work for 2001–03

| Country | Child Labor Protection | Labor Markets | Training | Pensions | Safety Nets and Transfers | Poverty Assessment/ Update | Microfinance Public Works | Social Protection Strategy |
|---|---|---|---|---|---|---|---|---|
| Algeria | | | 2003 | | | 2003 | | 2000 |
| Djibouti | | | | 2001 | | | | |
| Egypt, Arab Rep. of | 2001 | | 2003 | 2003 | | | 2001 | |
| Iran, Islamic Rep. of | | | | 2002 | 2003 | | | 2003 |
| Jordan | 2001 | | 2002 | 2003 | | 2001 | | |
| Lebanon | | | | 2001 | 2002 | 2001 | | 2002 |
| Morocco | 2002 | | | | | 2001 | | 2003 |
| Syrian Arab Rep. | | | | | | | | |
| Tunisia | | 2003 | | 2001 | | 2003 | | 2003 |
| West Bank and Gaza | | | | 2001 | | | | |
| Yemen, Republic of | 2002a | | | 2002 | | 2002 | | |
| Regional | 2001 | | | 2002 | | | | 2002 |

a. In conjunction with UNICEF.
**Source:** World Bank, Human Development Sector, MENA Region.

complementary manner with other sectors in areas such as social development, pensions, rural development, labor markets, and gender.

## 4.2. Directions for the Future

### Increased Emphasis on Social Insurance

Most regional economies are contemplating assessments of their pension systems. These include Algeria, Djibouti, Egypt, the Islamic Republic of Iran, Jordan, Lebanon, Morocco, Tunisia, and the Republic of Yemen. We should anticipate the need for support to our clients. A regional conference on pensions organized jointly with the World Bank Institute in March 2000 created sufficient interest and networking for follow-up operations. Because the international experience suggests that reforms in this area take a long time, entail heavy statistical and analytical work, and require substantial stakeholder consensus-building, we need to be proactive in this area and undertake good planning.

Social insurance systems that are important for development and poverty reduction go well beyond the more conventional or narrow social protection concerns. For example, the already large size and underperformance of social insurance systems have a significantly adverse effect on growth arising from poor outcomes in labor, product, insurance, and capital markets. The low returns in pension fund investments (and also the deficits in some funds) present a sizable obstacle to a more efficient and effective use of public social spending.

Key recommendations:

- Address fiscal and financial imbalances while there is a window of opportunity, before fiscal and financial imbalances reach a crisis stage as a result of changing demographics.

- Improve administrative and managerial efficiency of pension funds.

- Increase the coverage by developing a strong pay-as-you-go system. This would also improve equity.

Instruments to be used:

- Bank sector work, both formal and informal

- Country dialogue with both core ministries and technical ministries on the need to address pension problems before they reach a crisis stage

- Learning Investment Loans and Learning and Innovation Credits to support reforms and improve capacities of pension agencies

- Adjustment loans (when financial imbalances require them)

## Maintain and Expand Levels of Operations on Labor and Training Issues

Although training cannot be blamed for much of the high (and in some cases, still rising) unemployment rates in the regional economies, current training schemes tend to absorb considerable funds (often raised from payrolls), deprive the education and human development sector of valuable resources, and produce generally poor results. Regional systems tend to be publicly dominated, supply driven, and expensive, and they are often designed to act as a sponge for those who drop out from the formal education system. Training can help increase the employability of the youth or those who lost their jobs because of economic restructuring. The way skills are created, financed, and managed can, therefore, have important implications for productivity, employability and unemployment, and poverty. National reviews of the training systems and analyses of labor market data can pave the way for meaningful reforms with far-reaching effects on economic efficiency and poverty. Reforms in the training sectors would have sizable and deep effects on product and regional markets and productivity, on the one hand, and household earnings, unemployment, and poverty, on the other hand.

Key recommendations:

- Ensure better matching between job seekers and employers through greater involvement of the private sector.

- Increase private sector participation through regulatory and accreditation frameworks.

- Develop labor market information systems for better analysis and monitoring of the labor markets and employment programs.

- Adopt a comprehensive strategy that links the education system with the training system, and the public with the private sector, with a view to meeting emerging labor market requirements. This entails the adoption of policy frameworks for long-term development and reform. The frameworks should be objective driven and insulated against major policy shifts caused by changes in government.

- Improve the efficiency of the sector, and of individual institutions, by controlling and managing unit costs.

Instruments to be used:

- Continued sector work on labor market issues

- Loans and credits to support more market-based vocational training and to move existing supply-oriented vocational training systems to a demand orientation

- Loans and credits to finance retrenchment and retraining programs for displaced workers

### Introduce Innovations in Social Funds and Community Development (Including Gender and Children's Issues)

Social funds have historically been set up as emergency (reactive) institutions. But they also have a potential for evolving into broader developmental areas and applying community-based approaches beyond assistance programs and centrally administered schemes. Another emerging area of concern is child protection as the region starts exhibiting symptoms of a breakdown in traditional family networks, such as the existence of street children. Child protection (including child labor and disability) schemes, though embryonic in most regional economies, are promising developmental activities with strong participation of the civil society.

Issues to be addressed:

- Social funds can be more supportive of an approach based on community-driven development and follow a short- and long-term risk reduction strategy rather than individual investments or short-term job creation.

- Social funds need to define their long-term vision within the context of a national social protection strategy, and ensure their financial sustainability.

- Social funds can become nurseries for new approaches to development that, after development, may be spun off.

- Child protection needs to become comprehensive and community based, with less reliance on institutionalization.

Instruments to be used:

- Social funds would be supported by innovative loans and credits.

- The Bank will also provide technical support to social funds to increase their community orientation, develop new approaches, and develop their long-term vision.

- Specific Learning Investment Loans and Learning and Innovation Credits for child protection.

### Knowledge Management

The Bank has been very active in the compilation of knowledge in the area of social protection. Primers on pensions, labor markets, and safety nets have been produced. Recently, the social protection team has prepared a regional social protection primer that introduces the new Social Risk Management Framework. These and other products can be accessed at http://www1.worldbank.org/sp.

The new Social Risk Management Framework has imposed new demands in terms of analytical tools, and also new pieces of economic sector work to measure new constructs, such as vulnerability, and to operationalize new concepts. Some of these products include (a) risk and vulnerability assessments that identify vulnerable population groups and assess existing programs (such assessments have been prepared for countries in Latin America and the Caribbean and Sub-Saharan Africa), (b) a new methodology for Social Sector/Social Protection Expenditure and Financing Performance Reviews that is now being piloted to respond to the needs of the Social Risk Management Framework, (c) an alternative template for Labor Market Reviews that is under preparation, and (d) the new ISSUE, a simulation tool to assess unemployment support programs that is being developed and will be piloted in 2003.

### 4.3. Key Partnerships

The International Monetary Fund (IMF) is a key partner in implementing the Social Risk Management Framework and brings to the table its strengths in fiscal matters and strong macroeconomic policy advice, making the IMF an especially important partner when it comes to providing a conducive framework for risk reduction.

The regional development banks (such as the Islamic Development Bank and the African Development Bank) are already cooperating with the World Bank. A more strategic partnership with the regional banks would entail a combination of the World Bank's global knowledge base and the regional banks' in-depth knowledge of the region in which they are also operating. The regional banks bring substantial financial resources to the table. Such assistance needs to be closely coordinated among donors to make sure that support to countries is not fragmented. Greater cooperation will be sought.

The EU brings substantial resources and a growing interest in social protection issues to the table. It plays a large role in the region through various regional agreements and adjustment support programs. The World Bank has had good experiences in operational collaboration, but our joint efforts on the analytical front can be strengthened. In this respect, the World Bank intends to seek closer cooperation with regional think tanks, such as the Economic Research Forum and various national and regional institutes of economic and social research.

The International Labour Organization (ILO) brings to the table a long tradition of public-private partnerships, as demonstrated by its tripartite structure as well as years of experience in the implementation of labor standards. In recent years, the dialogue between the ILO and the World Bank has been strengthened, and a basis for good collaboration has been established. From a regional perspective, the World Bank expects to work closely with the ILO on areas of labor standards and child labor.

UNICEF brings a strong emphasis on and experience in community-based participatory programs as well as international advocacy on behalf of children. The social protection team has established links with the regional UNICEF offices, and the World Bank needs to build on past experiences and move forward in a coordinated fashion.

The UNDP can play a strong coordinating role. It has been instrumental in rallying support and organizing activities around the Egypt Social Protection Initiative on children. In Jordan, it facilitated the execution of the Training and Employment Support Project. As it begins to move toward implementing a more comprehensive approach to social protection, with more emphasis on institutions and governance, the social protection group is moving into areas where the UNDP clearly has comparative advantages, and closer coordination or partnerships will be necessary.

# Income and Key Human Development Indicators

TABLE A1.1

## Population and GNP Growth

| Country | Population (millions) 1999 | GNP (US$ billions) 1999 | GNP (world ranking) 1999 | GNP Average Annual Growth (%) 1998–99 | GNP per Capita (US$) 1999 | GNP per Capita (world ranking) 1999 | GNP per Capita Average Annual Growth (%) 1998–99 | GNP PPP[a] (US$ billions) 1999 | GNP PPP[a] per Capita (US$) 1999[b] | GNP PPP[a] per Capita (world ranking) 1999 |
|---|---|---|---|---|---|---|---|---|---|---|
| Algeria | 30 | 46.5 | 52 | 2.8 | 1,550 | 115 | 1.3 | 142.3 | 4,753 | 101 |
| Egypt, Arab Rep. of | 62 | 87.5 | 38 | 5.7 | 1,400 | 120 | 4.0 | 206.2 | 3,303 | 127 |
| Iran, Islamic Rep. of | 63 | 110.5 | 33 | 2.1 | 1,760 | 107 | 0.5 | 325.2 | 5,163 | 95 |
| Jordan | 5 | 7.0 | 97 | 0.8 | 1,500 | 119 | -2.0 | 16.6 | 3,542 | 124 |
| Lebanon | 4 | 15.8 | 75 | 1.0 | 3,700 | 76 | -0.4 | 17.6 | 4,129 | 113 |
| Morocco | 28 | 33.8 | 57 | 0.6 | 1,200 | 126 | -1.0 | 90.1 | 3,190 | 131 |
| Tunisia | 9 | 19.9 | 63 | 6.2 | 2,100 | 101 | 4.9 | 51.8 | 5,478 | 91 |
| Yemen, Republic of | 17 | 5.9 | 105 | -1.3 | 350 | 171 | -3.9 | 11.7 | 688 | 197 |

a. Purchasing power parity.
b. World Bank estimates.
**Source:** World Bank, *WDR 2000/2001*, 2001i.

TABLE A1.2

## Population and GNP Growth by Region

| | Population (millions) | GNP (US$ billions) | GNP[a] Average Annual Growth (%) | GNP per Capita (US$) | GNP[a] per Capita Average Annual Growth (%) | GNP PPP[b] (US$ billions) | GNP PPP[b] per Capita (US$) |
|---|---|---|---|---|---|---|---|
| Region | 1999 | 1999[c] | 1998–99 | 1999[c] | 1998–99 | 1999 | 1999 |
| East Asia and Pacific | 1837 | 1,833.0 | 7.2 | 1,000 | 6.0 | 6,424.0 | 3,500 |
| Europe and Central Asia | 475 | 1,022.0 | 0.0 | 2,150 | −0.1 | 2,654.0 | 5,580 |
| Latin America and the Caribbean | 509 | 1,955.0 | −0.9 | 3,840 | −2.4 | 3,197.0 | 6,280 |
| Middle East and North Africa | 291 | 599.3 | — | 2,060 | — | 1,338.0 | 4,600 |
| South Asia | 1329 | 581.1 | 6.2 | 440 | 4.2 | 2,695.0 | 2,030 |
| Sub-Saharan Africa | 642 | 320.6 | 2.0 | 500 | −0.3 | 929.3 | 1,450 |
| High income | 891 | 22,921.0 | 2.6 | 25,730 | 2.1 | 21,763.0 | 24,430 |

— Not available.

**Note: GNP** is the sum of value added by all resident producers, plus any taxes (less subsidies) not included in the valuation of output, plus net receipts of primary income (employee compensation and property income) from nonresident sources. Data are converted from national currency to current U.S. dollars by the World Bank Atlas method. **Average annual growth rate of GNP** is calculated from constant price GNP in national currency units. **GNP per capita** is GNP divided by midyear population. **GNP per capita average annual growth rate** is calculated from constant-price GNP per capita in national currency units. **GNP measured at PPP** is GNP converted to U.S. dollars by the purchasing power parity (PPP) exchange rate. At the PPP rate, one dollar has the same purchasing power over domestic GNP that the U.S. dollar has over U.S. GDP; dollars converted by this method are sometimes called international dollars.
a. The estimate is based on regression; others are extrapolated from the latest International Comparison Programme benchmark estimates.
b. Purchasing power parity.
c. World Bank estimates.
**Source:** World Bank, *WDR 2000/2001,* 2001i.

TABLE A1.3

## Population and Labor Force

| | Population Total (millions) | | Population Avg. Annual Growth Rate (%) | | Population Aged 15–64 (millions) | | Population Aged 15–64 Avg. Annual Growth Rate (%) | Labor Force Total (millions) | | Labor Force Growth Rate (%) | |
|---|---|---|---|---|---|---|---|---|---|---|---|
| Country | 1980 | 1999 | 1980–90 | 1990–99 | 1980 | 1999 | 1990–98 | 1980 | 1999 | 1980–90 | 1990–99 |
| Algeria | 19.0 | 30.5 | 2.9 | 2.2 | 9 | 18 | 3.6 | 5 | 10 | 3.7 | 4.0 |
| Egypt, Arab Rep of | 41.0 | 62.4 | 2.5 | 2.0 | 23 | 38 | 2.6 | 14 | 24 | 2.5 | 2.9 |
| Iran, Islamic Rep. of | 39.1 | 63.0 | 3.3 | 1.6 | 20 | 38 | 3.2 | 12 | 20 | 3.0 | 2.4 |
| Jordan | 2.2 | 4.7 | 3.7 | 4.4 | 1 | 3 | 5.1 | 1 | 1 | 4.8 | 5.2 |
| Lebanon | 3.0 | 4.3 | 1.9 | 1.8 | 2 | 3 | 2.5 | 1 | 1 | 2.9 | 3.1 |
| Morocco | 19.4 | 28.2 | 2.2 | 1.8 | 10 | 18 | 2.9 | 7 | 11 | 2.4 | 2.7 |
| Tunisia | 6.4 | 9.5 | 2.4 | 1.6 | 3 | 6 | 2.8 | 2 | 4 | 2.7 | 2.8 |
| Yemen, Republic of | 8.5 | 17.0 | 3.3 | 4.0 | 4 | 8 | 3.9 | 2 | 5 | 3.9 | 4.7 |

**Sources:** For population data—World Bank, *WDR 2000/2001,* 2001i; World Bank, *WDI,* 2000b and 2001h. (These are estimates produced by the Human Development Network and the Development Data Group based on national census provided by national statistical offices or the U.N. Population Division). For labor force data—World Bank, *WDR 2000/2001,* 2001i; World Bank, *WDI,* 2000b and 2001h. (These are estimates compiled by the ILO from census or labor force surveys. These were calculated by applying gender-specific activity rates from the ILO database to the World Bank's population estimates to create a labor force series consistent with those estimates.)

## TABLE A1.4

## Population and Labor Force by Region

| | Population Total (millions) | | Population Avg. Annual Growth Rate (%) | | Population Aged 15–64 (millions) | | Labor Force Total (millions) | | Labor Force Growth Rate (%) | |
|---|---|---|---|---|---|---|---|---|---|---|
| Region | 1980 | 1999 | 1980–90 | 1990–99 | 1980 | 1999 | 1980 | 1999 | 1980–90 | 1990–99 |
| East Asia and Pacific | 1397.0 | 1836.0 | 1.6 | 1.3 | 820 | 1220 | 719 | 1038 | 2.3 | 1.5 |
| Europe and Central Asia | 425.8 | 475.3 | 0.9 | 0.2 | 274 | 318 | 214 | 238 | 0.5 | 0.6 |
| Latin America and the Caribbean | 360.3 | 509.2 | 2.0 | 1.7 | 201 | 319 | 130 | 219 | 3.0 | 2.5 |
| Middle East and North Africa | 175.0 | 290.9 | 3.1 | 2.2 | 91 | 171 | 54 | 97 | 3.1 | 3.1 |
| South Asia | 902.0 | 1329.3 | 2.2 | 1.9 | 508 | 797 | 392 | 585 | 1.8 | 2.5 |
| Sub-Saharan Africa | 379.0 | 642.3 | 2.9 | 2.6 | 195 | 340 | 170 | 282 | 2.7 | 2.6 |
| High income | 789.1 | 890.9 | 0.6 | 0.6 | 505 | 596 | 357 | 433 | 1.1 | 0.9 |

**Note: Population total** includes all residents regardless of legal status or citizenship, except for refugees not permanently settled in the country of asylum, who are generally considered part of the population of their country of origin. **Population average annual growth rate** is calculated using the exponential end-point method. **Population aged 15–64** is the number of people in the age group that makes up the largest part of the economically active population, excluding children. **Labor Force total** comprises people who meet the definition established by the ILO for the economically active population: all people who supply labor for the production of goods and services during a specified period. It includes both employed and unemployed.
**Sources:** World Bank, *WDR 2000/2001,* 2001i; World Bank, *WDI,* 2000b and 2001h.

## TABLE A1.5

## Access to Education

| | Gross Enrollment Rates | | | | | | Net Enrollment Rates | | | |
|---|---|---|---|---|---|---|---|---|---|---|
| | Primary (% of relevant age group) | | Secondary (% of relevant age group) | | Tertiary (% of relevant age group) | | Primary (% of relevant age group) | | Secondary (% of relevant age group) | |
| Country | 1980 | 1998 | 1980 | 1998 | 1980 | 1998 | 1980 | 1998 | 1980 | 1998 |
| Algeria | 94 | 109 | 33 | 66 | 6 | 14 | 82 | 94 | 43 | 58 |
| Egypt, Arab Rep. of | 73 | 100 | 51 | 81 | 16 | 37 | 72 | 92 | 43 | 75 |
| Iran, Islamic Rep. of | 87 | 93 | 42 | 84 | — | 18 | 72 | 85 | 50 | 81 |
| Jordan | 82 | 89 | 59 | 80 | 13 | 19 | 73 | 83 | 53 | 72 |
| Morocco | 83 | 97 | 26 | 40 | 6 | 9 | 62 | 79 | 36 | 38 |
| Tunisia | 102 | 119 | 27 | 73 | 5 | 17 | 83 | 98 | 40 | 14 |
| Yemen, Republic of | — | 78 | — | 45 | 4 | 10 | — | 61 | — | 35 |

— Not available.
**Note:** The net enrollment rate for the Republic of Yemen is for the year 1998. The tertiary percent enrolled for the Islamic Republic of Iran and Jordan is for the year 1997.
**Sources:** Gross enrollment rates—World Bank, *WDI,* 2000b and 2001h; UNESCO 1997; World Bank database.

TABLE A1.6

## Access to Education by Region

| | Gross Enrollment Ratios | | | | | |
| | Primary (% of relevant age group) | | Secondary (% of relevant age group) | | Tertiary (% of relevant age group) | |
| Region | 1980 | 1997 | 1980 | 1997 | 1980 | 1997 |
|---|---|---|---|---|---|---|
| East Asia and Pacific | 111 | 119 | 44 | 69 | 4 | 8 |
| Europe and Central Asia | 99 | 100 | 86 | — | 30 | 32 |
| Latin America and the Caribbean | 105 | 113 | 42 | 60 | 14 | 20 |
| Middle East and North Africa | 87 | 95 | 42 | 64 | 11 | 16 |
| South Asia | 77 | 100 | 27 | 49 | 5 | 6 |
| Sub-Saharan Africa | 81 | 78 | 15 | 27 | 2 | 2 |
| High income | 106 | 104 | 81 | 108 | 25 | 49 |

— Not available.
**Note: Gross enrollment ratio** is the ratio of total enrollment, regardless of age, to the population of the age group that officially corresponds to the level of education.
**Source:** World Bank, *WDI,* 2000b and 2001h.

TABLE A1.7

## Educational Attainment

| | Percentage of Cohort Reaching Grade 5 | | | | Expected Years of Schooling | | | |
| | Male | | Female | | Male | | Female | |
| Country | 1980 | 1996 | 1980 | 1996 | 1980 | 1997 | 1980 | 1997 |
|---|---|---|---|---|---|---|---|---|
| Algeria | 90 | 94 | 85 | 95 | 10 | 12 | 7 | 10 |
| Egypt, Arab Rep. of | 92 | — | 88 | — | — | 12 | — | 10 |
| Iran, Islamic Rep. of | — | 92 | — | 89 | — | 12 | — | 11 |
| Jordan | 100 | — | 98 | — | 12 | — | 12 | — |
| Morocco | 79 | 76 | 78 | 74 | 8 | — | 5 | — |
| Tunisia | 89 | 90 | 84 | 92 | 10 | — | 7 | — |
| Yemen, Republic of | — | — | — | — | — | — | — | — |

— Not available.
**Note: Percentage of cohort reaching grade 5** is the share of children enrolled in primary school in 1980 and 1991 who reached grade 5 in 1994.
**Expected years of schooling** is the average number of years of formal schooling received.
**Source:** World Bank, *WDR 2000/2001,* 2001i.

## TABLE A1.8

### Adult Illiteracy Rate

| Country | Total (% of people 15+) | | | |
|---|---|---|---|---|
| | 1985 | 1990 | 1995 | 2000 |
| Algeria | 51.4 | 42.6 | 38.4 | 33 |
| Egypt, Arab Rep. of | 55.4 | 51.6 | 48.6 | 45 |
| Iran, Islamic Rep. of | 52.3 | 46.0 | 27.9 | 24 |
| Israel | 4.9 | — | — | 5 |
| Jordan | 25.8 | 19.9 | 13.4 | 10 |
| Lebanon | 23.2 | 19.9 | 15.0 | 14 |
| Morocco | 58.3 | 50.5 | 56.3 | 51 |
| Tunisia | 42.4 | 32.0 | 33.3 | 29 |
| Yemen, Republic of | 67.7 | 61.5 | — | 54 |

— Not available.
**Sources:** World Bank, *WDI 2001*, 2001h; UNESCO 2000.

## TABLE A1.9

### Adult Illiteracy Rate by Gender

| Country | Male (% of males 15+) | | Female (% of females 15+) | |
|---|---|---|---|---|
| | 1980 | 2000 | 1980 | 2000 |
| Algeria | 46 | 24 | 76 | 43 |
| Egypt, Arab Rep. of | 47 | 33 | 75 | 56 |
| Iran, Islamic Rep. of | 38 | 17 | 61 | 31 |
| Israel | 5 | 3 | 13 | 8 |
| Jordan | 18 | 5 | 46 | 16 |
| Lebanon | 17 | 8 | 37 | 20 |
| Morocco | 58 | 38 | 85 | 64 |
| Tunisia | 42 | 19 | 69 | 39 |
| Yemen, Republic of | 62 | 32 | 95 | 75 |

**Sources:** World Bank, *WDI 2001*, 2001h; UNESCO 2000.

## TABLE A1.10

### Adult Illiteracy Rate by Region

| Region | Male (% of males 15+) | | Female (% of females 15+) | |
|---|---|---|---|---|
| | 1980 | 2000 | 1980 | 2000 |
| East Asia and Pacific | 20 | 8 | 43 | 21 |
| Europe and Central Asia | 3 | 2 | 8 | 5 |
| Latin America and the Caribbean | 18 | 11 | 23 | 12 |
| Middle East and North Africa | 44 | 25 | 72 | 46 |
| South Asia | 48 | 34 | 75 | 57 |
| Sub-Saharan Africa | 51 | 30 | 72 | 47 |

**Note: Adult illiteracy rate** is the percentage of adults aged 15 and above who cannot, with understanding, read and write a short, simple statement about their everyday life.
**Sources:** World Bank, *WDI 2001*, 2001h; UNESCO 2000.

## TABLE A1.11

## Access to Health

| Country | Health Care (% of population with access) | | Safe Water (% of population with access) | | Sanitation (% of population with access) | |
|---|---|---|---|---|---|---|
| | 1980 | 1995 | 1980 | 1995 | 1982–85[a] | 1990–96[a] |
| Algeria | — | — | 77 | — | — | — |
| Egypt, Arab Rep. of | — | — | 90 | 64 | 70 | 11 |
| Iran, Islamic Rep. of | 50 | 73 | 50 | — | 65 | 67 |
| Jordan | — | 90 | 89 | 89 | 91 | 95 |
| Morocco | — | 62 | 32 | 52 | 50 | 40 |
| Tunisia | 95 | 90 | 72 | — | 52 | 96 |
| Yemen, Republic of | 16 | — | — | 52 | — | 19 |

— Not available.
**Note: Percentage of population with access to health care** is the share of the population that can expect treatment for common diseases and injuries, including essential drugs within one hour's walk or travel. **Percentage of population with safe water** is the share of the population with reasonable access to an adequate amount of safe water (including treated surface water and untreated but uncontaminated water, such as from springs, sanitary wells, and protected boreholes). **Percentage of population with access to sanitation** is the share of the population with at least adequate excreta disposal facilities that can effectively prevent human, animal, and insect contact with excreta.
a. Data are for the most recent year available.
**Sources:** World Bank, *WDI 2000*, 2000b; World Bank, *WDR 2000/2001*, 2001i; WHO 1996, 1997; WHO Programme of Immunization Information System; WHO; UNICEF; Water Supply and Sanitation Collaborative Council 1996.

## TABLE A1.12

## Child Immunization

| Country | Measles (% of children under 12 months) | DPT (% of children under 12 months) |
|---|---|---|
| | 1999 | 1999 |
| Algeria | 78 | 83 |
| Egypt, Arab Rep. of | 96 | 95 |
| Iran, Islamic Rep. of | 99 | 100 |
| Jordan | 83 | 85 |
| Morocco | 93 | 94 |
| Tunisia | 93 | 100 |
| Yemen, Republic of | 74 | 72 |

**Note: Child Immunization** is the rate of vaccination coverage of children under one year of age for four diseases—measles and DPT (diphtheria, pertussis or whooping cough, and tetanus). A child is considered adequately immunized against measles after receiving one dose of vaccine, and against DPT after receiving two or three doses of vaccine, depending on the immunization scheme.
**Source:** World Bank, *WDI 2001*, 2001h.

## TABLE A1.13

## Child Immunization by Region

| Region | Measles (% of children under 12 months) | DPT (% of children under 12 months) |
|---|---|---|
| | 1999 | 1999 |
| East Asia and Pacific | 83 | 82 |
| Europe and Central Asia | 97 | 97 |
| Latin America and the Caribbean | 90 | 87 |
| Middle East and North Africa | 91 | 92 |
| South Asia | 63 | 75 |
| Sub-Saharan Africa | 57 | 59 |
| High income | — | — |

— Not available.
**Sources:** World Bank, *WDI 2001*, 2001h.

TABLE A1.14

## Health Risk Factors

| Country | Prevalence of Anemia in Pregnant Women (%) | Low-Birthweight Babies | Prevalence of Child Malnutrition (% of children) | | Incidence of TB per 100,000 Population |
|---|---|---|---|---|---|
| | | | Weight for age (% of children under 5) | Height for age (% of children under 5) | |
| Country | 1985–99 | 1985–99 | 1985–98 | 1985–98 | 1997 |
| Algeria | 42 | 9 | 13 | 18 | 44 |
| Egypt, Arab Rep. of | 24 | 12 | 11 | 25 | 36 |
| Iran, Islamic Rep. of | 17 | 10 | 11 | 19 | 55 |
| Jordan | 50 | 2 | 5 | 8 | 11 |
| Morocco | 45 | 4 | 10 | 24 | 122 |
| Tunisia | 38 | 16 | 9 | 23 | 40 |
| Yemen, Republic of | — | 19 | 46 | 52 | 111 |

— Not available.
**Note: Prevalence of anemia,** or iron deficiency, is defined as hemoglobin levels at less than 11 grams per deciliter among pregnant women. **Low-birthweight babies** are newborns weighing less than 2,500 grams, with the measurement taken within the first hours of life, before significant postnatal weight loss has occurred. **Prevalence of child malnutrition** is the percentage of children under 5 whose weight for age is less than minus two standard deviations from the median of the reference population.
**Source:** World Bank, *WDI 2001,* 2001h.

TABLE A1.15

## Life Expectancy and Mortality

| Country | Life Expectancy at Birth (years) | | Infant Mortality Rate per 1,000 Live Births | | Under-5 Mortality Rate per 1,000 Live Births | | Child Mortality Rate per 1,000 Children, Aged 1–5 | | Adult Mortality Rate per 1,000 Adults, Aged 15–60 | |
|---|---|---|---|---|---|---|---|---|---|---|
| | | | | | | | Male | Female | Male | Female |
| Country | 1980 | 1999 | 1980 | 1999 | 1980 | 1999 | 1988–99[a] | 1988–99[a] | 1999 | 1999 |
| Algeria | 59 | 71 | 98 | 34 | 139 | 39 | — | — | 153 | 117 |
| Egypt, Arab Rep. of | 56 | 67 | 120 | 47 | 175 | 61 | 22 | 28 | 193 | 168 |
| Iran, Islamic Rep. of | 60 | 71 | 87 | 26 | 126 | 33 | — | — | 156 | 139 |
| Jordan | — | 71 | 41 | 26 | — | 31 | 7 | 5 | 156 | 118 |
| Morocco | 58 | 67 | 99 | 48 | 152 | 62 | 21 | 19 | 199 | 145 |
| Tunisia | 62 | 73 | 69 | 24 | 100 | 30 | 19 | 19 | 159 | 133 |
| Yemen, Republic of | 49 | 56 | 141 | 79 | 198 | 97 | 33 | 36 | 307 | 283 |

— Not available.
**Note: Child mortality rate** is the probability of dying between the ages of 1 and 5, if subject to current age-specific mortality rates.
a. Data for most recent year available.
**Sources:** World Bank, *WDI,* 2000b and 2001h; World Bank, *WDR 2000/2001,* 2001i; United Nations Department of Economic and Social Information and Policy Analysis, demographic and health surveys from national sources; UNICEF 1998.

## TABLE A1.16

## Life Expectancy and Mortality by Region

| | Life Expectancy at Birth (years) | | Infant Mortality Rate per 1,000 Live Births | | Under-5 Mortality Rate per 1,000 Live Births | | Adult Mortality Rate per 1,000 Adults, Aged 15–60 | |
|---|---|---|---|---|---|---|---|---|
| | | | | | | | Male | Female |
| Region | 1980 | 1999 | 1980 | 1999 | 1980 | 1999 | 1999 | 1999 |
| East Asia and Pacific | 65 | 69 | 55 | 35 | 82 | 44 | 184 | 141 |
| Europe and Central Asia | 68 | 69 | 41 | 21 | — | 26 | 289 | 127 |
| Latin America and the Caribbean | 65 | 70 | 59 | 30 | 78 | 38 | 207 | 122 |
| Middle East and North Africa | 59 | 68 | 96 | 44 | 136 | 56 | 183 | 151 |
| South Asia | 54 | 63 | 120 | 74 | 180 | 99 | 223 | 212 |
| Sub-Saharan Africa | 48 | 47 | 115 | 92 | 188 | 161 | 499 | 453 |
| High income | 74 | 78 | 13 | 6 | 15 | 6 | 125 | 63 |

— Not available.
Note: **Life expectancy at birth** is the number of years a newborn infant would live if prevailing patterns of mortality at the time of its birth were to stay the same throughout its life. **Infant mortality rate** is the number of infants who die before reaching one year of age, per 1,000 live births in a given year. **Under-five mortality rate** is the probability that a newborn baby will die before reaching age 5 if subject to current age-specific mortality rates. **Adult mortality rate** is the probability of dying between the ages of 15 and 60—that is, the population of 15-year olds who will die before their 60th birthday.
**Source:** World Bank, *WDI 2000,* 2000b.

## TABLE A1.17

## Fertility Transition in MENA between 1960 and 1995

| TFR (births per woman) | 2–3 | 3–4 | 4–5 | 5–6 | 6–7 | 7–8 |
|---|---|---|---|---|---|---|
| 1960 | | | | | | |
| | | | | Lebanon | Qatar<br>United Arab Emirates | Algeria<br>Bahrain<br>Egypt, Arab Rep. of<br>Iran, Islamic Rep. of<br>Iraq<br>Jordan<br>Kuwait<br>Libya<br>Morocco<br>Oman<br>Saudi Arabia<br>Syrian Arab Republic<br>Tunisia<br>Yemen, Republic of |
| 1995 | 2–3 | 3–4 | 4–5 | 5–6 | 6–7 | 7–8 |
| | Lebanon<br>Qatar<br>Tunisia | Algeria<br>Bahrain<br>Egypt, Arab Rep. of<br>Iran, Islamic Rep. of<br>Libya<br>Morocco | Iraq<br>Jordan<br>Kuwait<br>Syrian Arab Republic<br>United Arab Emirates | Saudi Arabia | Oman<br>Yemen, Republic of | |

Note: TFR is total fertility rate.

TABLE A1.18

## Water Availabilty and Access in MENA Countries

| Country | Freshwater Resources (cubic meters per capita) | | Access to Safe Water (% of population) | | | |
| | | | Urban | | Rural | |
| | 1999[a] | 2025 | 1990[b] | 2000[c] | 1990[b] | 2000[c] |
|---|---|---|---|---|---|---|
| Algeria | 477 | 323 | — | 98 | — | 88 |
| Egypt, Arab Rep. of | 930 | 649 | 97 | 96 | 91 | 94 |
| Iran, Islamic Rep. of | 1339 | 907 | 95 | 95 | 75 | 90 |
| Iraq | 3451 | 2198 | 92 | — | 22 | — |
| Israel | 377 | 264 | 100 | 100 | 100 | 100 |
| Jordan | 148 | 88 | 99 | 100 | 92 | 98 |
| Kuwait | 11 | 6 | 100 | 100 | 100 | 100 |
| Lebanon | 1124 | 833 | 95 | 100 | 85 | 100 |
| Libya | 148 | 94 | 72 | 72 | 68 | 68 |
| Morocco | 1062 | 764 | 94 | 100 | 58 | 60 |
| Oman | 426 | 251 | 41 | 41 | 30 | 30 |
| Syrian Arab Republic | 859 | 533 | 77 | 94 | 65 | 64 |
| Tunisia | 434 | 322 | 94 | 98 | 61 | 98 |
| United Arab Emirates | 71 | 48 | 100 | 100 | 100 | 100 |
| Yemen, Republic of | 241 | 123 | — | 74 | — | 75 |
| West Bank and Gaza | — | — | — | 95 | — | 85 |
| Middle East and North Africa | 1145 | 741 | 93 | 96 | 76 | 80 |

— Not available.
a. Data refer to 1999 except the Islamic Republic of Iran, Iraq, Israel, and the Syrian Arab Republic were cited from 1997 World Resources Institute data.
b. Data refer to the most recent year available in the period. Iraq, Lebanon, and the Syrian Arab Republic refer to 1985 data.
c. World Bank estimates.
**Source:** World Bank, *WDI 2001,* 2001h.

TABLE A1.19

## Net Renewable Water Distribution by Region and Per Capita, 1999–2000

| Region | Freshwater Resources (cubic meters per capita) | Access to Safe Water (% of population) | | | |
| | | Urban | | Rural | |
| | 1999 | 1990 | 2000 | 1990 | 2000 |
|---|---|---|---|---|---|
| East Asia and Pacific | — | 96 | 93 | 60 | 67 |
| Europe and Central Asia | 12,797 | — | — | — | — |
| Latin America and the Caribbean | 27,919 | 92 | 93 | 56 | 62 |
| Middle East and North Africa | 1,145 | 93 | 96 | 76 | 80 |
| South Asia | 2,854 | 93 | 92 | 75 | 85 |
| Sub-Saharan Africa | 8,257 | 81 | 82 | 37 | 41 |
| High income | — | 100 | — | 90 | — |

— Not available.
**Source:** World Bank, *WDI 2001,* 2001h.

TABLE A1.20

## Health Expenditures, 1995–98

| Country | Health Expenditure per Capita (US$) | Health Expenditure as Percent of GDP (US$) | | | Public Share of Health Expenditure (percent total) |
|---|---|---|---|---|---|
| | | Total | Public | Private | |
| Algeria | 58 | 3.6 | 2.6 | 1.0 | 72 |
| Egypt, Arab Rep. of | 38 | 3.8 | 1.8 | 2.0 | 47 |
| Iran, Islamic Rep. of | 107 | 5.8 | 2.4 | 3.4 | 42 |
| Jordan | 134 | 9.4 | 5.5 | 3.9 | 58 |
| Lebanon | 499 | 12.4 | 2.2 | 10.2 | 18 |
| Morocco | 58 | 4.0 | 1.1 | 2.9 | 28 |
| Tunisia | 105 | 5.9 | 3.0 | 2.9 | 51 |
| Yemen, Republic of | 19 | 5.0 | 2.2 | 2.8 | 43 |
| Middle East and North Africa Regional Average[a] | *285* | *5.8* | *2.9* | *2.7* | *55.8* |

**Note:** Data are for available year between 1995–1998.
a. Including Gulf countries.
**Sources:** World Bank estimates; WHO 2000.

TABLE A1.21

## Education Expenditures

| Country | Public Expenditure on Education (% of GNP) | | Expenditure per Student | | | | | |
|---|---|---|---|---|---|---|---|---|
| | | | Primary (% of GNP per capita) | | Secondary (% of GNP per capita) | | Tertiary (% of GNP per capita) | |
| | 1980 | 1997 | 1980 | 1997 | 1980 | 1997 | 1980 | 1997 |
| Algeria | 7.8 | 5.1 | 8.9 | 26.1 | 23.9 | — | — | — |
| Egypt, Arab Rep. of | 5.7 | 4.8 | — | — | — | 25.9 | 57.8 | — |
| Iran, Islamic Rep. of | 7.5 | 4.0 | 16.2 | 8.2 | — | 11.0 | 67.6 | 7.6 |
| Jordan | 6.6 | 6.8 | — | — | 24.5 | 112.4 | 59.9 | 81.0 |
| Lebanon | — | 2.5 | — | 18.5 | — | — | — | 22.3 |
| Morocco | 6.1 | 5.0 | 15.5 | 14.3 | 54.9 | — | 155.3 | 69.5 |
| Tunisia | 5.4 | 7.7 | 11.8 | 15.2 | 37.7 | — | 194.6 | 79.1 |
| Yemen, Republic of | — | 7.0 | — | — | — | — | — | — |

— Not available.
**Source:** World Bank, *WDI 2000,* 2000b.

TABLE A1.22

## Public Expenditures on Social Sectors
(as a percentage of GDP)

| Country | Food Subsidies | Cash & In-kind Transfers | Public Works | Public Pension | Housing | Public Health | Education | Total |
|---|---|---|---|---|---|---|---|---|
| Algeria | 0.0 | 0.4 | 0.2 | 4.6 | 5.5 | 2.6 | 6.1 | 19.4 |
| Egypt, Arab Rep. of | 1.3 | 0.2 | 0.3 | 2.5 | 2.0 | 1.8 | 4.8 | 12.9 |
| Iran, Islamic Rep. of | 2.7 | 1.2 | — | 1.5 | 1.5 | 2.4 | 4.0 | 13.3 |
| Jordan | 0.0 | 0.9 | — | 4.2 | 0.7 | 5.5 | 6.8 | 18.1 |
| Lebanon | 0.1 | 0.9 | — | — | — | 2.2 | 2.5 | 5.7 |
| Morocco | 1.6 | 0.1 | 0.2 | 1.8 | 0.1 | 1.2 | 5.9 | 10.9 |
| Tunisia | 1.7 | 0.5 | 0.1 | 2.6 | 1.7 | 3.0 | 6.9 | 16.5 |
| Yemen, Republic of | 0.0 | 1.0 | 0.2 | 0.1 | 0.7 | 2.2 | 7.0 | 11.2 |

— Not available.
**Note:** Social assistance includes cash and transfers but excludes public works.
**Source:** Various World Bank reports.

TABLE A1.23

## Functional Expenditures

(as a percentage of total government expenditure)

| Country | Year | General Public Services | Defense | Education | Health | Social Security and Welfare | Housing | Recreational | Fuel and Energy | Agriculture | Manufacturing Mining | Transport | Services | Total Functional Expenditures as a % Share of Total Government Expenditures |
|---|---|---|---|---|---|---|---|---|---|---|---|---|---|---|
| Algeria | 2000 | — | 3.90 | 20.30 | 10.30 | 29.00 | — | — | — | — | — | — | — | 20 |
| Egypt, Arab Rep. of | 1997 | 7.87 | 9.43 | 14.76 | 3.29 | 0.47 | 5.30 | 8.07 | 0.36 | 5.27 | 0.14 | 4.55 | 0.48 | 31 |
| Iran, Islamic Rep. of | 1998 | 7.08 | 8.50 | 15.99 | 6.43 | 13.57 | 5.64 | 3.14 | 10.70 | 2.00 | 0.68 | 5.18 | 11.31 | 27 |
| Jordan | 1997 | 14.42 | 17.90 | 14.58 | 10.24 | 17.77 | 2.03 | 2.10 | 0.38 | 3.79 | 0.08 | 3.79 | 0.66 | 34 |
| Morocco | 1995 | 17.31 | 13.56 | 16.55 | 3.12 | 6.96 | 0.36 | 0.92 | 0.69 | 4.15 | — | 4.33 | 0.77 | 33 |
| Tunisia | 1996 | 14.20 | 6.23 | 18.68 | 6.87 | 16.68 | 5.15 | 2.70 | — | 8.23 | 0.68 | 2.26 | 6.17 | 30 |
| Yemen, Republic of | 1999 | 30.30 | 18.77 | 21.81 | 4.40 | — | 1.63 | 2.82 | 0.30 | 7.82 | 0.07 | 3.10 | 0.19 | 42 |

— Not available.

**Source:** IMF 1999; World Bank 2002.

# Labor Market Indicators

TABLE A2.1

## Labor Force and Participation Rates

| Country | Population Total (millions) | | Population, Female (%) | Population Aged 15–64 (millions) | | Population, Female 15–64 (per 100 men) | Labor Force Total (millions) | | Participation Rates | | | |
|---|---|---|---|---|---|---|---|---|---|---|---|---|
| | | | | | | | | | (% of total) | | (% of aged 15–64) | |
| | 1980 | 1999 | 1998 | 1980 | 1999 | 1998 | 1980 | 1999 | 1980 | 1997 | 1980 | 1997 |
| Algeria | 19.0 | 30.5 | 49 | 9 | 18 | 115 | 5 | 10 | 26 | 33 | 56 | 56 |
| Egypt, Arab Rep of | 41.0 | 62.4 | 49 | 23 | 38 | 120 | 14 | 24 | 34 | 38 | 61 | 63 |
| Iran, Islamic Rep. of | 39.1 | 63.0 | 50 | 20 | 38 | 105 | 12 | 20 | 31 | 32 | 60 | 53 |
| Jordan | 2.2 | 4.7 | 48 | 1 | 3 | 79 | 1 | 1 | 45 | 21 | 100 | 33 |
| Lebanon | 3.0 | 4.3 | 51 | 2 | 3 | 117 | 1 | 1 | 33 | 23 | 50 | 33 |
| Morocco | 19.4 | 28.2 | 50 | 10 | 18 | 116 | 7 | 11 | 36 | 39 | 70 | 61 |
| Tunisia | 6.4 | 9.5 | 50 | 3 | 6 | 97 | 2 | 4 | 31 | 42 | 67 | 67 |
| Yemen, Republic of | 8.5 | 17.0 | 49 | 4 | 8 | 91 | 2 | 5 | 24 | 29 | 50 | 63 |

**Sources:** World Bank, *WDI 2000,* 2000b; World Bank, *WDR 2000/2001,* 2001i.

TABLE A2.2

## Labor Force and Participation Rates by Region

| Region | Population Total (millions) | | Population Aged 15–64 (millions) | | Labor Force Total (millions) | | Participation Rates | | | |
|---|---|---|---|---|---|---|---|---|---|---|
| | | | | | | | % of total | | (% of aged 15–64) | |
| | 1980 | 1999 | 1980 | 1999 | 1980 | 1999 | 1985 | 1996 | 1985 | 1996 |
| East Asia and Pacific | 1,398.0 | 1,837.0 | 820 | 1,220 | 719 | 1038 | 51 | 57 | 88 | 85 |
| Europe and Central Asia | 425.8 | 475.3 | 274 | 318 | 214 | 238 | 50 | 50 | 78 | 75 |
| Latin America and the Caribbean | 360.3 | 509.2 | 201 | 319 | 130 | 219 | 36 | 43 | 65 | 69 |
| Middle East and North Africa | 174.0 | 290.9 | 91 | 171 | 54 | 97 | 31 | 33 | 59 | 57 |
| South Asia | 903.0 | 1,329.0 | 508 | 797 | 392 | 585 | 43 | 44 | 77 | 73 |
| Sub-Saharan Africa | 380.5 | 642.3 | 195 | 340 | 170 | 282 | 45 | 44 | 87 | 83 |

**Note: Total labor force** comprises people who meet the ILO definition of the economically active population: all people who supply labor for the production of goods and services during a specified period. It includes both the employed and the unemployed. **Participation rates** are defined as percent share of the population economically active.
**Sources:** World Bank, *WDI 2000,* 2000b; World Bank, *WDR 2000/2001,* 2001i.

## TABLE A2.3

## Labor Force and GNP Growth by Region

| Region | GNP Average Annual Growth Rate, 1990–1999 (%) | Labor Force Average Annual Growth Rate, 1990–99 (%) |
|---|---|---|
| East Asia and Pacific | 7.2 | 1.5 |
| Europe and Central Asia | –2.3 | 0.6 |
| Latin America and the Caribbean | 2.9 | 2.5 |
| Middle East and North Africa | 3.7 | 3.1 |
| South Asia | 5.3 | 2.5 |
| Sub-Saharan Africa | 1.9 | 2.6 |
| High income | 2.3 | 0.9 |

**Sources:** World Bank, *WDR 2000/2001*, 2001i; World Bank, *WDI Database,* 2001g.

## TABLE A2.4

## Labor Force, Female, 1985–2000

(percentage of total labor force)

| Country | 1985 | 1990 | 1995 | 2000 |
|---|---|---|---|---|
| Algeria | 21 | 21 | 25 | 28 |
| Egypt, Arab Rep. of | 27 | 27 | 29 | 30 |
| Iran, Islamic Rep. of | 21 | 21 | 24 | 27 |
| Jordan | 16 | 18 | 21 | 25 |
| Lebanon | 25 | 27 | 28 | 30 |
| Morocco | 34 | 35 | 35 | 35 |
| Tunisia | 29 | 29 | 30 | 32 |
| Yemen, Republic of | 31 | 30 | 28 | 28 |

**Source:** World Bank, *WDI Database,* 2001g.

## TABLE A2.5

## Labor Force, Female, by Region

(percentage of total labor force)

| Region | 1985 | 1990 | 1995 | 2000 |
|---|---|---|---|---|
| East Asia and Pacific | 43 | 44 | 44 | 44 |
| Europe and Central Asia | 46 | 46 | 46 | 46 |
| Latin America and the Caribbean | 30 | 33 | 34 | 35 |
| Middle East and North Africa | 24 | 24 | 26 | 28 |
| South Asia | 33 | 32 | 33 | 33 |
| Sub-Saharan Africa | 42 | 42 | 42 | 42 |
| High income | 40 | 42 | 42 | 43 |

**Note: Females as a percentage of the labor force** shows the extent to which women are active in the labor force.
**Source:** World Bank, *WDI Database,* 2001g.

## TABLE A2.6

### Labor Force, Children 10–14
(percentage of age group)

| Country | 1990 | 1995 | 2000 |
|---|---|---|---|
| Algeria | 3 | 2 | 0 |
| Egypt, Arab Rep. of | 13 | 11 | 9 |
| Iran, Islamic Rep. of | 7 | 5 | 3 |
| Jordan | 1 | 1 | 0 |
| Lebanon | 0 | 0 | 0 |
| Morocco | 11 | 6 | 1 |
| Tunisia | 0 | 0 | 0 |
| Yemen, Republic of | 22 | 20 | 19 |

**Source:** World Bank, *WDI Database,* 2001g.

## TABLE A2.7

### Labor Force, Children 10–14, by Region
(percentage of age group)

| Region | 1990 | 1995 | 2000 |
|---|---|---|---|
| East Asia and Pacific | 14 | 11 | 8 |
| Europe and Central Asia | 3 | 2 | 1 |
| Latin America and the Caribbean | 11 | 10 | 8 |
| Middle East and North Africa | 8 | 6 | 4 |
| South Asia | 19 | 17 | 15 |
| Sub-Saharan Africa | 32 | 30 | 29 |
| High income | 0 | 0 | 0 |

**Note: Children 10–14** in the labor force is the share of that age group that is active in the labor force.
**Source:** World Bank, *WDI Database,* 2001g.

## TABLE A2.8

### Unemployment in the MENA Region

| Country | Total 1999–2000 (%) | Men 1995 | Women 1995 |
|---|---|---|---|
| Algeria | 30 | 22 | 17 |
| Djibouti | 40 | — | — |
| Egypt, Arab Rep. of | 11 | 6 | 28 |
| Iran, Islamic Rep. of | 15 | — | — |
| Jordan | 10 | 14 | 35 |
| Lebanon | 15 | — | — |
| Morocco | 20 | 12 | 13 |
| Tunisia | 15 | 15 | 22 |
| Yemen, Republic of | 11.5 | — | — |

— Not available.
**Sources:** Total Unemployment—Draft MENA Labor Market Study 1999 (not to be quoted). Unemployment by gender and region—Regional Perspectives on WDR 1995.

## TABLE A2.9

### Unemployment Rate by Region, 1999

| Region | % of Total Labor Force |
|---|---|
| OECD | 3.0 |
| Sub-Saharan Africa | 7.0 |
| South Asia | 5.0 |
| Middle East and North Africa | 15.0 |
| Latin America and the Caribbean | 9.2 |
| Europe and Central Asia | 11.1 |
| East Asia and Pacific | 3.8 |

**Source:** World Bank, MENA database.

FIGURE A2.1

## Unemployment in the MENA Region, 1999–2000

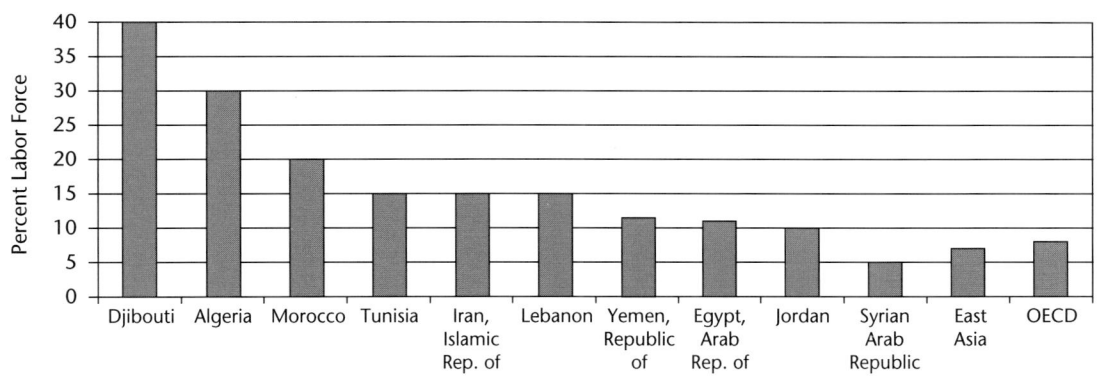

**Source:** World Bank, *WDI 2001,* 2001h.

FIGURE A2.2

## Many of the Unemployed Are Young

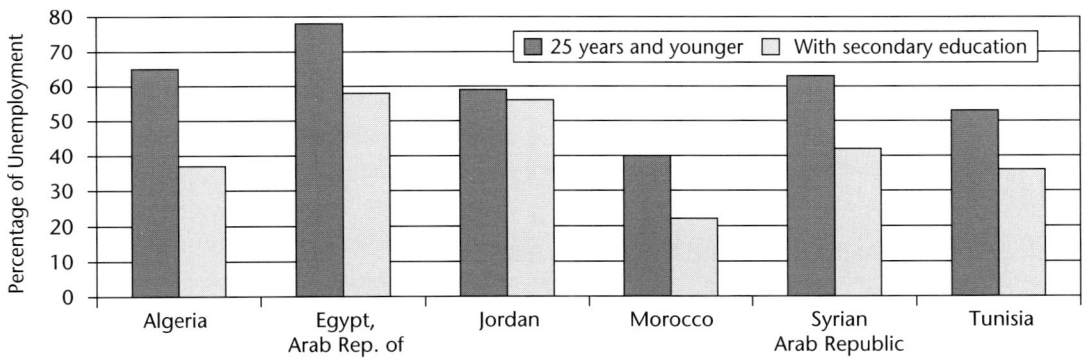

**Source:** World Bank, *WDI Database,* 2001g.

FIGURE A2.3

## Unemployment Rates by Region, 1999

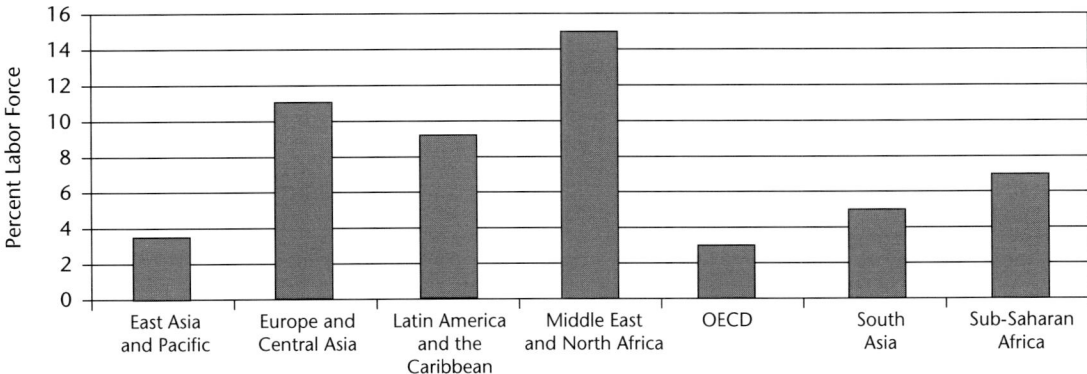

**Source:** World Bank, *WDI Database,* 2001g.

TABLE A2.10

## Employment by Major Economic Activity Categories

| | Agriculture | | | | Industry | | | | Services | | | |
|---|---|---|---|---|---|---|---|---|---|---|---|---|
| | Male (% of economically active male population) | | Female (% of economically active female population) | | Male (% of economically active male population) | | Female (% of economically active female population) | | Male (% of economically active male population) | | Female (% of economically active female population) | |
| Country | 1980 | 1992–97[a] | 1980 | 1992–97[a] | 1980 | 1992–97[a] | 1980 | 1992–97[a] | 1980 | 1992–97[a] | 1980 | 1992–97[a] |
| Algeria | 27 | 18 | 69 | 57 | 33 | 38 | 6 | 7 | 40 | 44 | 25 | 36 |
| Egypt, Arab Rep. of | 43 | 32 | 8 | 43 | 20 | 23 | 10 | 9 | 32 | 38 | 56 | 31 |
| Iran, Islamic Rep. of | 36 | 30 | 82 | 73 | 28 | 26 | 6 | 9 | 35 | 44 | 12 | 18 |
| Jordan | 11 | 10 | 58 | 41 | 27 | 28 | 3 | 4 | 62 | 63 | 39 | 55 |
| Lebanon | 13 | 6 | 20 | 10 | 29 | 34 | 21 | 22 | 58 | 59 | 59 | 68 |
| Morocco | 48 | 35 | 72 | 63 | 23 | 28 | 14 | 19 | 29 | 37 | 14 | 18 |
| Tunisia | 33 | 22 | 53 | 42 | 30 | 33 | 32 | 32 | 37 | 44 | 16 | 26 |
| Yemen, Republic of | 60 | 50 | 98 | 88 | 19 | 22 | 1 | 6 | 21 | 29 | 1 | 7 |

a. Data are for the most recent year available.
**Sources:** World Bank, *WDI,* 1998c and 2000b.

TABLE A2.11

## Employment by Major Economic Activity by Region

| | Agriculture | | | | Industry | | | | Services | | | |
|---|---|---|---|---|---|---|---|---|---|---|---|---|
| | Male (% of male population) | | Female (% of female population) | | Male (% of male population) | | Female (% of female population) | | Male (% of male population) | | Female (% of female population) | |
| Region | 1980 | 1992–97[a] | 1980 | 1992–97[a] | 1980 | 1992–97[a] | 1980 | 1992–97[a] | 1980 | 1992–97[a] | 1980 | 1992–97[a] |
| East Asia and Pacific | 69 | 67 | 75 | 72 | 15 | 16 | 12 | 13 | 15 | 17 | 13 | 15 |
| Europe and Central Asia | 25 | 23 | 27 | 22 | 45 | 43 | 31 | 30 | 30 | 33 | 42 | 48 |
| Latin America and the Caribbean | — | 29 | — | 12 | — | 28 | — | 16 | — | 42 | — | 71 |
| Middle East and North Africa | 39 | 29 | 53 | 55 | 25 | 26 | 10 | 11 | 35 | 43 | 29 | 29 |
| South Asia | 64 | 59 | 82 | 75 | 13 | 16 | 10 | 15 | 23 | 25 | 8 | 10 |
| Sub-Saharan Africa | 69 | 65 | 80 | 75 | 11 | 11 | 4 | 4 | 20 | 23 | 17 | 21 |
| High income | 8 | 6 | 8 | 4 | 41 | 35 | 23 | 18 | 47 | 56 | 66 | 75 |

— Not available.
a. Data are for the most recent year available.
**Sources:** World Bank, *WDI,* 1998c and 2000b.

TABLE A2.12

# Structure of Employment for Select Years

| | Total Employment (000) | % in Agriculture | % in Industry | % in Construction | % in Services | % in Nongovernment Services | % in Government Services (Administration) | % in Public enterprises |
|---|---|---|---|---|---|---|---|---|
| **Algeria** | | | | | | | | |
| YR85 | 5,622 | 18 | 9 | 12 | 30 | 14 | 16 | 2 |
| YR90 | 6,381 | 14 | 10 | 11 | 31 | 15 | 17 | 2 |
| YR95 | 6,737 | 16 | 8 | 10 | 32 | 14 | 18 | 1 |
| **Egypt, Arab Rep. of** | | | | | | | | |
| YR85 | 11,367 | 37 | 14 | 5 | 15 | 20 | 9 | 1 |
| YR90 | 13,032 | 34 | 14 | 6 | 15 | 11 | 20 | — |
| YR95 | 14,879 | 31 | 14 | 7 | 16 | 10 | 22 | — |
| YR97 | 15,825 | 30 | 14 | 7 | 16 | 10 | 23 | — |
| **Jordan** | | | | | | | | |
| YR85 | 286 | — | 13 | 2 | 43 | 10 | 32 | — |
| YR90 | 403 | — | 12 | 1 | 44 | 11 | 32 | — |
| YR93 | 541 | — | 14 | 1 | 42 | 13 | 30 | — |
| **Morocco** | | | | | | | | |
| YR85 | — | — | — | — | — | — | 323 | — |
| YR90 | 3,357 | 4 | 32 | 7 | 45 | 0 | 10 | — |
| YR93 | 3,614 | 3 | 31 | 7 | 48 | 0 | 11 | — |
| **Tunisia** | | | | | | | | |
| YR84 | 1,791 | 27 | 21 | 13 | 0 | 33 | 0 | 6 |
| YR89 | 1,948 | 26 | 21 | 13 | 0 | 40 | 0 | 0 |

— Not available.
**Sources:**
**ALGERIA**
Labor Force: Labor Force Sample Surveys. These have been carried out once a year from 1982 to 1985. No surveys were carried out from 1986 to 1988 to allow for the census and the household consumption survey carried out in 1988. The latest results are available for 1989/90/91/92, ONS (Office Nat. des Statistiques). World Bank 1997c.
Unemployment: ONS (Office Nat. des Statistiques), Labor force surveys; World Bank 1997c.
Employment: CNP (Conseil National de Planification); World Bank 1994b.
**EGYPT**
Labor Force Source: Ministry of Planning.
**JORDAN**
Employment surveys 1986–90. Statistical Yearbooks 1986, 1988, 1992, 1993, 1994.
Unemployment: Ministry of Labor Annual Reports; for 1994, Ministry of Planning; for 1995, The Department of Statistics: Employment, Unemployment and Income Survey 1995.
Data for 1980–89, *Jordan Poverty Assessment,* October 28, 1994; Data for 1991–95, Social Security Corporation, Annual 1995.
**MOROCCO**
For years 1985–1993, the data do not include rural employment; 1995 includes data for both urban and rural.
**TUNISIA**
Enquete Nationale Population et Emploi 1984, 1989; Institut National Statistique du Republique Tunisienne (INS) Statistical Yearbook (Annuaire Statistique De la Tunisie) 1989, 1992, 1994.

## TABLE A2.13

## Real Wage Indexes

| | Algeria | | Egypt, Arab Rep. of | | Jordan | | Morocco | | Tunisia | | Yemen, Republic of | |
|---|---|---|---|---|---|---|---|---|---|---|---|---|
| | DA/Month (1985 constant DA) | Base 1990 | Earnings per week (LE) | Base 1990 | Earnings per day (JD) | Base 1990 | Minimum DH/ monthly (unit) | | Industry average wage | | YR 000/ month | |
| Year | Real | Index | Real | Index | Real | Index | Real | Index | Real | Index | Real | Index |
| 1985 | — | — | — | — | — | — | 908 | 94 | 1,647 | 107 | — | — |
| 1986 | — | — | — | — | — | — | 843 | 88 | 1,458 | 95 | — | — |
| 1987 | — | — | — | — | — | — | 817 | 85 | 1,353 | 88 | — | — |
| 1988 | — | — | 36 | 111 | 5 | 140 | 0 | 0 | 1,381 | 90 | — | — |
| 1989 | — | — | 34 | 104 | 4 | 114 | 932 | 97 | 1,478 | 96 | — | — |
| 1990 | 1,291 | 100 | 33 | 100 | 3 | 100 | 962 | 100 | 1,533 | 100 | 6 | 100 |
| 1991 | 1,500 | 116 | 30 | 90 | 3 | 93 | 1,023 | 106 | 1,524 | 99 | 4 | 75 |
| 1992 | 1,673 | 130 | 28 | 86 | 3 | 96 | 1,064 | 111 | 1,547 | 101 | 3 | 47 |
| 1993 | 1,530 | 119 | 30 | 91 | 3 | 97 | 1,009 | 105 | 1,472 | 96 | 2 | 35 |
| 1994 | 1,419 | 110 | 30 | 91 | 4 | 106 | 960 | 100 | — | — | 1 | 21 |
| 1995 | 1,235 | 96 | 28 | 84 | 4 | 106 | 1,000 | 104 | — | — | 1 | 18 |
| 1996 | — | — | — | — | — | — | 1,064 | 111 | — | — | 1 | 15 |

— Not available.
**Note:** Real wages calculated using CPI deflator (1987=100).

## TABLE A2.14

## Wages and Salaries

(percentage of total public expenditure)

| Country | 1985 | 1990 | 1995 | 1999 |
|---|---|---|---|---|
| Algeria | — | — | 24.2 | 23.9 |
| Egypt, Arab Rep. of | 21.4 | 22.9 | 18.4 | — |
| Iran, Islamic Rep. of | 50.5 | 40.3 | 38.2 | 47.5 |
| Jordan | — | 43.7 | 45.5 | 47.0 |
| Lebanon | — | — | 21.2 | 22.6 |
| Morocco | 33.2 | 35.3 | 34.0 | — |
| Tunisia | 26.5 | 27.6 | 31.8 | 34.8 |
| Yemen, Republic of | — | 55.0 | 58.1 | 39.3 |

— Not available.
**Note: Wages and salaries** consist of all payments in cash, but not in kind, to employees in return for services rendered, before deduction of withholding taxes and employees' contributions to social security and pension funds. Data are shown for central government only.
**Source:** World Bank, *WDI Database*, 2001g.

# Formal Pension System Indicators

TABLE A3.1

## Total Dependents I: Share of Persons Aged 0–14 and 65+

(percent)

| Year | Algeria | Egypt, Arab Rep. of | Iran, Islamic Rep. of | Jordan | Lebanon | Morocco | Tunisia | Yemen, Republic of | France | United States |
|------|---------|---------|---------|--------|---------|---------|---------|---------|--------|--------|
| 1995 | 42.0 | 42.0 | 46.0 | 45.0 | 40.0 | 41.0 | 40.0 | 50.0 | 35.0 | 35.0 |
| 2000 | 39.0 | 39.0 | 41.0 | 41.0 | 38.0 | 38.0 | 37.0 | 51.0 | 35.0 | 34.0 |
| 2005 | 36.0 | 35.8 | 36.1 | 40.8 | 35.5 | 36.0 | 33.8 | 50.2 | 33.9 | 33.3 |
| 2010 | 34.2 | 33.8 | 34.7 | 39.4 | 32.2 | 33.3 | 31.3 | 49.0 | 33.5 | 33.2 |
| 2015 | 32.8 | 32.9 | 33.0 | 37.3 | 30.4 | 31.7 | 30.2 | 47.5 | 34.9 | 34.5 |
| 2020 | 31.6 | 32.4 | 31.2 | 33.4 | 30.4 | 30.7 | 30.8 | 45.7 | 36.6 | 36.6 |
| 2025 | 30.8 | 32.2 | 30.3 | 30.6 | 31.1 | 31.1 | 31.6 | 43.8 | 38.4 | 38.9 |
| 2030 | 31.4 | 32.2 | 30.4 | 30.0 | 32.1 | 31.8 | 32.4 | 41.1 | 40.1 | 40.6 |
| 2035 | 32.4 | 32.4 | 31.1 | 30.9 | 33.6 | 32.5 | 33.3 | 37.9 | 41.3 | 41.1 |
| 2040 | 33.4 | 32.7 | 32.1 | 32.7 | 34.8 | 33.4 | 34.3 | 34.4 | 42.3 | 40.9 |
| Change | −25.5 | −23.8 | −33.5 | −33.4 | −18.9 | −21.6 | −17.9 | −17.7 | 15.8 | 17.0 |

**Source:** World Bank 1999c.

TABLE A3.2

## Total Dependents II: Share of Persons Aged 0–19 and 60+

(percent)

| Year | Algeria | Egypt, Arab Rep. of | Iran, Islamic Rep. of | Jordan | Lebanon | Morocco | Tunisia | Yemen, Republic of | France | United States |
|------|---------|---------|---------|--------|---------|---------|---------|---------|--------|--------|
| 1995 | 53.6 | 52.4 | 56.7 | 57.2 | 49.4 | 51.9 | 50.1 | 60.8 | 41.3 | 41.3 |
| 2000 | 50.1 | 50.2 | 53.4 | 53.8 | 47.8 | 48.5 | 47.3 | 60.9 | 41.0 | 41.0 |
| 2005 | 46.5 | 46.8 | 48.4 | 50.9 | 45.3 | 46.0 | 43.9 | 61.0 | 40.3 | 40.3 |
| 2010 | 43.7 | 43.5 | 43.8 | 49.3 | 42.1 | 43.0 | 40.6 | 60.2 | 39.5 | 40.1 |
| 2015 | 41.7 | 41.6 | 41.8 | 47.1 | 39.3 | 40.5 | 38.5 | 58.8 | 40.8 | 41.1 |
| 2020 | 40.4 | 40.9 | 40.2 | 44.1 | 38.1 | 39.5 | 38.1 | 57.1 | 42.3 | 42.8 |
| 2025 | 39.4 | 40.4 | 38.9 | 40.3 | 38.3 | 38.8 | 38.9 | 55.0 | 43.8 | 45.0 |
| 2030 | 38.9 | 39.8 | 37.9 | 38.4 | 39.3 | 39.0 | 39.8 | 52.4 | 45.5 | 46.7 |
| 2035 | 39.4 | 39.7 | 38.1 | 38.1 | 40.8 | 39.7 | 40.5 | 49.2 | 46.9 | 47.3 |
| 2040 | 40.3 | 39.8 | 38.9 | 39.7 | 41.8 | 40.5 | 41.1 | 45.5 | 47.9 | 47.1 |
| Change | −27.4 | −24.0 | −33.1 | −32.9 | −20.4 | −24.7 | −20.6 | −13.8 | 10.3 | 13.1 |

**Source:** World Bank 1999c.

TABLE A3.3

## Old-Age Dependency Ratio I

(percent)

| Year | Algeria | Egypt, Arab Rep. of | Iran, Islamic Rep. of | Jordan | Lebanon | Morocco | Tunisia | Yemen, Republic of | France | United States |
|------|---------|---------|---------|--------|---------|---------|---------|---------|--------|--------|
| 1995 | 13.0 | 14.4 | 15.4 | 11.0 | 17.4 | 13.6 | 14.7 | 10.3 | 37.5 | 29.9 |
| 2000 | 12.2 | 14.3 | 14.5 | 10.6 | 16.6 | 13.5 | 14.9 | 9.9 | 37.4 | 29.7 |
| 2005 | 11.4 | 13.7 | 12.8 | 10.7 | 15.4 | 12.7 | 13.9 | 9.4 | 37.2 | 30.8 |
| 2010 | 12.0 | 14.2 | 11.9 | 11.5 | 15.0 | 13.0 | 13.7 | 8.8 | 41.5 | 34.6 |
| 2015 | 13.7 | 16.4 | 13.1 | 11.7 | 15.9 | 14.6 | 15.6 | 8.1 | 46.7 | 40.3 |
| 2020 | 16.1 | 19.1 | 15.4 | 12.2 | 18.0 | 17.3 | 19.2 | 8.0 | 51.8 | 47.8 |
| 2025 | 19.5 | 21.3 | 17.6 | 13.9 | 21.9 | 20.1 | 23.5 | 9.0 | 57.2 | 54.7 |
| 2030 | 23.1 | 23.6 | 20.3 | 16.5 | 28.1 | 23.7 | 28.3 | 9.9 | 62.5 | 58.3 |
| 2035 | 27.2 | 25.9 | 23.9 | 21.5 | 33.7 | 28.1 | 32.7 | 10.7 | 66.7 | 59.0 |
| 2040 | 32.4 | 29.4 | 28.8 | 26.5 | 37.2 | 33.1 | 37.3 | 11.3 | 68.3 | 58.7 |
| Change | **77.4** | **63.5** | **31.2** | **49.1** | **62.0** | **74.3** | **92.0** | **–3.5** | **66.6** | **95.2** |

Note: Persons aged 60+ divided by persons 20–59.
Source: World Bank 1999c.

TABLE A3.4

## Old-Age Dependency Ratio II

(percent)

| Year | Algeria | Egypt, Arab Rep. of | Iran, Islamic Rep. of | Jordan | Lebanon | Morocco | Tunisia | Yemen, Republic of | France | United States |
|------|---------|---------|---------|--------|---------|---------|---------|---------|--------|--------|
| 1995 | 6.5 | 7.4 | 7.5 | 4.9 | 9.1 | 7.0 | 7.3 | 4.8 | 23.2 | 19.2 |
| 2000 | 6.5 | 7.5 | 7.6 | 5.2 | 9.5 | 7.0 | 7.8 | 4.8 | 24.1 | 18.9 |
| 2005 | 6.4 | 7.4 | 7.1 | 5.5 | 9.1 | 7.3 | 8.2 | 4.6 | 24.2 | 18.6 |
| 2010 | 6.4 | 7.4 | 6.8 | 6.0 | 8.4 | 7.0 | 7.9 | 4.2 | 24.3 | 19.8 |
| 2015 | 7.1 | 8.2 | 6.9 | 6.5 | 8.6 | 7.5 | 8.1 | 4.0 | 27.8 | 23.1 |
| 2020 | 8.4 | 9.9 | 7.9 | 6.7 | 9.7 | 8.8 | 9.9 | 3.8 | 31.6 | 27.4 |
| 2025 | 10.2 | 11.8 | 9.6 | 7.1 | 11.6 | 10.9 | 12.5 | 3.8 | 35.5 | 32.6 |
| 2030 | 12.6 | 13.4 | 11.3 | 8.6 | 14.5 | 13.0 | 15.6 | 4.5 | 39.2 | 37.0 |
| 2035 | 15.3 | 15.1 | 13.4 | 10.8 | 18.6 | 15.4 | 18.7 | 5.1 | 42.0 | 38.7 |
| 2040 | 18.1 | 16.6 | 15.9 | 14.6 | 22.3 | 18.3 | 21.6 | 5.7 | 44.3 | 38.6 |
| Change | **94.6** | **82.1** | **51.4** | **76.8** | **58.7** | **85.4** | **112.2** | **–7.0** | **68.5** | **92.4** |

Note: Persons aged 65+ divided by persons 15–64.
Source: World Bank 1999c.

TABLE A3.5

## Pension Coverage and Replacement Rates

| Country | Year | Retirement Age | Coverage Contributors (% labor force) | System Dependency Ratio [a] (%) | Old-Age Dependency Ratio[b] (%) | Replacement Rates[c] (%) |
|---|---|---|---|---|---|---|
| **Algeria** | 1999 | 60/55 [d] | | | | |
| CNR | | | 26.6 | 25.4 | 43.6 | 50 |
| CASNOS | | | 3.5 | 30.0 | 30.0 | 33 |
| Total | | | 31.0 | 25.9 | 6.4 | — |
| **Djibouti** | 2001 | 55 | | | | |
| CNR (civil service) | | | 1.9 | 65.3 | 30.1 | 35 |
| OPS (priv./pub. employees) | | | 12.4 | 11.4 | 7.4 | 44 |
| CMR (military) | | | 1.0 | 59.6 | — | 47 |
| Total | | | 15.3 | 21.4 | 11.5 | 44 |
| **Egypt, Arab Rep. of** | 1998 | 60 | 94.0 | 37.9 | 14.4 | 80 |
| **Iran, Islamic Rep. of** | 2001 | 60 | | | | |
| CSRO (public employees) | | | 8.7 | 33.4 | — | 75 |
| SSO (private employees) | | | 34.0 | 18.8 | — | 60 |
| Total | | | 42.7 | 52.2 | 14.7 | — |
| **Jordan** | 2000 | 60/55[d] | | | | |
| SSC (private employees) | | | 23.8 | 20.3 | — | 40 |
| Public System (military) | | | 6.4 | 102.7 | — | — |
| Public System (civil serv.) | 1995 | | 7.9 | 17.3 | — | — |
| Total | | | 40.0 | 28.7 | 10.6 | — |
| **Morocco** | 1998 | 60 | | | | |
| CNSS (private employees) | | | 12.5 | 19.0 | — | 50 |
| CMR (civil serv./military) | | | 1.3 | 38.0 | — | 61 |
| RCAR (public entreprises) | | | 2.6 | 12.0 | — | 39 |
| CIMR (voluntary) | | | 2.7 | 29.0 | — | 44 |
| Total | | | 28.0 | 27.0 | 14.0 | 53 |
| **Tunisia** | 1997 | 60 | | | | |
| CNSS (private employees) | | | 74.6 | — | — | 80 |
| CNRPS (public employees) | | | 100.0 | — | — | 90 |
| Total | | | 80.7 | 20.4 | 41.4 | — |
| **Yemen, Republic of** | 1994 | 60/55[d] | — | — | 9.9 | — |

— Not available.
**Note:** Abbreviations and acronyms:
CASNOS: *Caisse d'Assurance Sociale des Non-salaries* (National Social Insurance Fund)
CIMR: *Caisse Interprofessionnelle Marocaine de Retraite* (Moroccan Interprofessional Pension Fund)
CMR : *Caisse Morocaine de Retraite* (Moroccan Pension Fund)
CNR : *Caisse Nationale de Retraite* (National Retirement Fund)
CNRPS : *Caisse Nationale de Retraite et de Prevoyance Sociale* (National Fund for Retirement & Social Protection)
CNSS : National Fund for Social Security
CSRO : Civil Servant Retirement Organisation
OPS: *Organisme Protection Sociale* (Social Protection Organization)
RCAR: *Regime Collectif d'Allocations de Retraite* (Retirement Benefits Collective Plan)
SSC : Social Security Corporation
SSO : Social Security Organisation
a. Pensioners/contributors.
b. Persons aged 60+ divided by persons aged 20–59.
c. Average pension/average wage.
d. Retirement age 60 for men and 55 for women.
**Sources:** World Bank 2001e, 2000a, 2001c; TAPR/USAID 1999.

TABLE A3.6

# Key Pension Fund Financial Indicators

| Country | Year | Pension Spending (% GDP) | Revenues from Contributions (% GDP) | Covered Wage Bill[a] (% GDP) | Contribution Rate as Share of Gross Wage Bill | | | | Reserves (% GDP) |
|---|---|---|---|---|---|---|---|---|---|
| | | | | | Emp'ee | Emp'er | Gov't | Total | |
| **Algeria** | | | | | | | | | |
| CNR (priv./pub. employees) | 1999 | 1.70 | 1.70 | 10.50 | 6.5 | 9.5 | 0.0 | 16.0 | — |
| CASNOS (self-employed) | | 1.20 | 0.10 | 1.00 | 7.5 | 7.5 | 0.0 | 15.0 | — |
| Total | | 2.90 | 1.80 | 11.50 | — | — | — | — | 1.2 |
| **Bahrain** | 1996 | 1.20 | 2.40 | 19.80 | 5.0 | 7.0 | 0.0 | 12.0 | |
| **Djibouti** | 1999 | | | | | | | | |
| CNR (civil service) | | 1.40 | 1.30 | 7.01 | 6,7,17[b] | 12,13,17[b] | 0.0 | 18,20,34[b] | — |
| OPS (priv./pub. employees) | | 1.30 | 0.04 | 0.50 | 4.0 | 4.0 | 0.0 | 8.0 | — |
| CMR (military) | | 0.70 | 0.40 | 2.10 | 7.0 | 13.0 | 0.0 | 20.0 | — |
| Total | | 3.40 | 1.80 | 9.60 | — | — | — | — | |
| **Egypt, Arab Rep. of** | 1998 | 2.90 | 3.60 | 11.60 | 13.0 | 17.0 | 1.0 | 31.0 | 40.6 |
| **Iran, Islamic Rep. of** | 2001 | | | 3.30 | | | | | |
| CSRO (public employees) | | 0.80 | 0.70 | 3.20 | 8.5 | 12.8 | 0.0 | 21.3 | 3.6 |
| SSO (private employees) | | 1.00 | 1.30 | 7.20 | 7.0 | 23.0 | 3.0 | 21.0[c] | 3.1 |
| Total | | 1.80 | 2.00 | 10.50 | — | — | — | — | 6.7 |
| **Jordan** | | | | | | | | | |
| SSC (private employees) | 2001 | 1.30 | 2.40 | 17.10 | 5.5 | 9.0 | 0.0 | 14.5 | 22.7 |
| Public System (military) | 1995 | 2.80 | — | — | 8.8 | 0.0 | 0.0 | 8.8 | 0.0 |
| Public System (civil serv.) | 1995 | 0.70 | — | — | 8.8 | 0.0 | 0.0 | 8.8 | 0.0 |
| Total | | 4.20 | 2.10 | 17.40 | — | — | — | — | 22.7 |
| **Kuwait** | 1996 | 5.90 | 8.50 | — | 5.0 | 10.0 | 10.0 | 25.0 | — |
| **Morocco** | 1998 | | | | | | | | |
| CNSS (private employees) | | 0.65 | 0.60 | 6.10 | 3.0 | 6.1 | 0.0 | 9.1 | 2.0 |
| CMR (civil serv./military) | | 1.00 | 1.30 | 9.50 | 7.0 | 7.0 | 0.0 | 14.0 | 1.0 |
| RCAR (public entreprises) | | 0.10 | 0.20 | 1.10 | 6.0 | 12.C | 0.0 | 18.0 | 3.9 |
| CIMR (voluntary) | | 0.30 | 0.20 | 3.00 | 3–6 | 3–6 | 0.0 | 6–12 | 1.0 |
| Total | | 2.00 | 2.30 | 19.70 | — | — | — | — | 9.0 |
| **Syrian Arab Republic** | 1999 | 0.60 | 1.30 | 6.20 | 7.0 | 14.0 | 0.0 | 21.0 | — |
| **Tunisia** | 1998 | | | | | | | | |
| CNSS (private employees) | | — | — | — | 6.3 | 17.5 | 0.0 | 23.8 | — |
| CNRPS (public employees) | | — | — | — | 7.5 | 9.7 | 0.0 | 17.2 | — |
| Total | | 4.80 | — | — | — | — | — | — | 6.9 |
| **Yemen, Republic of** | 1994 | 0.00 | 0.10 | 0.90 | 6.0 | 9.0 | 0.0 | 15.0 | 0.5 |

**Notes:** Pension spending includes some short-term benefits; revenues have been estimated assuming 1989 ratio of pension contribution to total contributions; government as employer.
CASNOS: *Caisse d'Assurance Sociale des Non-salaries* (National Social Insurance Fund)
CIMR: *Caisse Interprofessionnelle Marocaine de Retraite* (Moroccan Interprofessional Pension Fund)
CMR : *Caisse Morocaine de Retraite* (Moroccan Pension Fund)
CNR : *Caisse Nationale de Retraite* (National Retirement Fund)
CNRPS : *Caisse Nationale de Retraite et de Prevoyance Sociale* (National Fund for Retirement & Social Protection)
CNSS : National Fund for Social Security
CSRO : Civil Servant Retirement Organisation
OPS: *Organisme Protection Sociale* (Social Protection Organization)
RCAR: *Regime Collectif d'Allocations de Retraite* (Retirement Benefits Collective Plan)
SSC : Social Security Corporation
SSO : Social Security Organisation
a. Revenues from contributions (% GDP) / total contribution rate  x 100
b. Djibouti CNR: Contribution rates for functionaries, police, ministers, respectively.
c. Three percentage points of the contribution are allocated to the unemployment insurance and 9 points to the health branch.
**Sources:** World Bank 2001e, 2000a, 2001c, TAPR/USAID 1999.

TABLE A3.7

**Pension Fund Performance**

| Country | Reserves (% GDP) | Rate of Return (real) | Admin. Costs (% assets) | Public Sector Investment (%) | Short-Term Investment (%) |
|---|---|---|---|---|---|
| Algeria | 1.2 | highly negative | — | 100 | 100 |
| Egypt, Arab Rep. of | 40.6 | highly negative | — | 100 | — |
| Iran, Islamic Rep. of | 6.7 | –3% to 5% | 7.00 | 80 | 20 |
| Jordan | 22.7 | 2.50% | 0.70 | 52 | >50 |
| Morocco | 9.0 | 2.60% | 4.80 | >54 | 40 |
| Tunisia | 6.9 | slightly negative | 6.60 | 72 | — |

— Not available.

**Sources:** World Bank 1999c; Algeria Public Expenditure Review 2001; Djibouti, Islamic Republic of Iran, and Jordan Pension Reform Strategy Notes 2001; TAPR/USAID 1999.

# Poverty Indicators

## TABLE A4.1

### Population below National Poverty Lines

| Country | Survey Year | Rural | Urban | National | Survey Year | Rural | Urban | National |
|---|---|---|---|---|---|---|---|---|
| Algeria | 1988 | 16.6 | 7.3 | 12.2 | 1995 | 30.3 | 14.7 | 22.6 |
| Egypt, Arab Rep. of | 1981 | 24.2 | 22.5 | 26.0 | 1995–96 | 23.3 | 22.5 | 22.9 |
| Jordan | 1987 | 23.7 | 16.6 | 18.7 | 1997 | 18.2 | 10.0 | 11.7 |
| Morocco | 1990–91 | 18.0 | 7.6 | 13.1 | 1998–99 | 27.2 | 12.0 | 19.0 |
| Tunisia | 1990 | 13.1 | 3.5 | 7.4 | 1995 | 13.9 | 3.6 | 7.6 |
| Yemen, Republic of | 1992 | 19.2 | 18.6 | 19.1 | 1998 | 26.9 | 21.8 | 25.4 |

Note: **Rural poverty rate** is the percentage of the rural population living below the national rural poverty line. **Urban poverty rate** is the percentage of the urban population living below the national urban poverty line. **National poverty rate** is the percentage of the population living below the poverty line deemed appropriate for the country by its authorities.
**Sources:** World Bank 1991, 1999a, 2000a, 2001b, 2001c; Republic of Yemen: HBS 1992 and HBS 1998; FPRI 1997.

## TABLE A4.2

### International Poverty Lines

| Country | Survey Year | % Population below US$1 a day | Poverty gap at US$1 a day | % Population below US$2 a day | Poverty gap at US$2 a day |
|---|---|---|---|---|---|
| Algeria | 1995 | <2 | <0.5 | 15.1 | 3.6 |
| Egypt, Arab Rep. of | 1995 | 3.1 | 0.3 | 52.7 | 11.4 |
| Jordan | 1997 | <2 | <0.5 | 7.4 | 1.4 |
| Morocco | 1995 | <2 | <0.5 | 7.5 | 1.3 |
| Tunisia | 1990 | <2 | <0.5 | 11.6 | 2.9 |

Note: **International comparisons of extreme poverty** are based on a common international poverty line of $1 a person a day, expressed in 1985 international prices and adjusted to local currencies using PPP exchange rates. Most countries have their own poverty lines based on local views of minimum socially acceptable living standard. **Poverty gap** is the mean shortfall below the poverty line (counting the nonpoor as having zero shortfall) expressed as a percentage of the poverty line. This measure reflects the depth of poverty as well as its incidence.
**Source:** World Bank, *WDR 2000/2001*, 2001i.

## TABLE A4.3

### Population Living on Less Than US$1 a Day

| Region | Population (%) | | Population (millions) | |
|---|---|---|---|---|
| | 1987 | 1998 | 1987 | 1998 |
| East Asia and Pacific | 26.6 | 14.7 | 417.5 | 267.1 |
| Europe and Central Asia | 0.2 | 3.7 | 1.1 | 17.6 |
| Latin America and the Caribbean | 15.3 | 12.1 | 63.7 | 60.7 |
| Middle East and North Africa | 4.3 | 2.1 | 9.3 | 6 |
| South Asia | 44.9 | 40.0 | 474.4 | 521.8 |
| Sub-Saharan Africa | 46.6 | 48.1 | 217.2 | 301.6 |
| Total | 28.3 | 23.4 | 1,183.2 | 1,174.9 |

**Source:** World Bank estimates.

## TABLE A4.4

## Population Living on Less Than US$2 a Day

| Region | Population (%) | | Population (millions) | |
|---|---|---|---|---|
| | 1987 | 1998 | 1987 | 1998 |
| East Asia and Pacific | 67.0 | 48.7 | 1,052.3 | 884.9 |
| Europe and Central Asia | 3.6 | 20.7 | 16.3 | 98.2 |
| Latin America and the Caribbean | 35.5 | 31.7 | 147.6 | 159.0 |
| Middle East and North Africa | 30.0 | 29.9 | 65.1 | 85.4 |
| South Asia | 86.3 | 83.9 | 911.0 | 1,094.6 |
| Sub-Saharan Africa | 76.5 | 78.0 | 356.6 | 489.3 |
| Total | 61.0 | 56.1 | 2,549.0 | 2,811.5 |

**Note: Population below $1 a day and $2 a day** are the percentages of the population living on less than $1 a day and $2 a day at 1985 international prices, adjusted for PPP.
**Source:** World Bank estimates.

## TABLE A4.5

## Share of Income or Consumption

| Country | Survey Year | Gini Index | Percentage Share of Income or Consumption[a] | | | | | | |
|---|---|---|---|---|---|---|---|---|---|
| | | | Lowest 10% | Lowest 20% | Second 20% | Third 20% | Fourth 20% | Highest 20% | Highest 10% |
| Algeria | 1995 | 35.3 | 2.8 | 7.0 | 11.6 | 16.1 | 22.7 | 42.6 | 26.8 |
| Egypt, Arab Rep. of | 1996 | 28.9 | 4.4 | 9.8 | 13.2 | 16.6 | 21.4 | 39.0 | 25.0 |
| Jordan | 1997 | 36.4 | 3.3 | 7.6 | 11.4 | 15.5 | 21.1 | 44.4 | 29.8 |
| Morocco | 1998–99 | 39.5 | 2.6 | 6.5 | 10.6 | 14.8 | 21.3 | 46.6 | 31.2 |
| Tunisia | 1990 | 40.2 | 2.3 | 5.9 | 10.4 | 15.3 | 22.1 | 46.3 | 30.7 |
| Yemen, Republic of | 1992 | 39.5 | 2.3 | 6.1 | 10.9 | 15.3 | 21.6 | 46.1 | 30.8 |

**Note: Percentage share of income or consumption** is the share that accrues to subgroups of population indicated by deciles or quintiles. Percentage shares by quintiles may not add up to 100 because of rounding.
a. Ranked by per capita income.
**Source:** World Bank, *WDR 2000/2001,* 2001i.

## TABLE A4.6

## Income Shares of Lowest and Highest Quintiles by Region

| Region | 1960 | | 1970 | | 1980 | | 1990 | |
|---|---|---|---|---|---|---|---|---|
| | Lowest | Highest | Lowest | Highest | Lowest | Highest | Lowest | Highest |
| East Asia and Pacific | 6.4 | 45.9 | 6.0 | 46.5 | 6.3 | 45.5 | 6.9 | 44.3 |
| Europe and Central Asia | 9.7 | 36.3 | 9.8 | 34.5 | 9.8 | 34.6 | 8.8 | 37.8 |
| Latin America and the Caribbean | 3.4 | 61.6 | 3.7 | 54.2 | 3.7 | 54.9 | 4.5 | 52.9 |
| Middle East and North Africa | 5.7 | 49.0 | — | — | 6.6 | 46.7 | 6.9 | 45.4 |
| South Asia | 7.4 | 44.1 | 7.8 | 42.2 | 7.9 | 42.6 | 8.8 | 39.9 |
| Sub-Saharan Africa | 2.8 | 62.0 | 5.1 | 55.8 | 5.7 | 48.9 | 5.2 | 52.4 |
| High income | 6.4 | 31.2 | 6.3 | 41.1 | 6.7 | 39.9 | 6.3 | 39.8 |

— Not available.
**Source:** World Bank, *WDR 1997,* 1997d.

# Social Protection and Rural Development in Select MENA Countries

## Morocco

Despite average agriculture sector growth of 4 percent annually over the past 10 years, Morocco is making inadequate progress toward reducing absolute and relative rural poverty. The path that rural sector policy is on is unlikely to improve this. The objective of Bank strategy is to assist the government to define and implement a set of policies and programs conducive to successful rural development based on efficient, sustainable, and equitable growth in rural areas.

Agricultural policy has come through a period of structural adjustment, but the agenda is unfinished. Success has been greater in fiscal savings than in production efficiency or progress on agricultural incomes in rainfed areas. Cost recovery for goods, particularly inputs such as fertilizers and seeds, has been the area of greatest progress. The government now recovers most of the costs of inputs where it continues to deliver these, compared with earlier heavy subsidization. Privatization of veterinary services has progressed rapidly and successfully. However, problems continue in the areas listed below.

### Key Issues

- Irrigation water continues to be a particularly difficult case. Collection of water and pumping charges cover less than half of operations and maintenance costs for the irrigation systems operated by the *Office Régional de mise en valeur agricole* (Regional Authority for Agricultural Development). Although this compares favorably with many other countries, it remains one of the most costly services provided to farmers and does not encourage the water use efficiency that the agricultural sector will increasingly need to achieve as other sectors demand greater quantities of scarce national resources.
- Output price distortions and irrigation water subsidies continue to encourage crop production in which Morocco has little comparative

advantage while other crop production with clearer comparative advantage receives little public support. Producer protection through import tariffs has been persistently high for wheat (hard and soft), sugar (sugar beet and sugar cane), oilseeds (mainly sunflower), beef, and dairy products without bringing Morocco closer to its stated objective of food self-sufficiency. Trade agreements within the World Trade Organization framework and the existing Free Trade Agreement with the European Community will have no impact on these protection levels over the next two years. Discussions of agricultural trade with the European Community reopened in the year 2000. Meanwhile, domestic market liberalization has gained some momentum since July 1996, beginning with cereal markets, and these are bringing greater competition to domestic marketing and processing chains for some agricultural commodities.

- Public investment and agricultural services focus on irrigated agriculture despite the majority of farmers practicing rainfed agriculture. Natural resource management policy is only tentatively encouraging decentralized and participatory approaches that will be essential to sustainable resource management and sectoral growth.

## Implications for Social Protection Needs

If, as anticipated, the Moroccan government moves to implement a new rural development strategy involving, in particular, price liberalization through import tariff reduction to make the sector more efficient, productive, and competitive, there is likely to be a significant rise in short-term unemployment for unskilled rural workers and subsistence cereal farmers as domestic production loses ground to cheaper imports. Subsistence farmers, who according to surveys, earn one-third of their income as wage laborers on large cereal farms, could be particularly hard hit until absorbed by growing sectors of the rural and urban economies.

The transitional impact of a liberalization-based growth strategy is a serious concern. Not only are the magnitudes important, but Morocco is singularly ill equipped with social safety net mechanisms to assist households and workers through such an adjustment phase. Existing government programs include PN and EN. PN is putting in place reforms under the Social Priorities Project in Morocco's poorest provinces to refocus on its original mandate of job creation in public works in poor communities. EN, which has experience in operating a range of social safety net programs, has a smaller network now than when it had access to donor food aid, and it is struggling to increase its capacity to design and implement alternative programs. NGOs and religious organizations exist in rural areas, but they currently work only on a limited scale in partnership with the government for provision of social programs.

# Republic of Yemen

The Republic of Yemen is predominantly a rural country where agriculture still provides more than one-half of employment. Today, most value in the rural sector comes from market-oriented irrigation, but most rural people still depend on rainfed and livestock husbandry systems. There are many potential sources of future growth in agriculture, and markets are expanding. However, natural resources are already fully utilized, so productivity improvements are the key, and growth has to be matched by conservation of the resource base. In addition, the terms of trade are moving against agriculture.

Within 20 years, the rural population will increase by 8 million. Twenty percent of the rural population is already poor, and unless ways to absorb the increased labor into the rural economy can be found, rural poverty will continue to increase. The broad challenge for agriculture is to create sustainable growth in productivity when natural resources are overstrained and public services are weak. This needs to be complemented by the development of alternative employment, social infrastructure, water supply, and communications to improve living standards and avert a rush to the cities.

## Key Issues

- *Unsustainability and low productivity of irrigated agriculture.* Irrigation is under threat from shrinking margins, depleting groundwater, and deteriorating public services. In recent years, there has been no improvement in factor productivity for most crops. The Yemeni government is changing relative prices, and the cost of groundwater is going up. Once adjustments are complete, incentives to overuse groundwater will have dropped, but so will incomes unless efficiency improvements are made.
- *Low incomes in rainfed and livestock systems.* The counterpart to the rapid growth of the irrigated sector has been the decline of traditional rainfed and livestock systems, to which the government's policy of subsidizing imported cereal has contributed. Yet these systems support the poorest rural people and are in the long run the more sustainable. The consequences are felt not just in the incomes of poorer people but also in the accompanying decline of traditional systems of natural resource management and conservation.
- *Lack of rural development policy.* Public policy and investment concentrate on urban areas. Up to now, rural exodus has been stemmed by the high profitability of qat production and groundwater mining, but as resources dwindle and the population grows, a positive approach to rural investment and off-farm employment creation will be essential.

## Policy

The Yemeni government's policy goal is to create sustainable and equitable growth in output and incomes from agriculture, particularly for the poor. Together with the International Development Association (IDA), the government has developed the following strategy: (a) promoting growth with sustainability in irrigated agriculture through the removal of the subsidy to groundwater, technology development and dissemination to improve productivity, and increased farmer participation in spate and groundwater irrigation; (b) alleviating poverty with sustainability in poor rainfed and livestock farming through the removal of policy disincentives to grain production, improving research and farmer education, and increasing community participation in management of natural resources; and (c) restructuring public services and promoting the role of the private and cooperative sectors.

## Implications for Social Protection Needs

The demographic pressure and the natural resource constraint represent the twin threats to the Republic of Yemen's rural economy. The risk is rural pauperization and this can be exacerbated by structural adjustment, particularly trade liberalization and the removal of subsidies on diesel and credit. A recent exercise created a static model to assess the impact of these policy changes on principal fruit and vegetable products. Assuming subsidies were removed in one step without any change in farmer behavior, the model showed a reduction in income of 13 percent for three products, equivalent to a drop in agricultural GDP of 3 percent.

There will be a difficult transition period, and there is a need for a three-pronged approach. First, support on the supply side to improve agricultural productivity is planned under several projects. Second, support through poverty alleviation programs is in place through the Social Fund, including off-farm employment creation, the Public Works Project, and the Southern Governorates Project. But it is on the third prong that emphasis needs to placed; a more aggressive rural development policy. Areas of particular emphasis include rural roads (a rural access study is just starting), rural water and sanitation (an IDA project is under preparation), rural telecommunications, rural energy, income diversification, natural resource management, and rural organization, including administrative decentralization.

## Tunisia

The Bank's Rural Development Strategy in Tunisia seeks to improve growth and reduce poverty, especially in rural areas. This is to be achieved through (a) agricultural growth and improved sector competitiveness through further liberalization, diversification, and greater involvement of the private sector; (b) the strengthening of sector institutions in key public functions and facilitation of their retrenchment from those to be carried out by the private sector in line with the new vision; (c) greater efficiency in the use of scarce water resources; and (d) protection of the natural resource base and the environment. A number of lending and nonlending activities support these measures. In particular, significant changes are expected in the medium-term as a result of policy changes in the water sector pending trade liberalization as a result of negotiations with the EU.

The early results of the ongoing Agricultural Competitiveness Study signal an anticipated social problem in the cereals sector in that small- and medium-size farms, which constitute a majority of farms in Tunisia, are not competitive and would be adversely affected by liberalization of cereal production and trade. While the results of liberalization are positive on the overall economy in terms of GDP growth and budget deficits, the costs of this increase in welfare are borne entirely by the agricultural and agroindustrial sectors. For example, in the specific case of the long-term effects of total liberalization while European subsidies are being maintained, agricultural production decreases by 13 percent as compared to the reference scenario, investment decreases by 40 percent, and employment by 16 percent. Agricultural exports increase by 50 percent, while imports increase by 80 percent. The only subsector that shows any improvement is oil production under agroindustry. Cereal production in particular falls by 15 percent, while employment in cereal production declines by 23 percent.

Even if these magnitudes appear excessive and could be interpreted as the general direction of changes rather than absolute changes, the implications are severe. It would be very difficult under Tunisian sociopolitical conditions to consider that such drastic changes would receive wide acceptance. The large transfers of resources out of agriculture, particularly in labor, would not be politically palatable to Tunisian and European decisionmakers. The implicit transfer and adaptation costs would also be quite large. A comprehensive approach to social protection would therefore have to be developed. It could include few options of social protection for the rural areas, targeting old farmers, unemployed farmers and farm workers, reconversion and training programs, and so forth.

## Algeria

According to the results of the Poverty Assessment Study for Algeria, poverty is essentially a rural phenomenon, compounded by a high incidence of unemployment in rural areas as well as underemployment due to the seasonality of agricultural activities. This study indicates that up to 6.4 million people live in poverty (up to 22.6 percent of the population). Furthermore, the study shows that (a) 70 percent of the poor live in rural areas, and 30.3 percent of the rural population live below the poverty line; (b) the rural poor have larger families with high dependency ratios; (c) the poor have low levels of education, are mainly wage earners, and have a higher incidence of unemployment (the unemployment rate among the rural poor is 35 percent versus 24 percent among the non-poor); (d) the incidence of poverty *and* unemployment is highest among the rural young (the 16- to 34-year-old age group); and (e) social indicators are low for the rural poor, especially in access to potable water from public services, education (particularly for females), and health services.

## Producer Support Policies As an Instrument of Social Protection in Rural Areas

Algeria uses producer price supports, currently exclusively for wheat, as an instrument of social policy as well as economic policy. Price supports are a major budgetary expenditure, recently amounting to between a third and a half of public expenditures in the budget of the Ministry of Agriculture and Fisheries. Historically, support prices have been around $100 per metric ton over reference prices for wheat, implying nominal rates of protection of 50 to 100 percent.

It is estimated that approximately 500,000 small farmers in Algeria depend on cereal production. On average, farm production is approximately two metric tons, and below that more than half the time. Furthermore, other crop production options are limited in these dry, rain-fed areas. Hence, for a large part of the cereal-producing farm families, the potential for productivity increases is limited. Producer supports for wheat will not have the desired effect of yield and production increases for these farm families. The average impact is less than DA 10 per day per person in an average small-farm family involved in wheat.

Another modality for social transfers is the implicit subsidy on irrigation water in large-scale irrigation schemes, whereby current tariffs are equivalent to 1 to 7 percent of the marginal cost of water, depending on source and loss assumptions. However, little is known about the beneficiaries of these transfers in terms of farm characteristics, product mix, costs of production, and so on. Hence, it is not clear if such transfers are justified as a tool of economic or social policy.

The impact of the austerity measures under the macroeconomic stabilization, economic reform, and structural adjustment programs since 1994 have been hard on the agricultural sector as demand has fallen with an almost 50 percent drop in real incomes. Social protection measures to buffer the impact of this recession have focused largely on urban families and have neglected interventions in the rural areas. Instead, distortionary economic policies continue to be the main instrument of social policy in rural areas, along with labor-intensive civil works in certain areas. It is preferable to provide social protection in rural areas in the context of social programs. Such support should be decoupled from programs for specific crops. However, the potential issues associated with such an option for social protection in rural areas have not been assessed.

TABLE A5.1

# MENA: Matrix of Rural Sector Issues and Action Plan

| Issues and Background | Progress | Future Action |
|---|---|---|
| **Water**<br>Agriculture has to adjust to using less and more expensive water more efficiently:<br>• Water is scarce.<br>• Agriculture is a high and inefficient user.<br>• Water charges are low; O&M is inadequate.<br>• Intersectoral water transfers are inevitable and entail political and policy decisions backed by sound information.<br>• User participation is weak. | • Irrigation investments and increasing focus on improving efficiency and the user's role of existing systems.<br>• Water Sector Investment Loan in Jordan, Morocco, Tunisia, and the Republic of Yemen is under preparation.<br>• SAL and AGSECAL in Algeria for O&M.<br>• Policy dialogue for integrated water resource management.<br>• AGSECAL in Jordan began sector adjustment.<br>• The Republic of Yemen water strategy: participatory policy work is under way. | • Water Sector Investment Loan.<br>• Integrated water resource management studies and projects.<br>• Specific irrigation, drainage, and sanitation projects.<br>• Sector adjustment loans and economic and sector work for policy dialogue on water pricing and O&M.<br>• Water action plan: establishing a MENA water fund. |
| **Rural development and poverty alleviation**<br>• Poverty is higher in rural areas.<br>• A politically sensitive issue.<br>• Extensive development, despite progress.<br>• Limited access to land and insecurity of tenure.<br>• Poor access to basic infrastructure and productive and social services, especially health, education, and potable water.<br>• Poor rural women are even more disadvantaged.<br>• Poor social development indicators. | • Regional projects targeting rural poverty alleviation (for example, Tunisia Northwest Project, Yemen Southern Governorates, Egypt Matruh Resource Management)<br>• Poverty reduced substantially in some countries but remains an issue in others, and more so in rural areas in terms of access to services (health and education in particular). | • Increased lending for rural participatory development, including poverty alleviation.<br>• Rural development and employment strategy and projects.<br>• Increased private sector involvement.<br>• Emphasis on rural health and education, particularly for women, as well as other services (roads, electrification, potable water).<br>• Mountainous areas development.<br>• Rainfed agriculture development. |
| **Competitiveness of agriculture**<br>*Rural finance*<br>• Inadequate agricultural and rural credit from official sources.<br>• System finances itself, but at a high cost including inefficiency.<br><br>Food price stability for urban consumers has led to:<br>• Distortions due to market controls and subsidies;<br>• Dominance of state enterprises in agricultural marketing and transformation;<br>• Inadequate marketing organization and infrastructure for domestic and export market development;<br>• Inefficient price formation and transmission; | • Projects to increase productivity and efficiency.<br>• Research and extension projects<br>• AGSECAL have made significant progress in addressing these issues, but there are remaining issues on the agenda, depending on the country.<br>• Irrigation investments. | • Redefine public goods: focus on institutions and incentives to promote the private sector (services, marketing, agribusiness, exports).<br>• New approaches need to revitalize rural finance projects.<br>• New instruments need to be utilized along with investment projects (guarantees, nonbalance of payment support sector adjustment loans, targeting private sector development— for example, industrial renovation project in Tunisia).<br>• Adjustment lending on the decline; needs to be resuscitated. |

| Issues and Background | Progress | Future Action |
|---|---|---|
| • Rent-seeking intermediaries; and <br> • Inefficient product and market diversification. <br><br> *Food security* <br> • Region is net importer of basic foodstuffs (cereals, milk, sugar, cooking oil). <br> • Food self-sufficiency is low and concern about food security is increasing in the face of rising cereal prices as a consequence of trade liberalization. <br><br> *Support to cereal production* <br> • Targets mainly in low rainfall areas. <br> • Heavy budgetary burden. <br> • No incentive to increase productivity due to inadequate research and extension. <br> • These supports entail social subsidies to producers who have few alternatives to cereal production. <br><br> *EU agenda* <br> • Proximity of EU has advantages, but EU trade barriers limit diversification toward higher-value crops for export. | | • Need to increase lending for private sector development, competitiveness in agriculture, marketing, and agroindustry in light of increased global trade liberalization. <br> • Rainfed agriculture needs special focus, especially research and extension, and needs balance between production support and social transfers. <br> • Close coordination needed with EU/European Investment Bank, Germany, the Netherlands, and France. <br> • Macro agenda should include liberalization of internal and external marketing, privatization of state marketing companies. |
| **Natural resource management and environment** <br> • Arable land resources have reached their limit under current irrigation and rainfed water availability. <br> • Productivity increases are the only way to increase production. <br> • Requires efficient and sustainable use. <br> • Common land resources (steppes, ranges, fallow) are overexploited for livestock production (links land tenure). <br> • Soil erosion is a major environmental problem (importance of forestry). <br> • Desert encroachment and desertification is a problem. <br> • Overexploitation of groundwater is a major problem in some countries. <br> • Watershed management is inadequate; new approaches are particularly needed because top-down approaches are not effective. | • Forestry and watershed management projects. <br> • Increased national and donor resources for environmental problems. <br> • Implementation capacity development. | • Soil, watershed, and rangeland projects. <br> • Natural resource management and environmental lending need to be maintained. <br> • Participatory approaches need to be an integral part of project. <br> • Rainfed agriculture should not be overlooked. <br> • Governments need to reassert control over groundwater. <br><br><br> *(Table continues on the following page.)* |

**TABLE A5.1    (continued)**

| Issues and Background | Progress | Future Action |
|---|---|---|
| **Land tenure**<br>• Politically sensitive.<br>• Small landholders predominate. For many, farm size may be economically inadequate, especially with fragmentation.<br>• Insecurity of tenure and lack of land titles cause inefficient and unsustainable exploitation, as well as constraints in access to official credit (collateral issue).<br>• Historical and social factors lead to smaller farm sizes through division of inheritance.<br>• Common lands are exploited without any title but through customary right.<br>• Much of the agricultural land has not been surveyed for cadastre, and this process moves slowly because of the cadastre techniques used.<br>• Land markets are virtually nonexistent and are encumbered by costly and time-consuming bureaucratic processes. | • Cadastre projects.<br>• Pilot components for land consolidation in some projects. | • Bank is timid in this area, including policy dialogue.<br>• Should the Bank get involved? If the Bank decides not to get involved, we have to live with the consequences, in that what we do in other areas may have limited effectiveness as a result of constraints posed by land tenure. |

TABLE A5.2

## Implications for the Bank

| How to Meet Challenges and Improve Performance | Bank Process and Resource Implications | Indicators |
|---|---|---|
| • Diversify overall rural economic growth, not just agriculture.<br>• Coordinate rural strategy and economic and sector work with Country Assistance Strategy (CAS) and macro policies.<br>• Focus on rural employment and incomes.<br>• Set realistic objectives.<br>• Use selectivity, small-scale, "staged" projects as part of long-term program.<br>• Lending on parallel track with macro (potable water).<br>• Empower and strengthen local institutions.<br>• Donor coordination. | • Coordination with central management units and other sector units (for example, Morocco Rural Development Strategy).<br>• Flexibility in process management post-CAS (cut steps but reinstate technical review).<br>• Control of divisions through adherence to CAS and total budget allocations (not micromanagement of individual operations).<br>• Skill shifts, not necessarily increased budgets:<br>  ▪ Operations management<br>  ▪ Water resource planning<br>  ▪ Participatory development<br>  ▪ Marketing, agribusiness, finance<br>• Need to strengthen intersectoral country team approach.<br>• Need to constitute thematic teams for, for example, water.<br>• Greater use of local technical assistance capacity and local staff in resident missions.<br>• Cofinanciers (and clients) pay more of direct processing and management costs. | *Caveat*<br>• Must take long-term perspective.<br>• Very significant weather risk.<br><br>*Impact indicators*<br>• Baseline data critical.<br>• Rural development performance indicators.<br>• Coverage of basic services.<br>• Rural poverty reduction.<br>• Rural employment generation.<br>• Export growth—diversification.<br>• Agricultural GDP/water used.<br>• Income-consumption stability.<br>• Level participation.<br><br>*Bank quality control indicators*<br>• Portfolio improvements.<br>• Progress toward staffing profile changes.<br>• Improvement in delivery times.<br>• Monitoring of processing costs. |

# Social Safety Nets in Select MENA Countries

TABLE A6.1

# Social Safety Nets in Select MENA Countries

| Program/Measure | Population Affected, 1999–2000 | Overall Impact | Budgetary Cost (% of GDP in 1999–2000) | Leakage |
|---|---|---|---|---|
| **Algeria** | | | | |
| Family allowance | 1.3 million families or about 5 million children | Cover 14 percent of the population and benefit only families that contribute to the formal social security system | 0.8% | Large; it is inequitable because its coverage is limited to wage earners in the formal sector, and there is no link between family income and eligibility |
| School allowance | All families with children aged 6–21 | Small; benefit only families that contribute to the formal social security system | 0.2% | Large; no link between family income and eligibility |
| Public works and cash transfers | Public works provide compensation to those able to work, and cash transfers provide financial support to those unable to work (elderly and handicapped) | Cover about 4 percent of population (or 20 percent of the poor) | 0.6% | Moderate; some people may receive multiple benefits, while a large share of the poor is not covered |
| Unemployment insurance | Was introduced in July 1994 to facilitate industrial restructuring | Targeted to the retrenched workers; in 2000, 183,000 received the benefit | 0.3% | None; however, financial sustainability of the system may be jeopardized because reserves have been diverted to new active labor market initiatives |
| **Egypt, Arab Rep. of** | | | | |
| Food subsidies | 87 percent of the population | Large, because they are self-targeted; these food subsidies benefit the poor | 1.30% | Moderate; in urban areas the richest 20 percent of the population receives 17 percent of food subsidies, while the bottom 20 percent receives 21 percent |
| Social assistance | 2.7 million beneficiaries | Small; payment is only 5 percent of the absolute poverty line | 0.15% | Moderate; administrative costs account for some 12 percent of total costs |
| Casual workers scheme | 771,000 beneficiaries | Total number of beneficiaries represents only 30 percent of the poor | 0.16% | None |

| | | | |
|---|---|---|---|
| **Iran, Islamic Republic of** | | | |
| Consumer subsidies (universal for food items, and specific coupon goods) | Mostly available to all through controlled prices on food items exchanged in official markets (overvalued exchange rates) | Large, although scaled down through reform in light of fiscal constraints | 2.7% | Large and not well targeted to the poor. In urban areas, the top decile consumes 30 percent more subsidized bread than the first decile; leakage ranges from 15 percent for coupon goods to 40 percent for building materials. |
| **Jordan** | | | |
| Cash transfers to the unemployed poor | 45,000 households | The program relies on individual assessment and self-selection of the chronically poor unemployed | 0.2% | Limited because extensive documentation is required, and monitoring activities ensure that all beneficiaries deserve the cash transfers |
| Cash transfers | Poor handicapped, household heads (widows, elderly) | Covers 3.6 percent of the population | 0.7% | Moderate, because of the shift from general food subsidies (regressive) toward targeted cash transfers (progressive) |
| **Morocco** | | | |
| Activities of national mutual aid (*Entraide Nationale*) | 80,000 people | Targets needy populations through preschool education, literacy for poor mothers, basic training for illiterate girls, shelters for school-age children and orphans. | 0.1% | Small; programs are self-targeted because they do not attract the nonpoor: about 70 to 80 percent of their budget reaches the poor, but the coverage is small (only 1.6 percent of the poor are covered); programs are inefficiently run; administration is highly centralized and overstaffed, and there is no monitoring |
| Public Works Program (*Promotion Nationale*) | Creates about 40,000 person years' employment, and majority of beneficiaries are unskilled workers | Creates temporary employment for under- or unemployed and income-earning opportunities for rural poor, although the urban programs are targeted to first-job seekers, not necessarily poor; however, about 40 percent of total employment created is labor intensive | 0.2% | Moderate; over half of the resources are supporting local government wage payments rather than helping the low-income communities through labor-intensive activities |
| Food subsidy | Available to all; covers edibles oils, sugar, and flour | Only 25 percent of subsidies reach the poor, but they account for higher proportion of poors' expenditures | 1.6% | Large; close to half of expenditures in subsidies is a transfer to producers and processors and generates significant economic distortions in agriculture sector |

*(Table continues on the following page.)*

**TABLE A6.1** (continued)

| Program/Measure | Population Affected, 1999–2000 | Overall Impact | Budgetary Cost (% of GDP in 1999–2000) | Leakage |
|---|---|---|---|---|
| **Tunisia** | | | | |
| Food subsidies | Available to all | Large because they are self-targeted; these food subsidies benefit the poor effectively | 1.70% | Moderate; the richest 20 percent of the population receives 18 percent of the food subsidies, while the bottom 20 percent receives 21 percent |
| Direct transfers | Targeted through indicators and include food aid in schools and food rations for preschoolers; financial aid to the handicapped and the elderly poor; cash transfers to poor families | Services 300,000 preschoolers, 5,000 handicapped people, 4,700 elderly poor, and 101,000 needy families | 0.50% | Large; eligibility lists are rarely updated, and eligibility criteria are very general; some people receive multiple benefits |
| Public Works Program | Aimed to provide employment for the poor in urban and rural areas | The largest and most effective programs for unskilled workers | 0.12% (as of 1994) | Moderate; in addition to helping the low-income communities through labor-intensive activities, the program also supports local government wage payments |
| **Yemen, Republic of** | | | | |
| Food subsidy | Available to all but eliminated in 1999 | Small due to various leakages that lead to an estimated 80 percent of domestic supply of food items such as wheat being sold on the parallel market due to smuggling | 3% | Large because of faulty distribution channels, gross inefficiencies in port operations, and external payment systems |
| Social Welfare Fund | 300,000 people | Small; cash transfers to orphans; women without providers; handicapped; poor families without income | 1% | Large; geographic coverage does not match distribution of the poor; selection methods are not transparent; mainly centralized; level of transfers is low; no monitoring system in place |

# Notes

1. The MENA region in the World Bank includes Algeria, Djibouti, the Arab Republic of Egypt, Jordan, the Islamic Republic of Iran, Lebanon, Morocco, Tunisia, the West Bank and Gaza, and the Republic of Yemen (active borrowers), as well as Bahrain, Iraq, Kuwait, Libya, Malta, Oman, Saudi Arabia, the Syrian Arab Republic, and the United Arab Emirates. This report focuses primarily on the former group.

2. In economic terms, the Iran-Iraq and Gulf wars and the Algerian, Yemeni, and Lebanese civil wars are estimated to have cost more than US$1 trillion. Lebanon alone lost one-third of its population through emigration; 65,000 were killed, and many more were wounded or disabled.

3. In fact, using an adapted method of national accounting that takes into account the depletion of natural resources, even real GDP growth rates for the period 1970–80 become negative, suggesting that oil resources were not used efficiently.

4. The six leading types of disease are acute respiratory infections, diarrheal diseases, intestinal helminthes, malaria, trachoma, and tropical cluster (including schistosomiasis, trypanosomiasis, and filariasis). Five of these six types are waterborne diseases.

5. The measurement of poverty is based on the per capita spending of US$1 a day (or US$2 a day) at 1993 purchasing power parity terms.

6. For poverty calculations, the MENA region comprises Algeria, Egypt, the Islamic Republic of Iran, Jordan, Lebanon, Morocco, the Syrian Arab Republic, Tunisia, and the Republic of Yemen.

7. The 1998–99 National Household Survey (*Enquête Nationale sur les Niveaux de Vie des Ménages [ENNVM]*) was conducted over 12 months,

from February 12, 1998, to February 11, 1999, and covered 5,131 house-holds from different regions. The survey is comparable to the one conducted in 1990–91, which had a sample size of 3,400 households.

8. The most widely used measure of inequality in the Gini coefficient. It is derived from the cumulative distribution of expenditure across the population, or from the Lorenz curve. The Lorenz curve shows the cumulative fraction of expenditures as a function of the cumulative fraction of the population, arranged in order of increasing expenditures. The closer the Lorenz curve is to the diagonal, the more equitable is the distribution. The Gini coefficient is the ratio of the area between the Lorenz curve and the 45 degree line to the whole area beneath the 45 degree line. A value of zero represents perfect equality and a value of one perfect inequality.

9. Informal systems are by nature private systems.

10. *Zakat* is a contribution required by Islam for charity paid according to wealth. *Waqfs* are endowments encouraged by Islam whereby wealthy people finance social services.

11. The Schengen Agreement allows for one visa for travel anywhere in Europe.

12. A rough estimation of the effects of wheat price supports in Algeria during the mid-1990s arrived at a figure of 15 Algerian dinars per capita per day for an average wheat-producing farm family, the equivalent of around US$0.25 at the exchange rates prevailing then.

13. Losses are defined as the difference between the volume of water delivered into a supply system and the volume of water accounted for by legitimate consumption, whether metered or not.

14. Microfinance practitioners generally use the household as the unit of analysis because household activity and microenterprise activity are closely intertwined. It is also a common rule that not more than one member of a household should be eligible for a microloan.

15. The Alexandria Business Association Program and the National Bank for Development Program, both in Egypt.

16. These include the spun-off Save the Children Programs in Lebanon, the West Bank and Gaza, and Jordan (Al Majmoua, JDWS, and Faten, respectively); the UNRWA Program in the West Bank and Gaza; Zakoura and Al Amana in Morocco; and two programs in Egypt (Cairo, Sharkia) designed along the lines of the Alexandria Business Association. Another seven are designed and implemented according to best-practice guidelines, but their sustainability cannot yet be evaluated.

17. In Algeria, Egypt, Morocco, Tunisia, and the Republic of Yemen, rates of return have been negative for long periods of time.

18. In the Islamic Republic of Iran there are also noncontributory systems. It has been estimated that 60 percent of the population aged 15 to 59 is covered.

19. In the Republic of Yemen coverage is even lower than in Morocco. A recent study has found that less than one-third of eligible private sector employees participate in the pension scheme, and that the informal sector is likely to be very large.

20. These figures refer to total payroll tax rates as a share of gross wage plus employer payroll contributions.

21. Important differences emerge, however, when considering details such as whether there is a ceiling on taxable earnings. There is such a ceiling in Egypt and Morocco, but not in Algeria, Jordan, and Tunisia.

22. A PWP's labor cost share must exceed 60 to 70 percent to be considered high. For example, in Chile, which operates one of the best PWPs in the world, labor cost was set at a minimum of 80 percent of total cost, virtually mandating selection of labor-intensive activities. Wages were also maintained at about 70 percent of the minimum wage, thus facilitating self-targeting of the poor.

23. The productive assets created by a PWP are maintained either by the program itself or by some other mechanism.

24. This review broadly defines SIFs as agencies that finance small projects in several sectors. The projects are targeted to benefit a country's poor and vulnerable groups, based on demand generated in a participatory manner by local groups and organizations and screened against a set of eligibility criteria.

25. These observations do not apply to programs that support small and microenterprises, where the nature of working with individual clients is by definition highly demand driven and participatory.

26. These figures are for net job creation.

27. Improving targeting in the allocation of subsidies will be a recurring topic in the discussion about social protection systems and will be developed in subsequent sections.

# Bibliography

Adams, R., Jr. 1991. *The Effects of International Remittances on Poverty, Inequality and Development in Rural Egypt.* Research Report 86. Washington, D.C.: International Food Policy Research Institute.

————. 1995. *Sources of Income Inequality and Poverty in Rural Pakistan.* Research Report 102. Washington, D.C.: International Food Policy Research Institute.

————. 1998. "Remittances, Investment and Rural Asset Accumulation in Pakistan." *Economic Development and Cultural Change* 47 (October): 155–73.

Ahmad, Z. 1994. "Islamic Banking: State of the Art." *Islamic Economic Studies* 1 (2).

Aiyer, S. R. 1997. "Pension Reform in Latin America: Quick Fixes or Sustainable Reform?" Working Paper 1865, World Bank, Washington, D.C.

Amerah, M. S. 1990. "Major Employment Issues in Arab Countries." The Royal Scientific Society, Jordan, paper presented at the Policy Seminar on Employment Policy in Arab Countries, Amman, Jordan.

Arrau, P., and K. Schmidt-Hebbel. 1994. "Pension System and Reforms: Country Experiences and Research Issues." *Revista Analisis Economico* 9 (1).

Asher, M. G. 1998. "Investment Policies and Performance of Provident Funds in Southeast Asia." Paper presented at the Workshop on Pension System Reform, Governance, and Fund Management, January.

Azam, J. P. 1992. "The Agricultural Minimum Wage and Wheat Production in Morocco, 1971–1989." Processed.

Banque Centrale de Tunisie. 1994. "Tunisian Financial System." *Journal of Economic Cooperation*, 15 (3–4).

Birks, J. S., A. Holt, and C. A. Sinclair. 1990. *Employment and Unemployment in Jordan: A Review.* Geneva: International Labour Office.

Bisat, A., M. A. El-Erian, and T. Helbling. 1997. "Growth, Investment, and Saving in the Arab Economies." IMF Working Paper 97/8, International Monetary Fund, Washington, D.C.

Bonnerjee, A., and M. Moretti. 1997. "Kingdom of Morocco: A Simulation Analysis of the Long-Term Pension System of CNSS." Social Protection Team, Human Development Network, World Bank, Washington, D.C.

Börsch-Supan, A. 1992. "Population Aging, Social Security Design, and Early Retirement." *Journal of Institutional and Theoretical Economics* 148: 583–657.

————. 1998a. "Capital Productivity and the Nature of Competition." Brookings Papers on Economic Activity, Microeconomics. Brookings Institution, Washington, D.C.

————. 1998b. "Germany: A Social Security System on the Verge of Collapse." In Horst Siebert, ed., *Redesigning Social Security.* Tübingen: Mohr.

————. 1998c. "Incentive Effects of Social Security in Germany and Across Europe." *Journal of Public Economics.*

Börsch-Supan, A., and P. Schmidt. 1996. "Early Retirement in East and West Germany." In R. Riphahn, D. Snower, and K. Zimmermann, eds., *Employment Policy in the Transition to Free Enterprise: German Integration and Its Lessons for Europe.* London.

Börsch-Supan, A., and Reinhold Schnabel. 1998. "Social Security and Declining Labor Force Participation in Germany." *American Economic Review.*

Bos, E., M. T. Vu, E. Massiah, and R. Bulatao. 1994. *World Population Projections, 1994–1995.* Washington, D.C.: World Bank.

Botka, A. U. 1994. "Some Features on Current Pension System Reform in Latin America." *Revista Analisis Economico* 9 (1).

Caisse Nationale de Sécurité Sociale. 1996. *Rapport d'activite 1995*. Royaume du Maroc.

Cashin, P., and C. J. McDermott. 1995. "Informational Efficiency in Developing Equity Markets." IMF Working Paper 95/58. International Monetary Fund, Washington, D.C.

Charmes, J. 1991. "Employment and Income in the Informal Sector of Maghreb and Mashreq Countries." Cairo Papers in Social Sciences. The American University in Cairo Press, Cairo.

Corsetti, G. 1994. "An Endogenous Growth Model of Social Security and the Size of the Informal Sector." *Revista Analisis Economico* 9 (1).

Corsetti, G., and K. Schmidt-Hebbel. 1995. "Pension Reform and Growth." Policy Research Department, World Bank, Washington, D.C.

Cox, D., and E. Jimenez. 1992. "Social Security and Private Transfers in Developing Countries: The Case of Peru." *World Bank Economic Review* 6 (1): 155–70.

Dar, A., and Z. Tzannatos. 1999. "Active Labor Market Programs: A Review of the Evidence from Evaluations." Social Protection Discussion Paper 9901. World Bank, Washington, D.C.

Davis, E. P. 1996. "The Role of Institutional Investors in the Evolution of Financial Structure and Behavior." Proceedings of a Conference on the Development of Financial Systems. Reserve Bank of Australia.

————. 1997. "Public Pensions, Pension Reform and Fiscal Policy." Staff Paper 5. European Monetary Institute, Frankfurt.

de Soto, Hernando. 2000. "The Mystery of Capital."

Diamond, P. 1994. "Privatization of Social Security: Lessons from Chile." *Revista Analisis Economico* 9 (1).

————. 1998. "The Economics of Social Security Reform." Paper presented at the National Academy of Social Insurance conference, March.

Disney, R. 1996. *Can We Afford to Grow Older?* London: Cambridge University Press.

Diwan, I., and L. Squire. 1992. "Economic and Social Development in the Middle East and North Africa." Discussion Paper Series 3. World Bank, Washington, D.C.

Easterly, W., and others. 1993. "Good Policy or Good Luck? Country Growth Performance and Temporary Shocks." *Journal of Monetary Economics.* 32: 459–83.

Economic Research Forum. 1996. *ERF Indicators: Economic Trends in the MENA Region.* Cairo.

————. 1998. *Economic Trends in the MENA Region.* Cairo.

El-Erian, M. A., and M. S. Kumar. 1995. "Emerging Equity Markets in Middle Eastern Countries." *IMF Staff Papers* 42 (2). Washington, D.C.: International Monetary Fund.

Feiler, G. 1991. "Migration and Recession: Arab Labor Mobility in the Middle East." *Population and Development Review* 17 (March): 134–55.

Feldstein, M. 1977. "Social Security and Private Savings: International Evidence in an Extended Life-Cycle Model." In M. Feldstein and R. Inman, eds., *The Economics of Public Services.* International Economic Association.

————. 1995. "Social Security and Savings: New Time Series Evidence." NBER Working Paper 5054.

Gilani, Ijaz, M. Khan, and I. Munawar. 1981. "Labor Migration from Pakistan to the Middle East and Its Impact on the Domestic Economy." Research Report 126. Pakistan Institute of Development Economics, Islamabad.

Gelos, G. 1995. "Investment Efficiency, Human Capital and Migration: A Productivity Analysis of the Jordanian Economy." Discussion Paper 14. World Bank, Washington, D.C.

Government of Egypt. 1995. *Population Policy Report.*

Government of Iran. 1998. *Population Policy Report.*

Gruber, J., and D. Wise, eds. 1998. *International Social Security Comparisons.* Chicago: University of Chicago Press.

Hall, R. E., and C. I. Jones. 1996. "The Productivity of Nations." NBER Working Paper 5812.

Handoussa, H. 1991. "Crisis and Challenge: Prospects for the 1990s." In H. Handoussa and G. Potter, eds., *Employment and Structural Adjustment: Egypt in the 1990s*. Cairo: The American University in Cairo Press.

Heller, P. S., J. Amieva-Huerta, B. Clements, and P. Tinios. 1996. *Jordan: Pension Reform Issues*. Washington, D.C.: International Monetary Fund.

Holzmann, R. 1994. "Funded and Private Pensions for Eastern European Countries in Transition?" *Revista Analisis Economico* 9 (1).

————. 1995. "Pension Reform, Financial Market Development and Endogenous Growth: Preliminary Evidence from Chile." International Monetary Fund, Washington, D.C. (Updated and shortened version was published as an IMF Staff Paper in 1997.)

————. 1999. *Financing the Transition from PAYG to Fully Funded Pension Schemes*. Washington, D.C.: World Bank.

————. 2002. "Risk and Vulnerability: The Forward Looking Role of Social Protection in a Globalizing World." In E. Dowler and P. Mosely, eds., *Poverty and Social Exclusion in North and South*. London and New York: Routledge.

Holzmann, R., and Jorgensen, S. 1999. "Social Protection as Social Risk Management: Conceptual Underpinnings for the Social Protection Sector Strategy Paper." *Journal of International Development* 11: 1005–1027.

————. 2000. "Social Risk Management: A New Conceptual Framework for Social Protection, and Beyond." Social Protection Discussion Paper 0006. World Bank, Washington, D.C. (Revised version published in 2001 in International Tax and Public Finance, Volume 8 pages 529–556.

Hsin, P. L., and O. S. Mitchell. 1994. "The Political Economy of Public Pensions: Pension Funding, Governance, and Fiscal Stress." *Revista Analisis Economico* 9 (1).

IFPRI (International Food Policy Research Institute). 1997. *A Profile of Poverty in Egypt.* Washington, D.C.

Iglesias, A., and R. Palacios. 1998. "Public Management of Pension Reserves." Social Protection Working Paper Series. World Bank, Washington, D.C.

ILO (International Labour Organization). 1998. *Yearbook of Labor Statistics.*

————. 2000. *World Labor Report.*

IMF (International Monetary Fund). 1999. *Government Finance Statistics Yearbook.* Washington, D.C.

International Bank for Reconstruction and Development. 1997. "Contractual Savings Development Loan to the Kingdom of Morocco." Report No. P-7176-MOR. World Bank, Washington, D.C.

International Development Association. 1996. "Country Assistance Strategy of the World Bank Group for the Republic of Yemen." Report No. 15286-Yem. World Bank, Washington, D.C.

International Finance Corporation. 1997. *Emerging Stock Markets Factbook.* Washington, D.C.: World Bank.

Jbili, A., K. Enders, and V. Treichel. 1997. "Financial Sector Reforms in Algeria, Morocco, and Tunisia: A Preliminary Assessment." IMF Working Paper 97/81. International Monetary Fund, Washington, D.C.

Keely, C., and B. Tran. 1989. "Remittances from Labor Migration: Evaluations, Performance and Implications." *International Migration Review* 23 (fall): 500–25.

Khan, M. F. 1994. "Comparative Economics of Some Islamic Financing Techniques." *Islamic Economic Studies* 1 (2).

Kim, J. I., and L. J. Lau. 1994. "The Sources of Economic Growth of the East Asian Newly Industrialized Countries." *Journal of the Japanese and International Economies* 8: 235–71.

Klevser, H. 1004. "Financial Structure of Egypt." *Journal of Economic Cooperation* 15 (3–4).

Knowles, J., and R. Anker. 1981. "An Analysis of Income Transfers in a Developing Country: The Case of Kenya." *Journal of Development Economics* 8 (April): 205–26.

Levine, R., and S. Zervos. 1996. "Stock Market Development and Economic Growth." *The World Bank Economic Review* 10 (2).

McKinsey Global Institute. 1996. *Capital Productivity.* Washington, D.C.

Ministère des Finances et des Investissements Extérieurs, Royaume du Maroc. 1997. *Développement de l'Epargne Institutionelle en vue de la Dynamisation des Marches de Capitaux.* Bossard Consultants.

Ministry of Planning. 1997. *Report to the Ministry of Planning on Provident Funds in the Hashemite Kingdom of Jordan.* Provident Funds Working Group.

Mitchell, Deborah. 1999. "Coping Mechanisms of Poor Communities in Yemen."

Musalem, A. 1999. *Contractual Savings and the Capital Markets.*

————. 1996. *Reforming Public Pensions.* Paris.

Newberry, D. M. G., and J. E. Stiglitz. 1981. *The Theory of Commodity Price Stabilization.* Oxford: Clarendon Press.

OECD (Organisation for Economic Co-operation and Development). 1988. *Reforming Public Pensions.* Paris.

————. 1994. *The OECD Jobs Study: Evidence and Explanations.* Paris: OECD.

Ogaki, M., J. D. Ostry, and C. M. Reinhart. 1996. "Saving Behavior in Low- and Middle-Income Developing Countries." *IMF Staff Papers* 43 (1). Washington, D.C.: International Monetary Fund.

Palacios, R., and R. Rocha. 1998. "The Hungarian Pension System in Transition." Social Protection Discussion Paper 9805. World Bank, Washington, D.C.

Palacios, R., and E. Whitehouse. 1998. "The Role of Choice in a Shift from PAYG to Fully Funded Pension Schemes." Social Protection Discussion Paper 9815. World Bank, Washington, D.C.

Pissarides, Ch. A. 1993. "Labor Markets in the Middle East and North Africa." Discussion Paper 5. World Bank, Washington, D.C.

Queisser, M. 1996. "Pensions in Germany." Working Paper 1664. World Bank, Washington, D.C.

———. 1998. *Financial Liberalization in Asia: Analysis and Prospects.* Washington, D.C.: World Bank.

Ravallion, M. 1998. "Reaching poor areas in a federal system." Policy Research Working Paper 1901. World Bank, Washington, D.C.

Ribe, F. 1994. "Funded Social Security Systems: A Review of Issues in Four East Asian Countries." *Revista Analisis Economico* 9 (1).

Rodriguez, Edgard. 1998. "International Migration and Income Distribution in the Philppines." *Economic Development and Cultural Change* 46 (January): 329–50.

Rodrik, Dani. 1999. "Where Did All the Growth Go? External Shocks, Social Conflict and Growth Collapses." *Journal of Economic Growth* 4 (December): 385–412.

Russell, Sharon. 1986. "Remittances from International Migration: A Review in Perspective." *World Development* 14 (June): 677–96.

Sachs, J., and A. Werner. 1996. "Achieving Rapid Growth in the Transitional Economies of Central Europe." Harvard Institute of Economic Development. Processed.

Said, M. 1995. "Public Sector Employment and Labor Markets in Arab Countries: Recent Developments and Policy Implications." Workshop on Labor Markets and Human Resources Development, Economic Research Forum, Cairo.

Schiavo-Campo, S., G. de Tommaso, and A. Mukherjee. 1997. "Government Employment and Pay: A Global and Regional Perspective." World Bank, Washington, D.C.

Schmidt-Hebbel, K. 1998. "Chile's Takeoff: Facts, Challenges, Lessons." *Economic Development.* World Bank, Washington, D.C. Processed.

———. 1998. "Does Pension Reform Really Spur Productivity, Saving, and Growth?" Processed.

Schwarz, A. 1998. *The Moroccan Pension System*. World Bank, Washington, D.C. Processed.

Serven, L., K. Schmidt-Hebbel, and A. Solimano. 1994. *Saving, Investment, and Growth in Developing Countries: An Overview*. Washington, D.C.: Policy Research Department, World Bank.

Shaban, Radwan, and Dina Abu Ghaida. 2000. "Poverty by Age in Jordan." Processed.

Social Security Administration. 1997. "Social Security Programs throughout the World." Research Report 65, SSA Publication 13-11805.

Social Security Corporation. 1997. *Annual Report 1996*. Amman, Jordan.

Social Security Research Group. 1997. *Social Security in Iran*. Tehran, Iran.

Stark, O. 1991. *The Migration of Labor*. Cambridge, Mass: Blackwell Press.

Stark, O., J. E. Taylor, and S. Yitzhaki. 1986. "Remittances and Inequality." *Economic Journal* 96 (September): 722–40.

Swamy, Gurushri. 1981. "International Migrant Workers' Remittances: Issues and Prospects." Working Paper 481. World Bank, Washington, D.C.

Tanzi, Vito, and Ken-Young Chu. 2000. "Social Protection in a Globalizing World: The Role of the International Community." Paper presented at the Rockefeller and Russell Sage Foundations conference, Welfare State Policies in Emerging Market Economies, New York, March 24–25.

TAPR/USAID. 1999. *Enhancing Egypt's Social Insurance System*.

Tharakan, G., and T. Wolden. 2000. "West Bank and Gaza Transport Sector Strategy Review." World Bank, Washington, D.C.

UNESCO (United Nations Educational, Scientific, and Cultural Organization). 1997. *Statistical Yearbook*.

———. 2000. *World Education Report*. Paris.

UNICEF (United Nations Children's Fund). 1998. *The State of the World's Children*.

Vittas, D. 1993. "Options for Pension Reform in Tunisia." Policy Research Working Paper 1154.

———. 1997a. *The Case for Partial Privatization of Pensions in Jordan.* Washington, D.C.: World Bank.

———. 1997b. "The Argentine Pension Reform and Its Relevance for Eastern Europe." Working Paper 1819. World Bank, Washington, D.C.

———. 1998. "The Role of Non-Bank Financial Intermediaries (with Particular Reference to Egypt)." Working Paper 1892. World Bank, Washington, D.C.

Water Supply and Sanitation Collaborative Council. 1996. "Water Supply and Sanitation Sector Monitoring Report."

Whiteford, P. 1995. "The Use of Replacement Rates in International Comparisons of Benefit Systems." *International Social Security Review* 48 (2).

Whitehouse, E. 1997. "Pension Reform in Britain." World Bank, Washington, D.C. Processed.

WHO (World Health Organization). 1996. *World Health Report.*

———. 1997. *World Health Report.*

———. 2000. *World Health Report.*

World Bank. Various years. *World Development Report.* Washington, D.C.

———. 1991. *Egypt: Alleviating Poverty during Structural Adjustment.* Washington, D.C.

———. 1993. "Republic of Tunisia: The Social Protection System." Report 11376-TUN. Washington, D.C.

———. 1994a. *Averting the Old Age Crisis: Policies to Protect the Old and Promote Growth.* London: Oxford University Press.

———. 1994b. "The Democratic and Popular Republic of Algeria, Country Economic Memorandum: The Transition to a Market Economy." Report 12048 DZ. Washington, D.C.

————. 1994c. "Hashemite Kingdom of Jordan: Poverty Assessment." Report 12675-JO. Washington, D.C.

————. 1995a. "Kingdom of Morocco, Country Economic Memorandum: Towards Higher Growth and Employment." Report 14155-MOR. Washington, D.C.

————. 1995b. "Tunisia: Poverty Alleviation: Preserving Progress while Preparing for the Future." Report 13993-TUN (August). Washington, D.C.

————. 1996. *Report on Social Security Corporation of Jordan.* Washington, D.C.

————. 1997a. "Arab Republic of Egypt, Country Economic Memorandum: Issues in Sustaining Economic Growth." Summary Report 16207-EGT. Washington, D.C.

————. 1997b. *Democratic and Popular Republic of Algeria: Growth, Employment and Poverty Reduction.* Washington, D.C.

————. 1997c. *Growth, Employment and Poverty Reduction* II (June).

————. 1997d. *World Development Report 1997.* Washington, D.C.

————. 1998a. *Education in the Middle East and North Africa: A Strategy toward Learning for Development.* Washington, D.C.

————. 1998b. "Macroeconomic Development and Employment in Egypt." Washington, D.C. Processed.

————. 1998c. *World Development Indicators 1998.* Washington, D.C.

————. 1999a. *Algeria: Poverty Assessment.* Washington, D.C.

————. 1999b. "Consumer Food Subsidies Program in MENA." Report 19561-MNA. Washington, D.C.

————. 1999c. *Pension Systems in the Middle East and North Africa: A Window of Opportunity.* Washington, D.C.

————. 1999d. "Yemen Social Fund for Development Project Midterm Review." Washington, D.C.

————. 2000a. "Republic of Tunisia: Social Conditions Update." Report 21503-TUN (August). Washington, D.C.

————. 2000b. *World Development Indicators 2000*. Washington, D.C.

————. 2000c. Yemen Social Fund for Development Project Appraisal Document. Washington, D.C.

————. 2001a. *Iran: Trade and Foreign Exchange Policies in Iran*. Washington, D.C.

————. 2001b. *Jordan: Poverty Alleviation Report*. Washington, D.C.

————. 2001c. "Kingdom of Morocco: Poverty Update." Report 21506-MOR (March). Washington, D.C.

————. 2001d. "Renewable Water Resources." *World Development Indicators*. Washington, D.C.

————. 2001e. *Republic of Djibouti: Pension System Reform*. Washington, D.C.

————. 2001f. *Social Protection Sector Strategy—From Safety Net to Springboard*. Washington, D.C.: The World Bank.

————. 2001g. *World Development Indicators Database*. Washington, D.C.

————. 2001h. *World Development Indicators 2001*. Washington, D.C.

————. 2001i. *World Development Report 2000/2001*. Washington, D.C.

————. 2002. *Algeria Public Expenditure Review of the Social Sector*. Washington, D.C.

WRI (World Resources Institute). 1998. *World Resources 1998–1999*. Washington, D.C.: Oxford University Press.